Legendlore

VOLUME THREE   **THE REALM CHRONICLES**

CALIBER
COMICS

Legendlore

VOLUME THREE THE REALM CHRONICLES

PLOT & WRITTEN BY
RALPH GRIFFITH
STUART KERR

PENCILS
GUY DAVIS

INKS
SANDY SCHREIBER

LETTERS
LEX MORRIS
GEORGE McVEY

THIS BOOK CONTAINS *THE REALM* VOLUME ONE ISSUES 8 - 11
Originally published by Arrow Comics

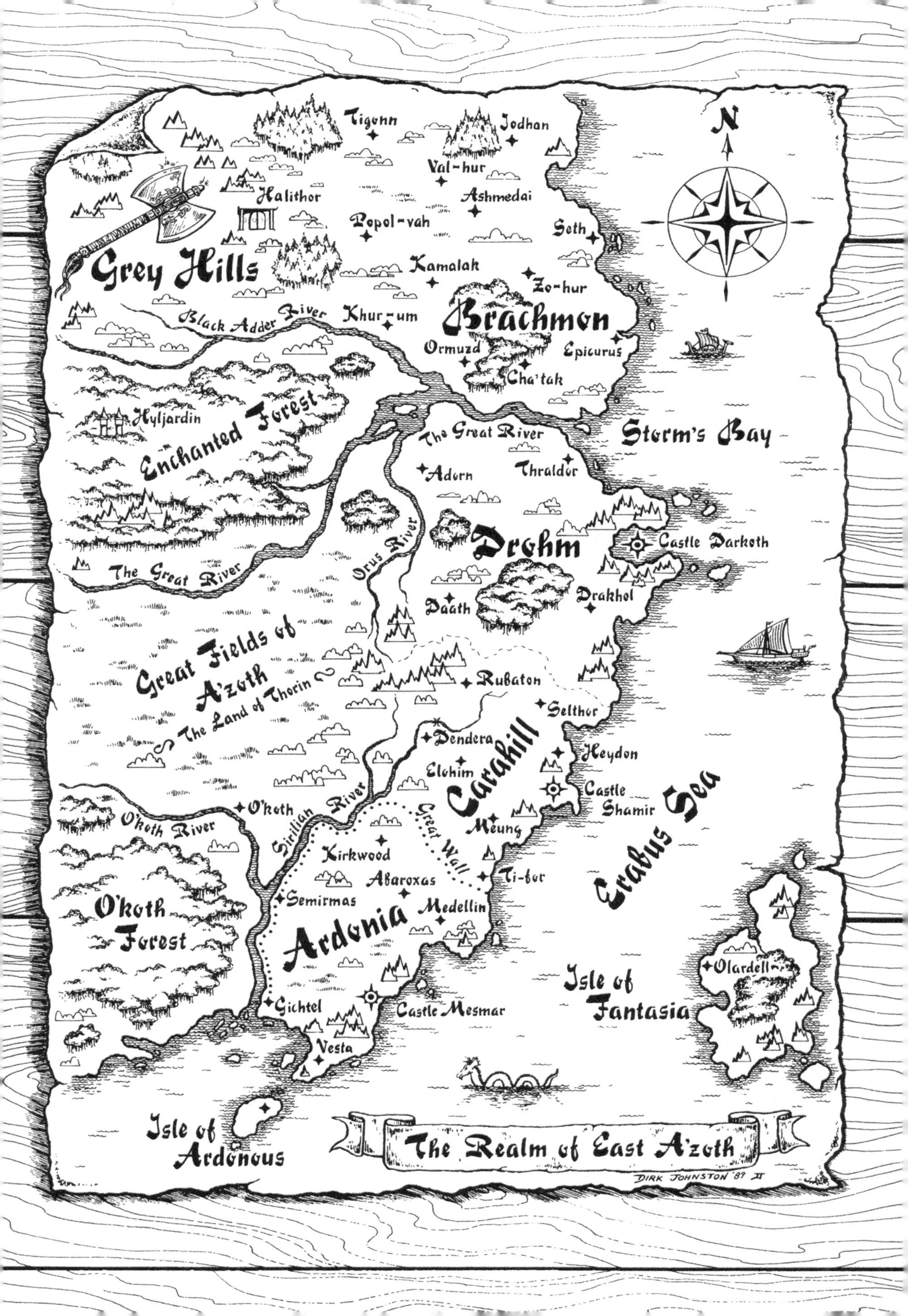
Tigonn
Jodhan
N
Val-hur
Halithor
Ashmedai
Popol-vah
Seth
Grey Hills
Kamalah
Zo-hur
Black Adder River
Khur-um
Brachmon
Ormuzd
Epicurus
Cha'tak
Hyljardin
Enchanted Forest
Storm's Bay
The Great River
Adorn
Thraldor
Orus River
Drohm
Castle Darkoth
The Great River
Drakhol
Daath
Great Fields of A'zoth
The Land of Thorin
Rubaton
Selthor
Dendera
Carahill
Heydon
Elohim
Castle Shamir
O'koth
O'koth River
Sirilian River
Great Wall
Meung
Erabus Sea
Kirkwood
Ti-for
Abaroxas
Semirmas
Medellin
O'koth Forest
Ardonia
Isle of Fantasia
Olardell
Gichtel
Castle Mesmar
Vesta
Isle of Ardonous
The Realm of East A'zoth
DIRK JOHNSTON '89

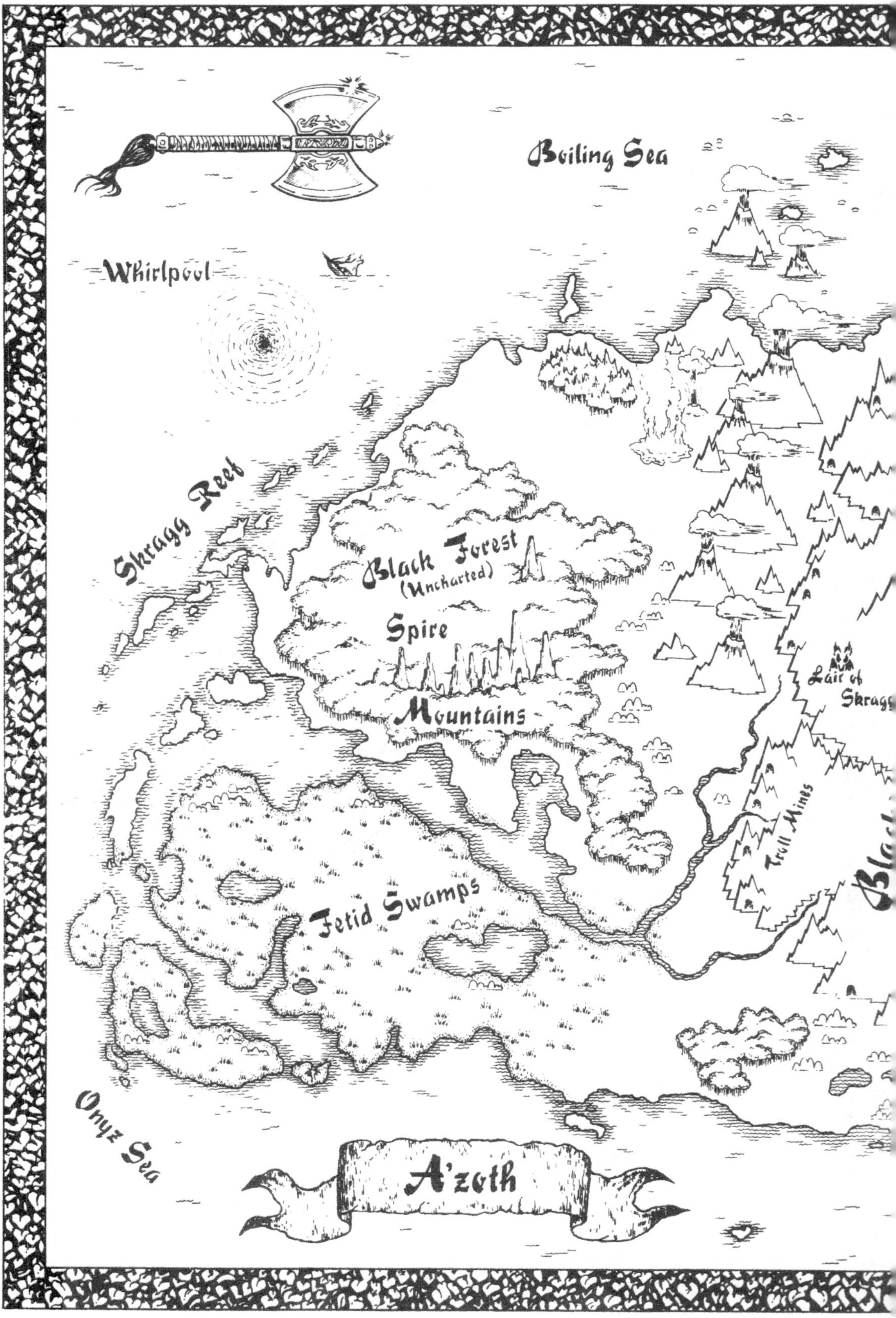
Boiling Sea
Whirlpool
Skragg Reef
Black Forest
(Uncharted)
Spire
Mountains
Lair of
Skragg
Troll Mines
Fetid Swamps
Onyz Sea
A'zoth

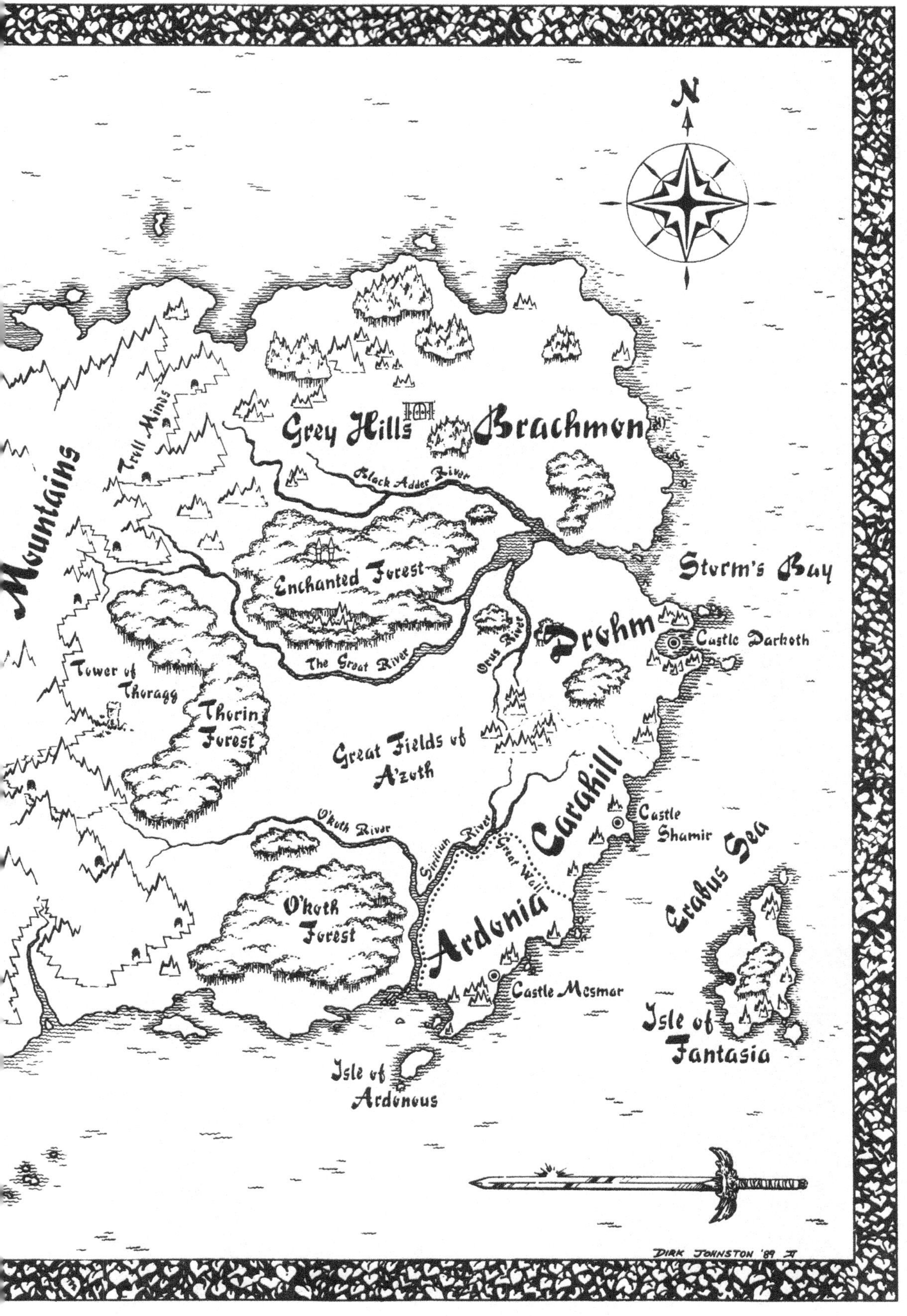
N
Mountains
Troll Mines
Grey Hills
Brachmon
Black Adder River
Enchanted Forest
Storm's Bay
Drohm
Castle Darkoth
Orus River
The Great River
Tower of Thoragg
Thorin Forest
Great Fields of A'zoth
Carahill
Castle Shamir
Erabus Sea
O'koth River
Sirilion River
Great Wall
O'koth Forest
Ardonia
Castle Mesmar
Isle of Fantasia
Isle of Ardonous
DIRK JOHNSTON '89

CHARACTER PORTFOLIO

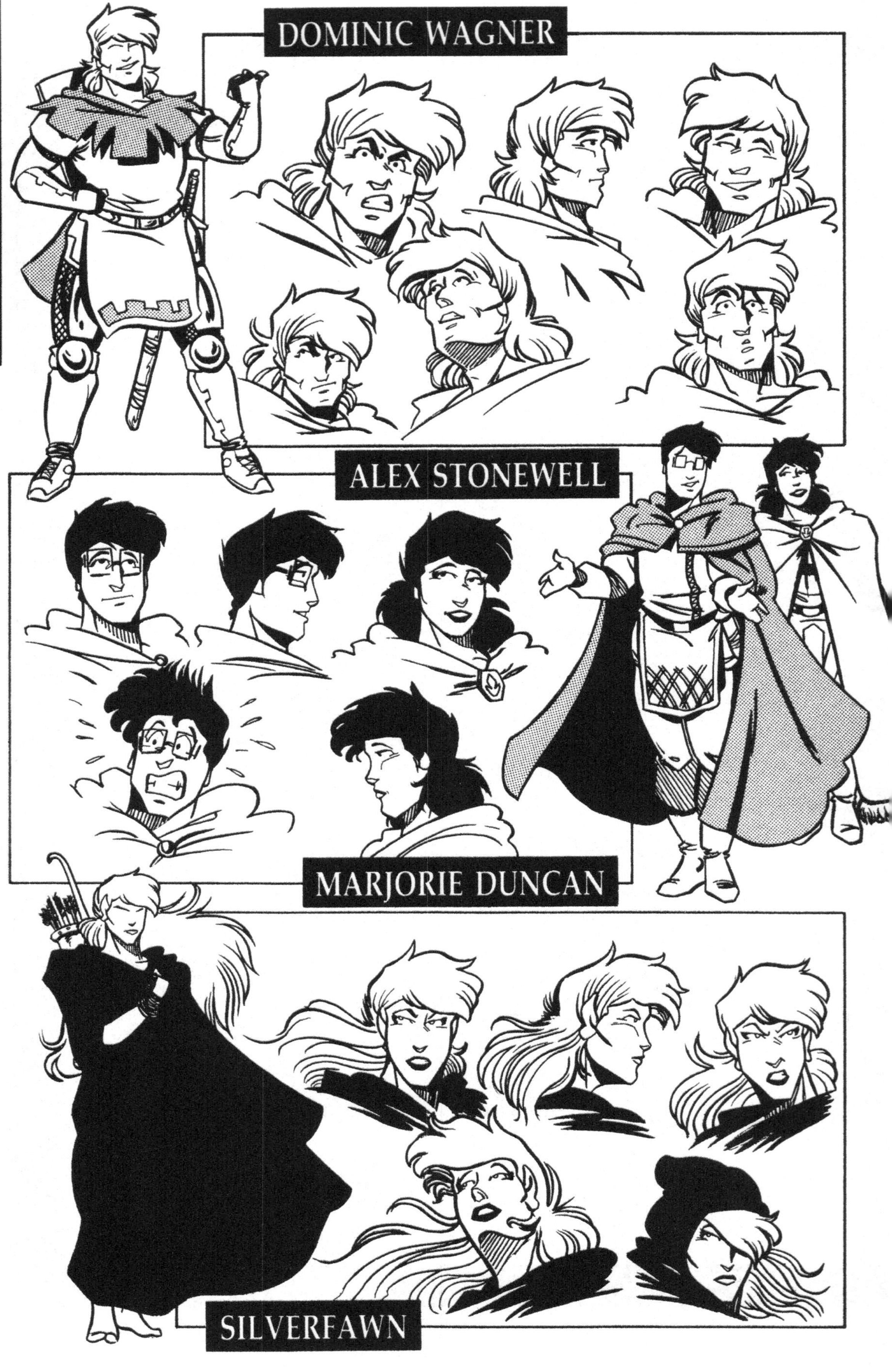
DOMINIC WAGNER
ALEX STONEWELL
MARJORIE DUNCAN
SILVERFAWN

DIGGORRUS GOREY

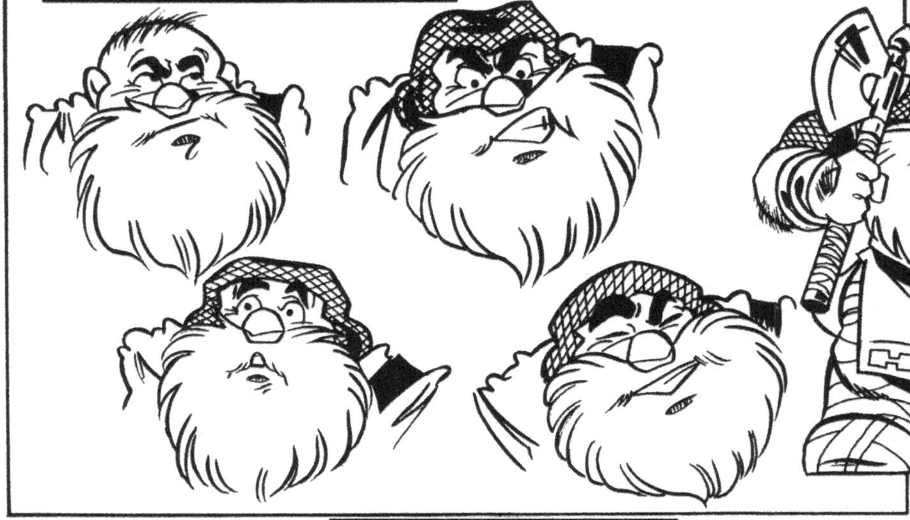

GRAPPO PILDEN

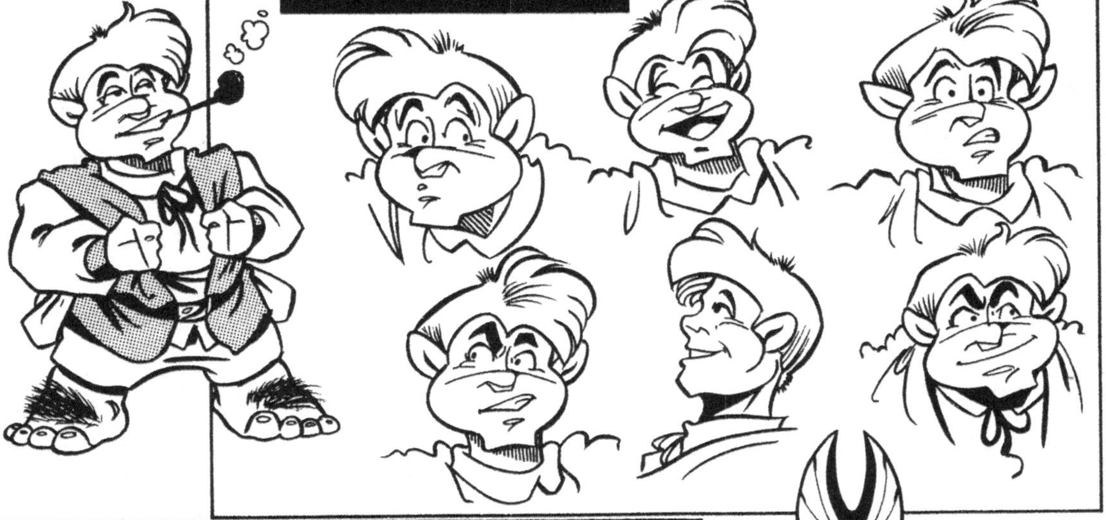

LORD DARKOTH • SANDRA BEACH

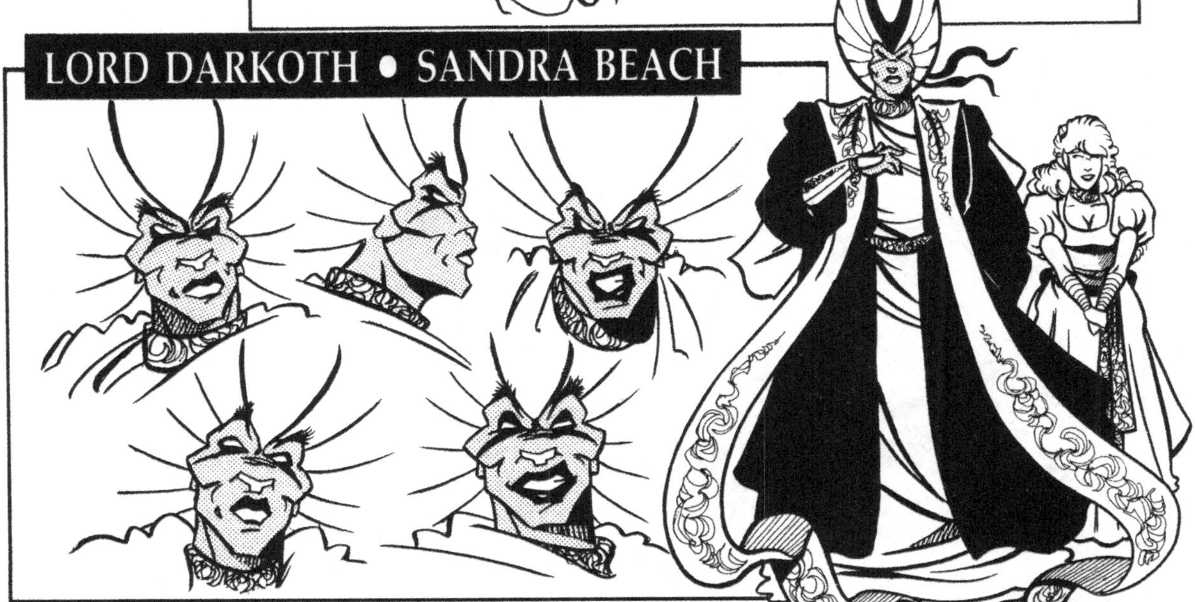

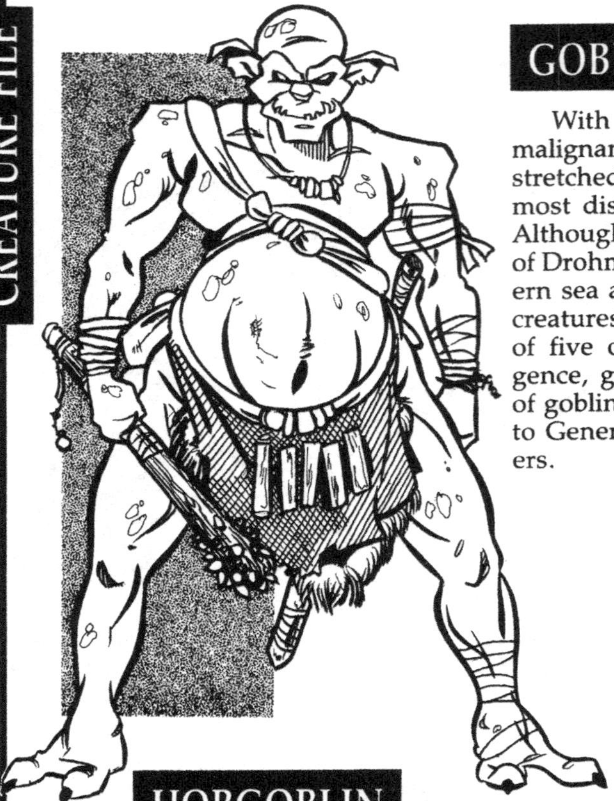

GOBLIN

With a skull-like face twisted into an eternal, malignant grin and sickly mottled green skin stretched over a blotted stomach, the goblin is the most disgusting and common of the sub-creatures. Although most heavily concentrated in the darklands of Drohm, there are tribes scattered between the eastern sea and the Black Mountains. They are nomadic creatures and will usually be encountered in packs of five or more. Limited only by their low intelligence, goblins are fierce barbaric fighters. The chief of goblins in Drohm is BoneCrack who answers only to General Ramus, one of Darkoth's most able leaders.

HOBGOBLIN

Hobgoblins are one of the most feared humanoid creatures in Azoth. Evolved from goblins, they have a much higher intelligence while retaining their cousins' savagery and strength in battle. They are very rare outside of Drohm and the vast majority of them have been drafted into Lord Darkoth's army. Serving only the cause of death and destruction, hobgoblins can tolerate most any other creature sharing the same goal. Hobgoblins have some martial arts abilities, and are greenish yellow with vari-colored markings around the eyes.

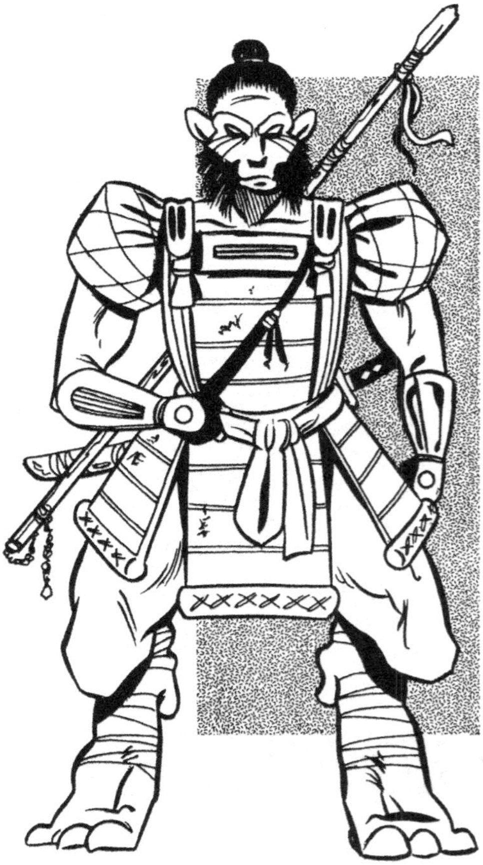

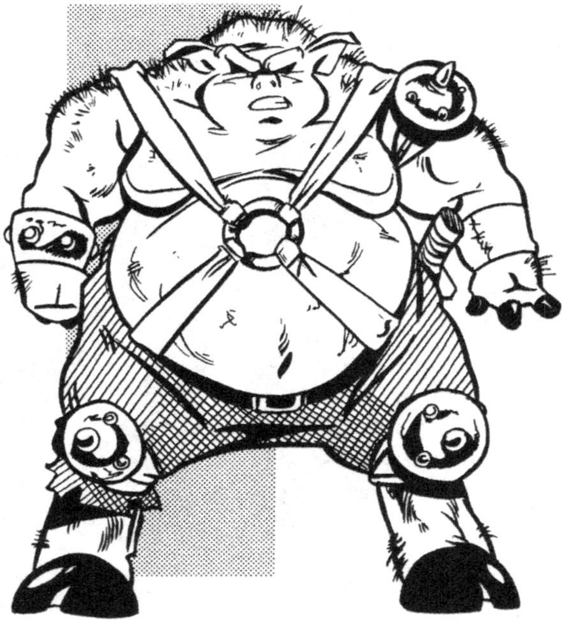

ORC

One of the most vile races of Azoth is the orc. Brown, black or green, with splotches of pink, orcs fight only for wealth or power. They detest all races, including other tribes of their own species. They are numerous and scattered all across Azoth. One particularly large and powerful tribe, the Orcs of the Bloody Hills, are found in the region east of the Orus River. There is a legend of a Crown of Orc-Controlling, the possessor of which has total control of every orc in the land. This artifact has been lost for hundreds, if not thousands, of years.

LEGENDLORE

THE REALM - VOLUME ONE

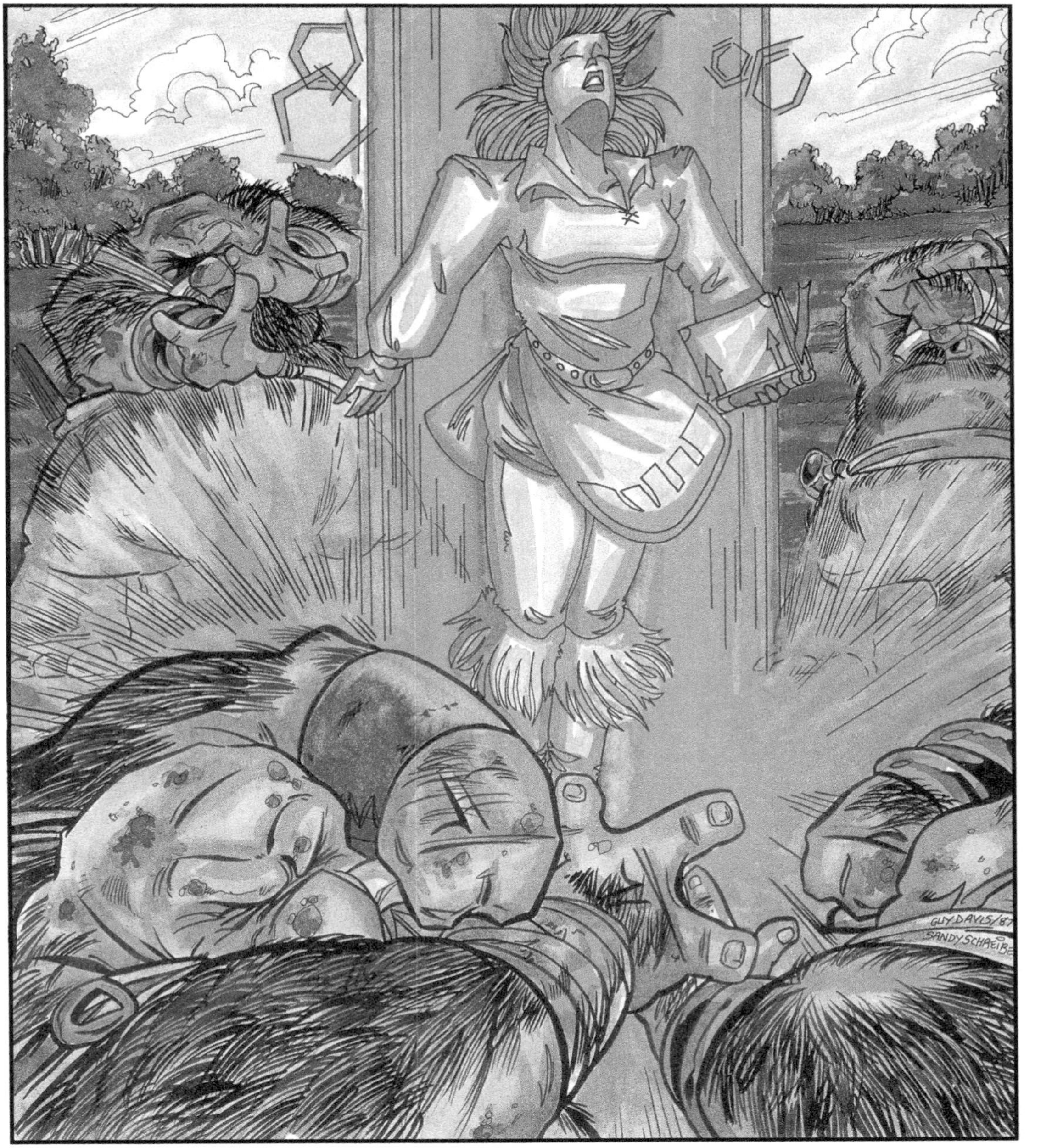

ISSUE EIGHT

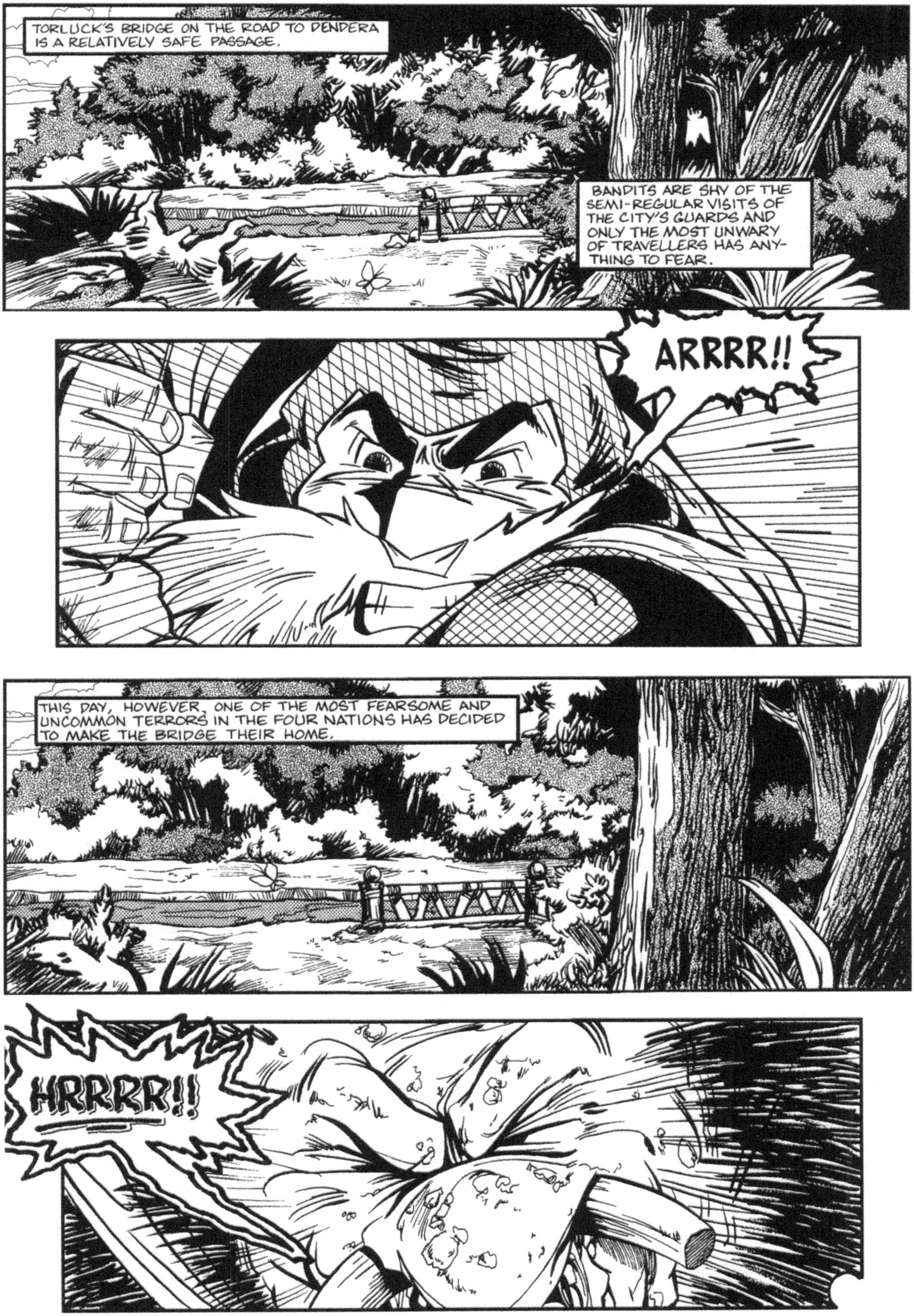

TORLUCK'S BRIDGE ON THE ROAD TO DENDERA IS A RELATIVELY SAFE PASSAGE.
BANDITS ARE SHY OF THE SEMI-REGULAR VISITS OF THE CITY'S GUARDS AND ONLY THE MOST UNWARY OF TRAVELLERS HAS ANYTHING TO FEAR.
ARRRR!!
THIS DAY, HOWEVER, ONE OF THE MOST FEARSOME AND UNCOMMON TERRORS IN THE FOUR NATIONS HAS DECIDED TO MAKE THE BRIDGE THEIR HOME.
HRRRR!!

RIVER TROLLS, NEARLY UNSTOPPABLE DUE TO A VERY SPECIAL ABILITY THAT THEY POSSESS, AS ONE DIGGORUSS GOREY IS ABOUT TO DISCOVER...

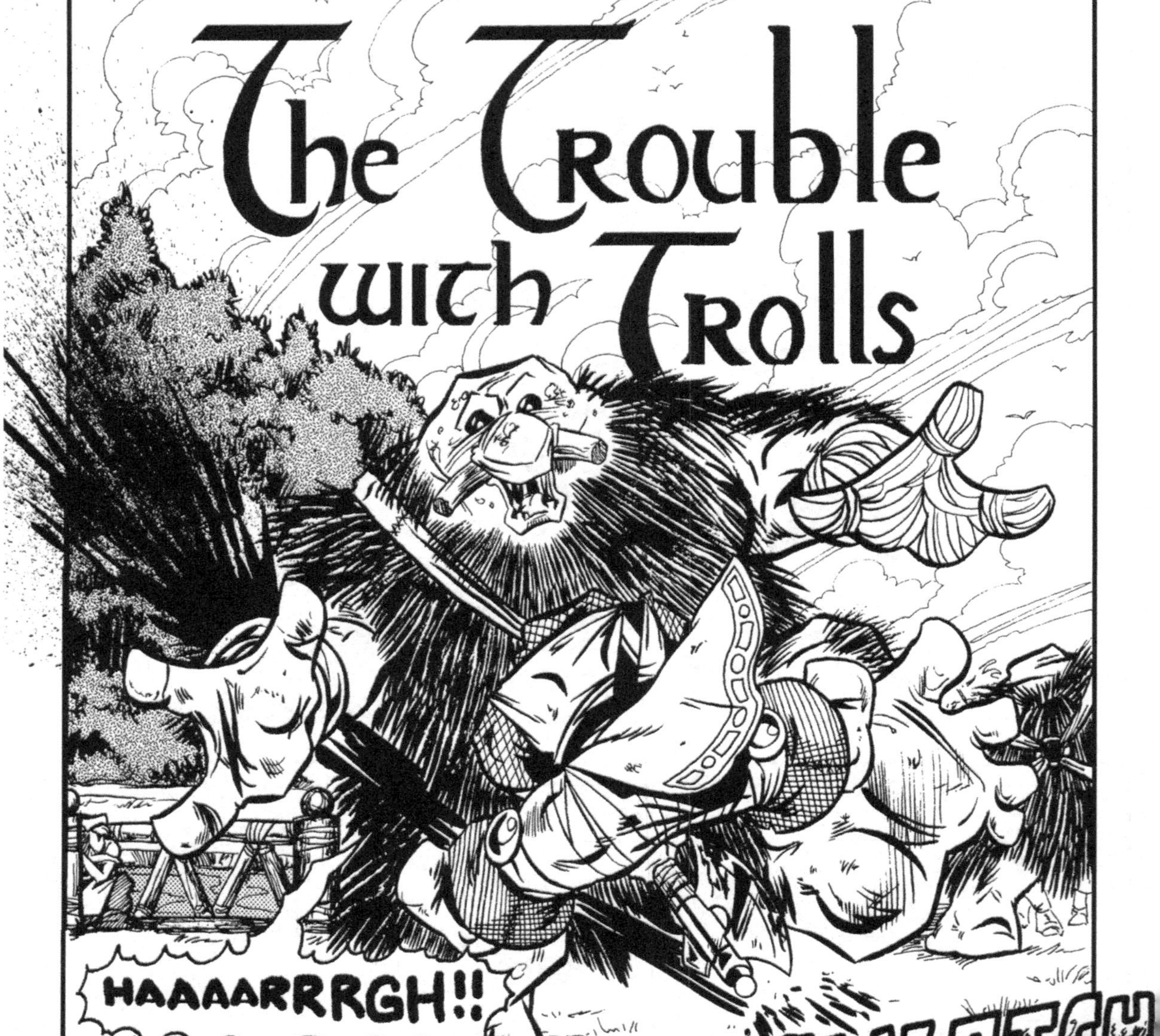
The Trouble with Trolls
HAAAARRRGH!!
SWLATCH

PLOT GRIFFITH

SCRIPT KERR

PENCILS DAVIS

INKS SCHREIBER

LETTERS MORRIS

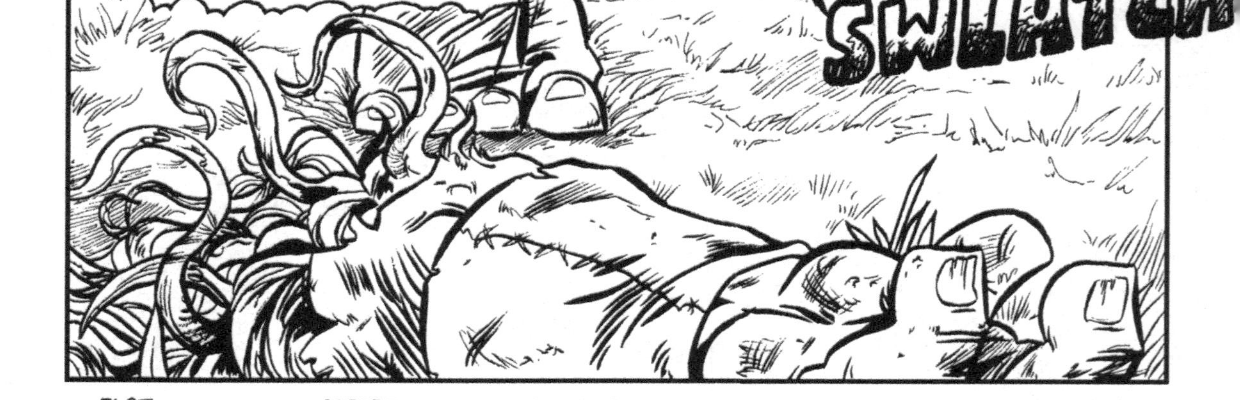

YOUR AXE WILL DO NO GOOD AGAINST THESE CREATURES, DWARF. THEY HEAL THEMSELVES.

"ONLY FIRE WILL STOP THEM."

HEH·HEH HEH!

I'LL FIND A WAY.

WELL IF YOU CAN'T CUT THEM...

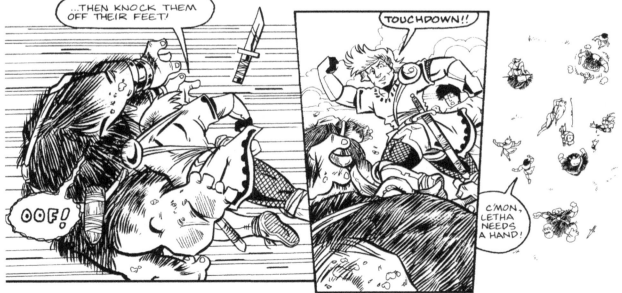

...THEN KNOCK THEM OFF THEIR FEET!

OOF!

TOUCHDOWN!!

C'MON, LETHA NEEDS A HAND!

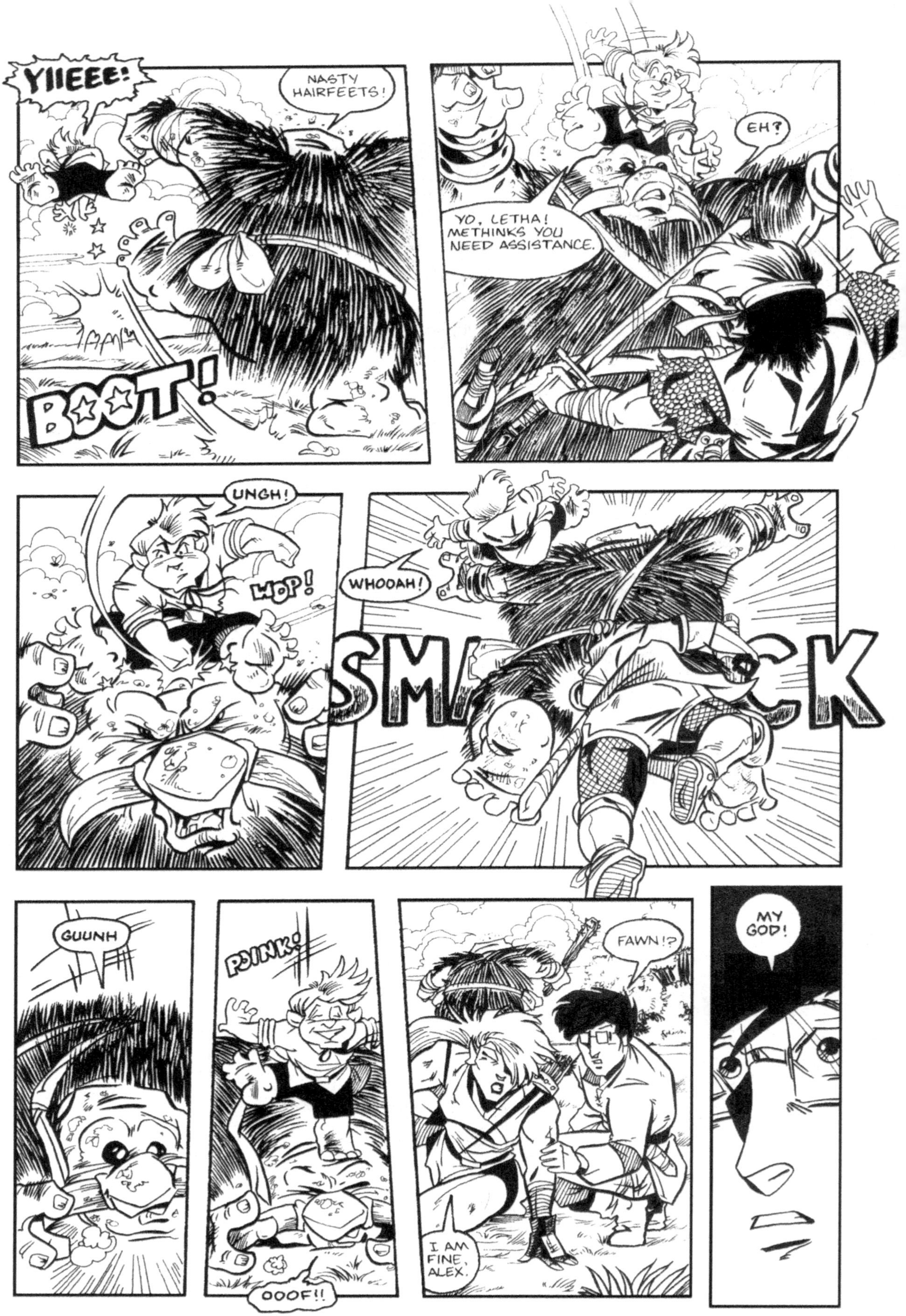
YIIEEE!
NASTY HAIRFEETS!
BOOT!
EH?
YO, LETHA! METHINKS YOU NEED ASSISTANCE.
UNGH!
WOP!
WHOOAH!
SMACK
GUUNH
PINK!
OOOF!!
FAWN!?
I AM FINE, ALEX.
MY GOD!

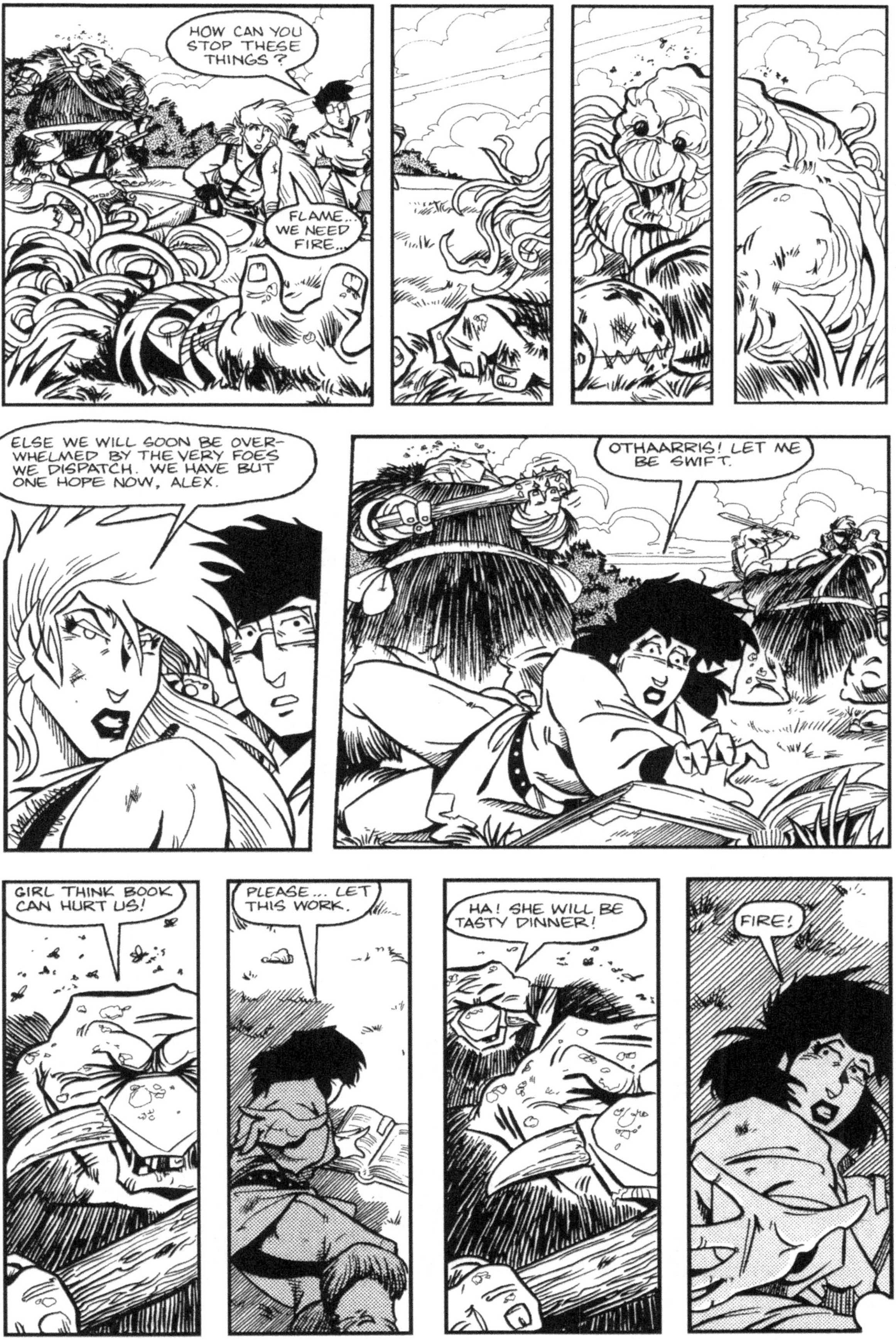
HOW CAN YOU STOP THESE THINGS?
FLAME... WE NEED FIRE...
ELSE WE WILL SOON BE OVER-WHELMED BY THE VERY FOES WE DISPATCH. WE HAVE BUT ONE HOPE NOW, ALEX.
OTHAARRIS! LET ME BE SWIFT.
GIRL THINK BOOK CAN HURT US!
PLEASE... LET THIS WORK.
HA! SHE WILL BE TASTY DINNER!
FIRE!

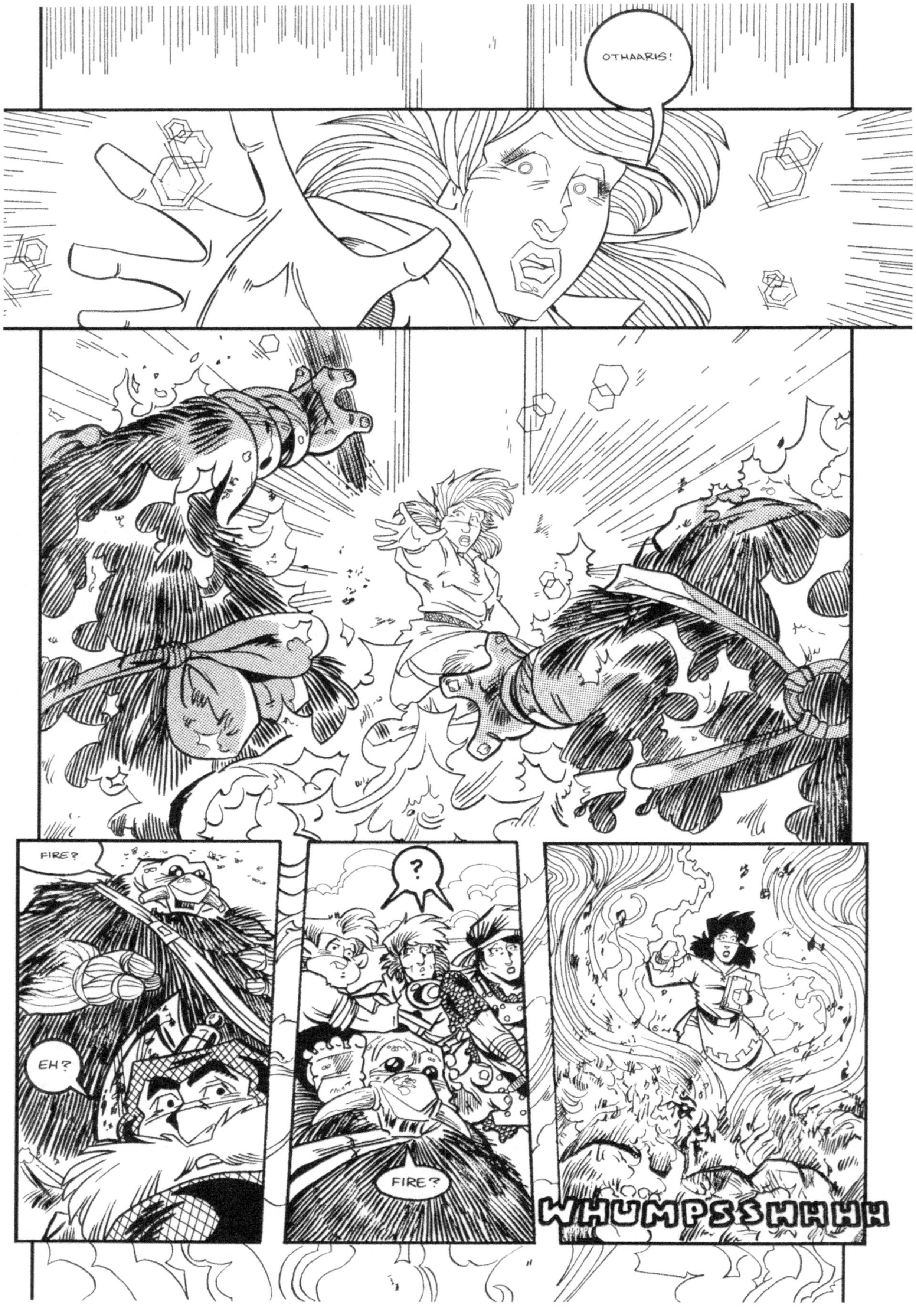
OTHAARIS!
FIRE?
EH?
?
FIRE?
WHUMPSSHHHHH

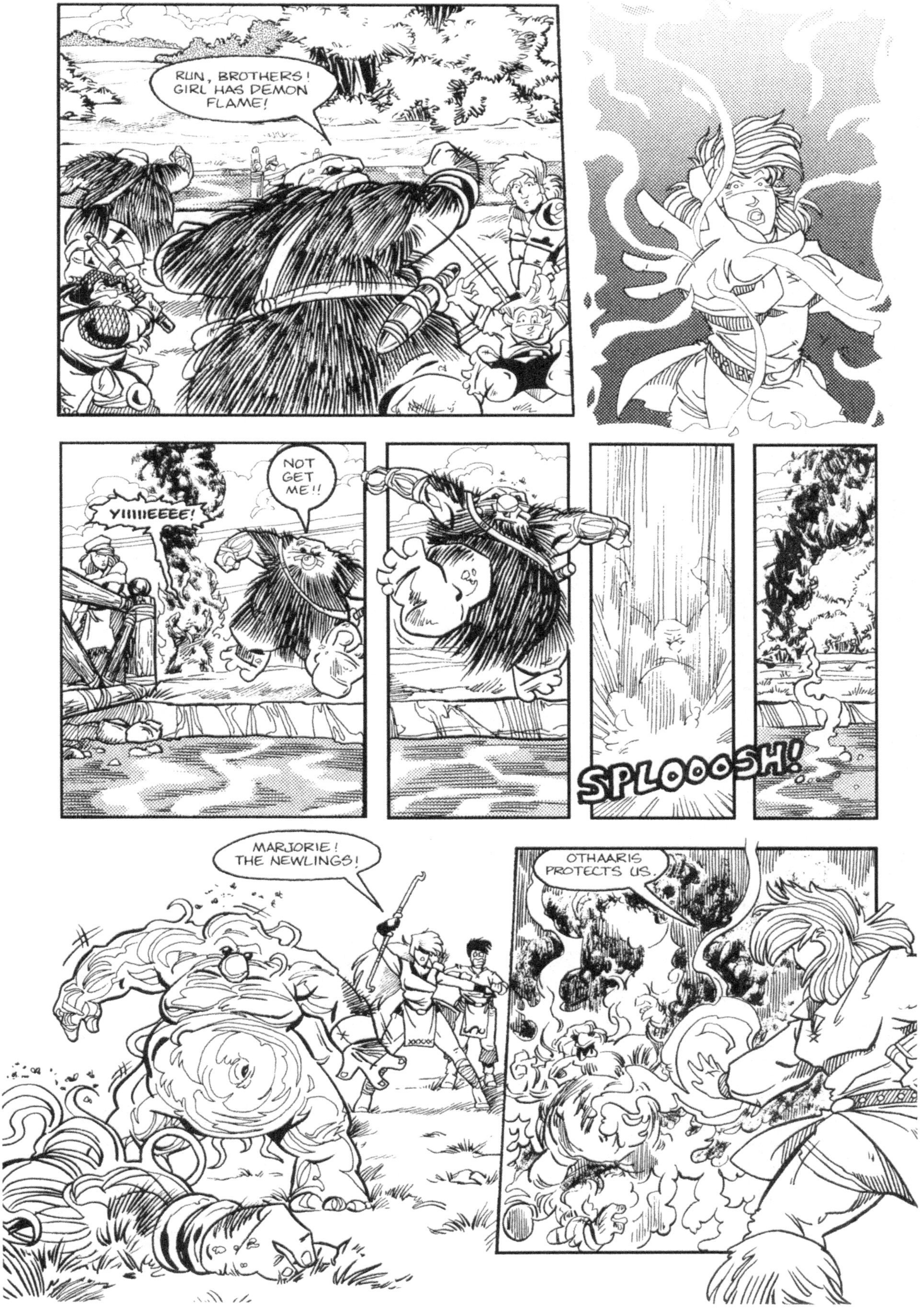
RUN, BROTHERS! GIRL HAS DEMON FLAME!
YIIIIEEEE!
NOT GET ME!!
SPLOOOSH!
MARJORIE! THE NEWLINGS!
OTHAARIS PROTECTS US.

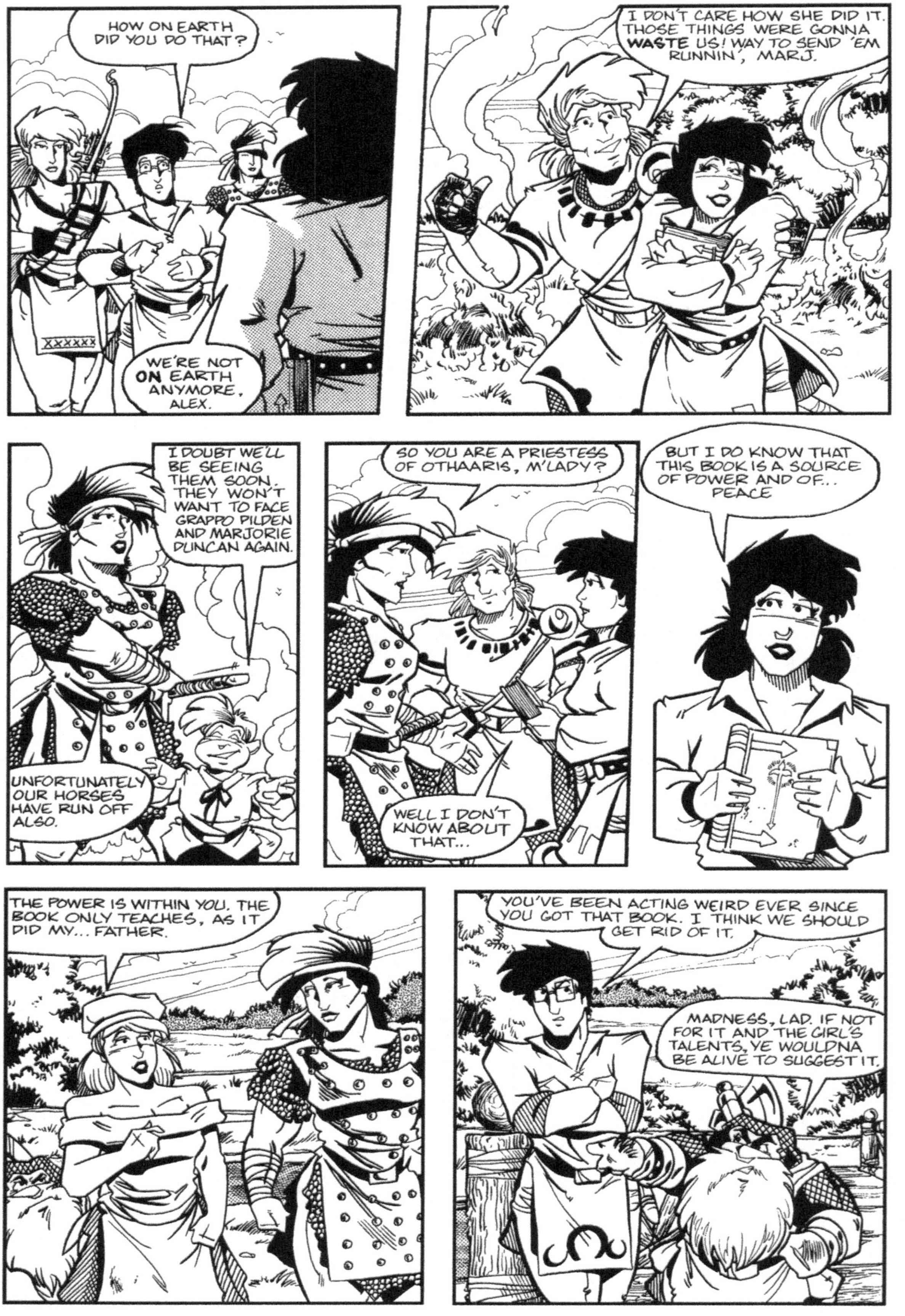

HOW ON EARTH DID YOU DO THAT?
WE'RE NOT **ON** EARTH ANYMORE, ALEX.
I DON'T CARE HOW SHE DID IT. THOSE THINGS WERE GONNA **WASTE** US! WAY TO SEND 'EM RUNNIN', MARJ.
I DOUBT WE'LL BE SEEING THEM SOON. THEY WON'T WANT TO FACE GRAPPO PILDEN AND MARJORIE DUNCAN AGAIN.
UNFORTUNATELY OUR HORSES HAVE RUN OFF ALSO.
SO YOU ARE A PRIESTESS OF OTHAARIS, M'LADY?
WELL I DON'T KNOW ABOUT THAT...
BUT I DO KNOW THAT THIS BOOK IS A SOURCE OF POWER AND OF... PEACE
THE POWER IS WITHIN YOU. THE BOOK ONLY TEACHES, AS IT DID MY... FATHER.
YOU'VE BEEN ACTING WEIRD EVER SINCE YOU GOT THAT BOOK. I THINK WE SHOULD GET RID OF IT.
MADNESS, LAD. IF NOT FOR IT AND THE GIRL'S TALENTS, YE WOULDNA BE ALIVE TO SUGGEST IT.

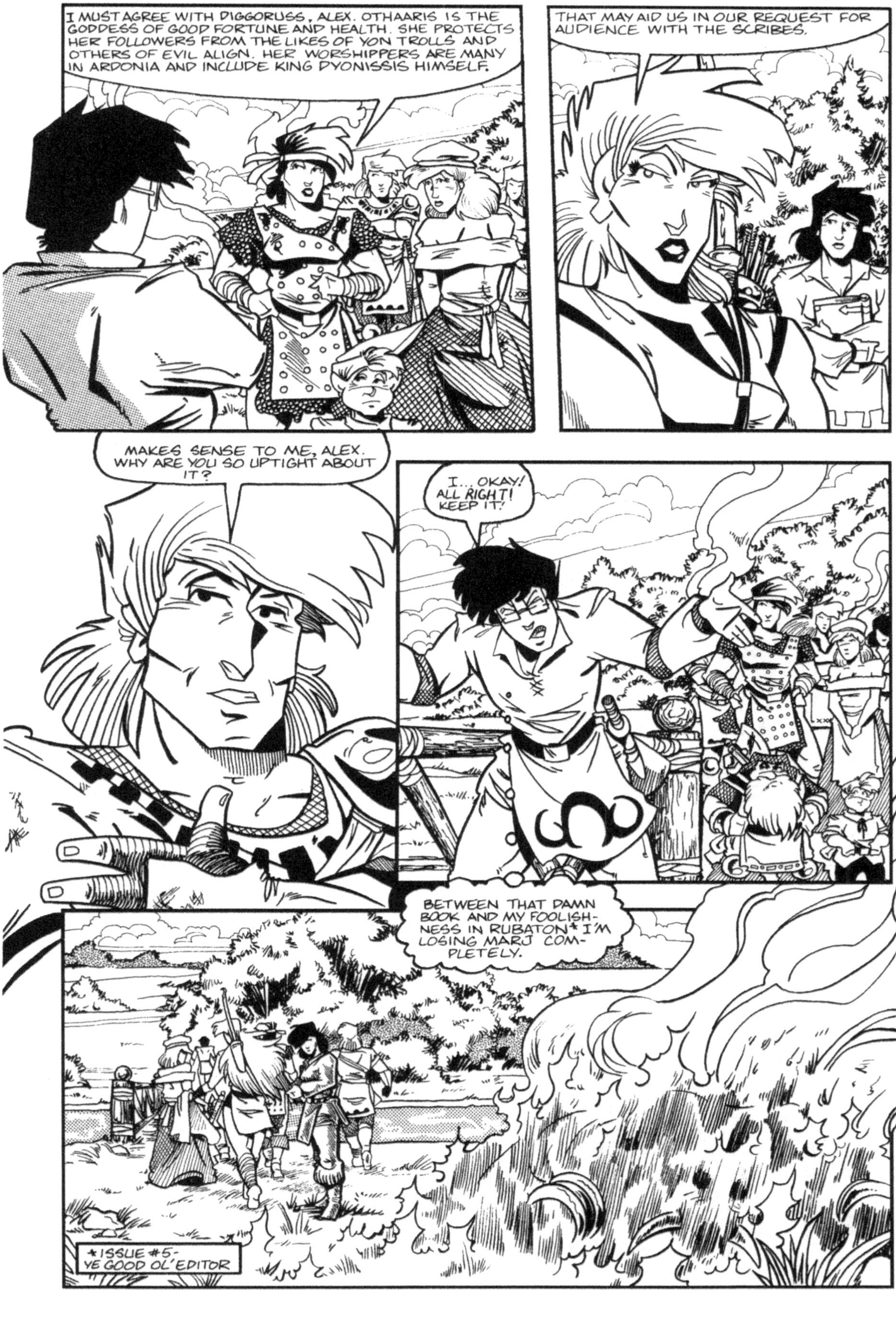
I MUST AGREE WITH DIGGORUSS, ALEX. OTHAARIS IS THE GODDESS OF GOOD FORTUNE AND HEALTH. SHE PROTECTS HER FOLLOWERS FROM THE LIKES OF YON TROLLS AND OTHERS OF EVIL ALIGN. HER WORSHIPPERS ARE MANY IN ARDONIA AND INCLUDE KING DYONISSIS HIMSELF.
THAT MAY AID US IN OUR REQUEST FOR AUDIENCE WITH THE SCRIBES.
MAKES SENSE TO ME, ALEX. WHY ARE YOU SO UPTIGHT ABOUT IT?
I... OKAY! ALL RIGHT! KEEP IT!
BETWEEN THAT DAMN BOOK AND MY FOOLISHNESS IN RUBATON* I'M LOSING MARJ COMPLETELY.
*ISSUE #5- YE GOOD OL' EDITOR

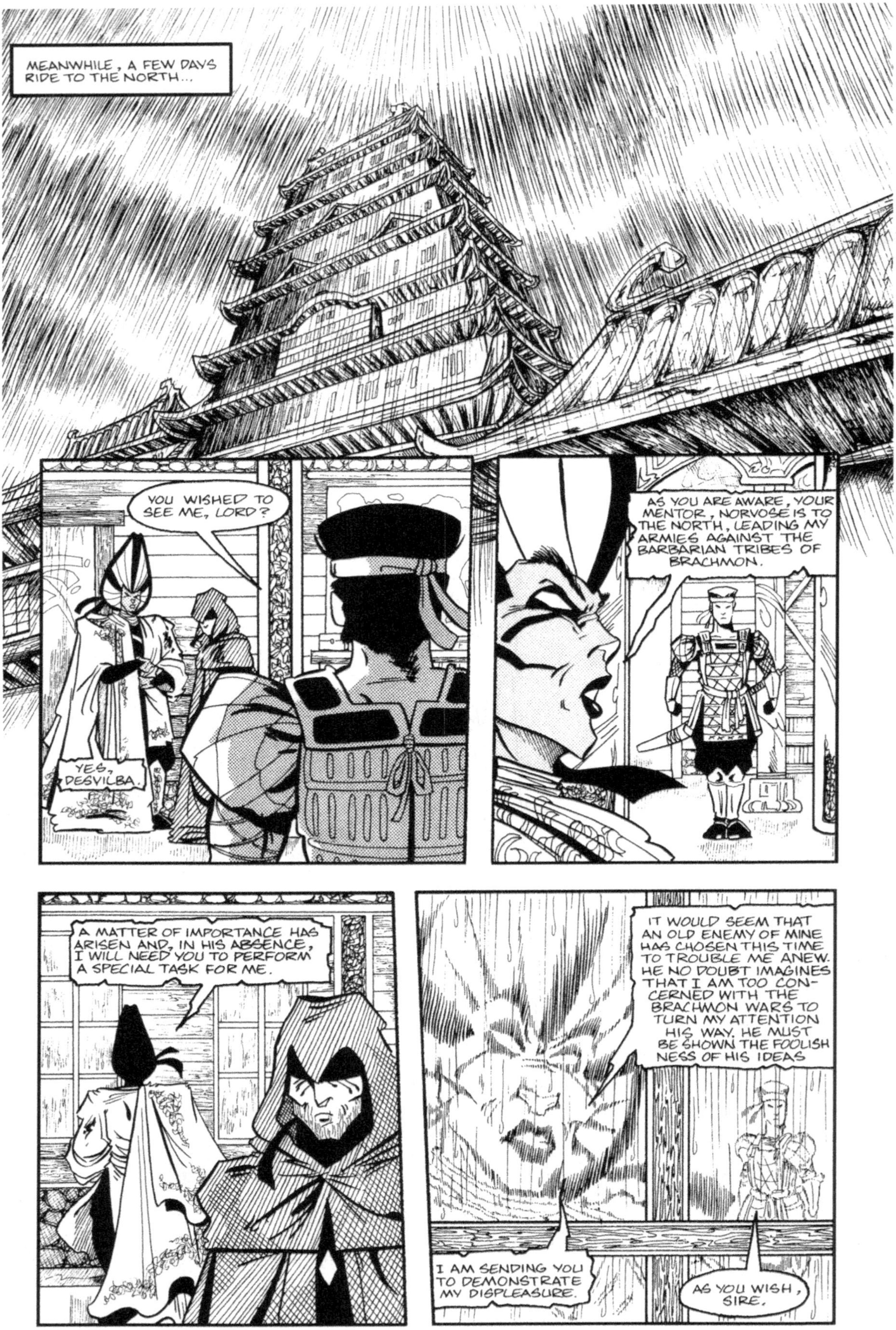
MEANWHILE, A FEW DAYS RIDE TO THE NORTH...
YOU WISHED TO SEE ME, LORD?
YES, DESVILBA.
AS YOU ARE AWARE, YOUR MENTOR, NORVOSE IS TO THE NORTH, LEADING MY ARMIES AGAINST THE BARBARIAN TRIBES OF BRACHMON.
A MATTER OF IMPORTANCE HAS ARISEN AND, IN HIS ABSENCE, I WILL NEED YOU TO PERFORM A SPECIAL TASK FOR ME.
IT WOULD SEEM THAT AN OLD ENEMY OF MINE HAS CHOSEN THIS TIME TO TROUBLE ME ANEW. HE NO DOUBT IMAGINES THAT I AM TOO CON-CERNED WITH THE BRACHMON WARS TO TURN MY ATTENTION HIS WAY. HE MUST BE SHOWN THE FOOLISH NESS OF HIS IDEAS
I AM SENDING YOU TO DEMONSTRATE MY DISPLEASURE.
AS YOU WISH, SIRE.

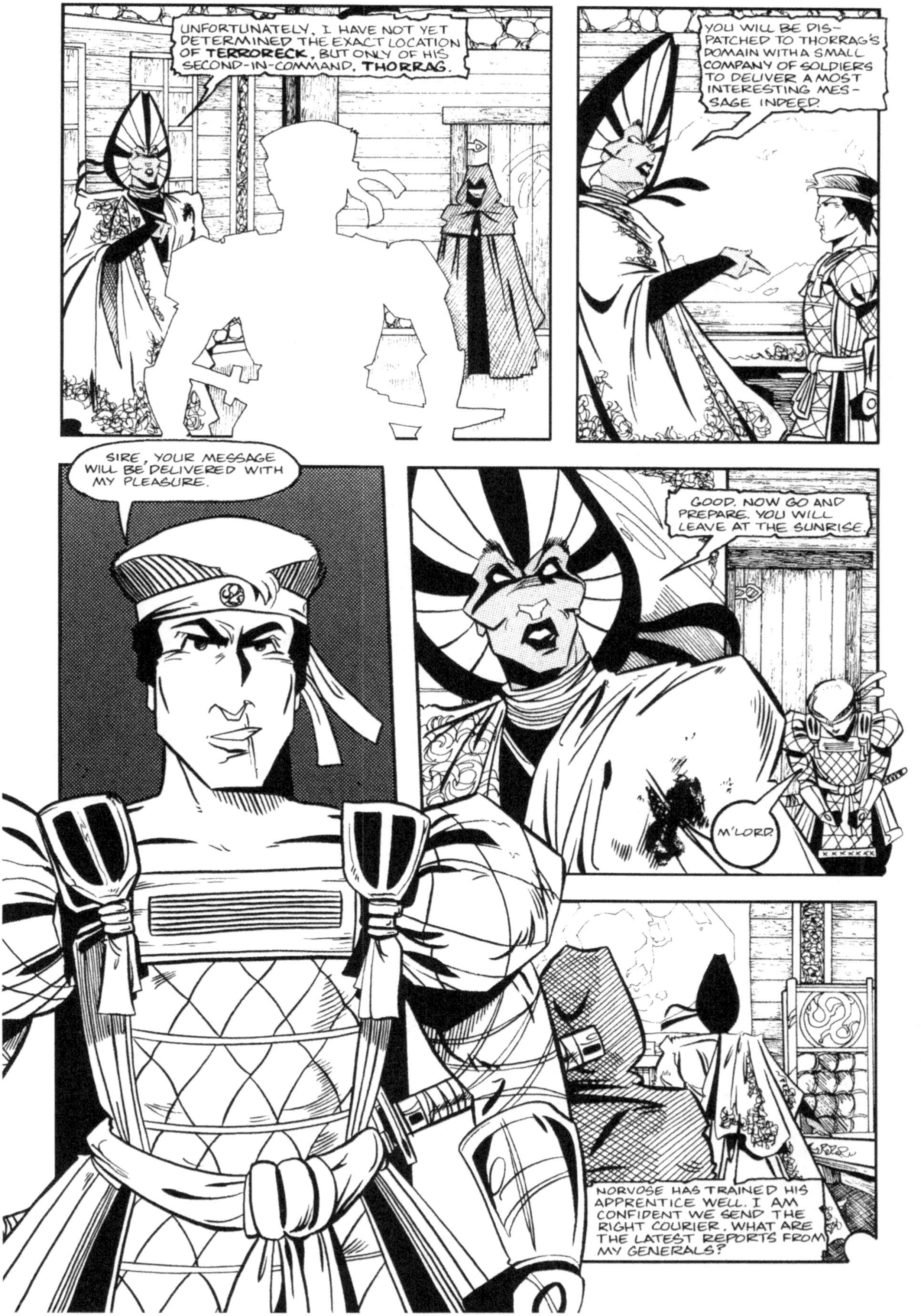
UNFORTUNATELY, I HAVE NOT YET DETERMINED THE EXACT LOCATION OF **TERRORECK**, BUT ONLY OF HIS SECOND-IN-COMMAND, **THORRAG**.
YOU WILL BE DISPATCHED TO THORRAG'S DOMAIN WITH A SMALL COMPANY OF SOLDIERS TO DELIVER A MOST INTERESTING MESSAGE INDEED.
SIRE, YOUR MESSAGE WILL BE DELIVERED WITH MY PLEASURE.
GOOD. NOW GO AND PREPARE. YOU WILL LEAVE AT THE SUNRISE.
M'LORD.
NORVOSE HAS TRAINED HIS APPRENTICE WELL. I AM CONFIDENT WE SEND THE RIGHT COURIER. WHAT ARE THE LATEST REPORTS FROM MY GENERALS?

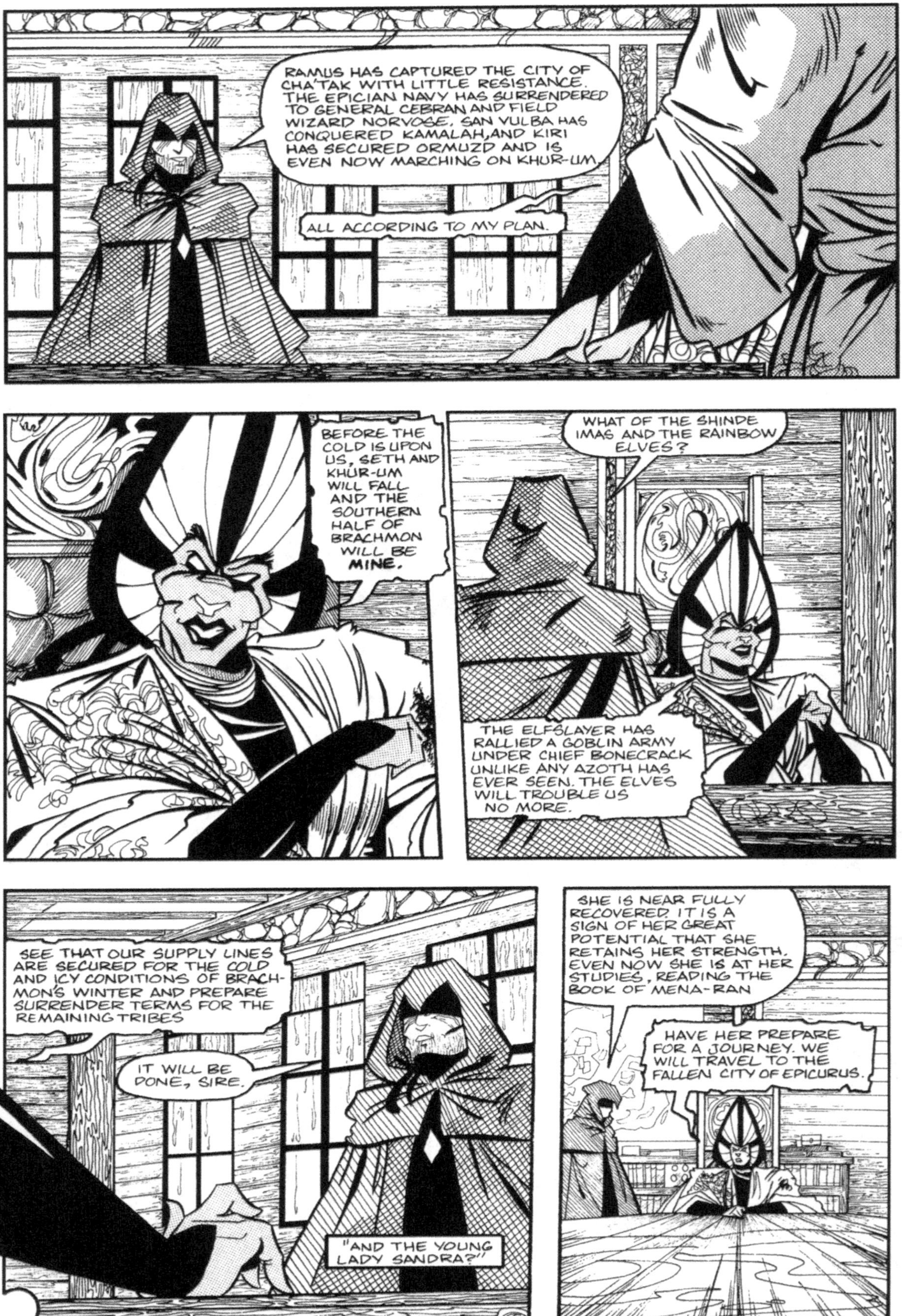
RAMUS HAS CAPTURED THE CITY OF CHA'TAK WITH LITTLE RESISTANCE. THE EPICIAN NAVY HAS SURRENDERED TO GENERAL CEBRAN AND FIELD WIZARD NORVOSE, SAN VULBA HAS CONQUERED KAMALAH, AND KIRI HAS SECURED ORMUZD AND IS EVEN NOW MARCHING ON KHUR-UM.
ALL ACCORDING TO MY PLAN.
BEFORE THE COLD IS UPON US, SETH AND KHUR-UM WILL FALL AND THE SOUTHERN HALF OF BRACHMON WILL BE **MINE.**
WHAT OF THE SHINDE IMAS AND THE RAINBOW ELVES?
THE ELFSLAYER HAS RALLIED A GOBLIN ARMY UNDER CHIEF BONECRACK UNLIKE ANY AZOTH HAS EVER SEEN. THE ELVES WILL TROUBLE US NO MORE.
SEE THAT OUR SUPPLY LINES ARE SECURED FOR THE COLD AND ICY CONDITIONS OF BRACHMON'S WINTER AND PREPARE SURRENDER TERMS FOR THE REMAINING TRIBES
IT WILL BE DONE, SIRE.
"AND THE YOUNG LADY SANDRA?"
SHE IS NEAR FULLY RECOVERED. IT IS A SIGN OF HER GREAT POTENTIAL THAT SHE RETAINS HER STRENGTH. EVEN NOW SHE IS AT HER STUDIES, READING THE BOOK OF MENA-RAN
HAVE HER PREPARE FOR A JOURNEY. WE WILL TRAVEL TO THE FALLEN CITY OF EPICURUS.

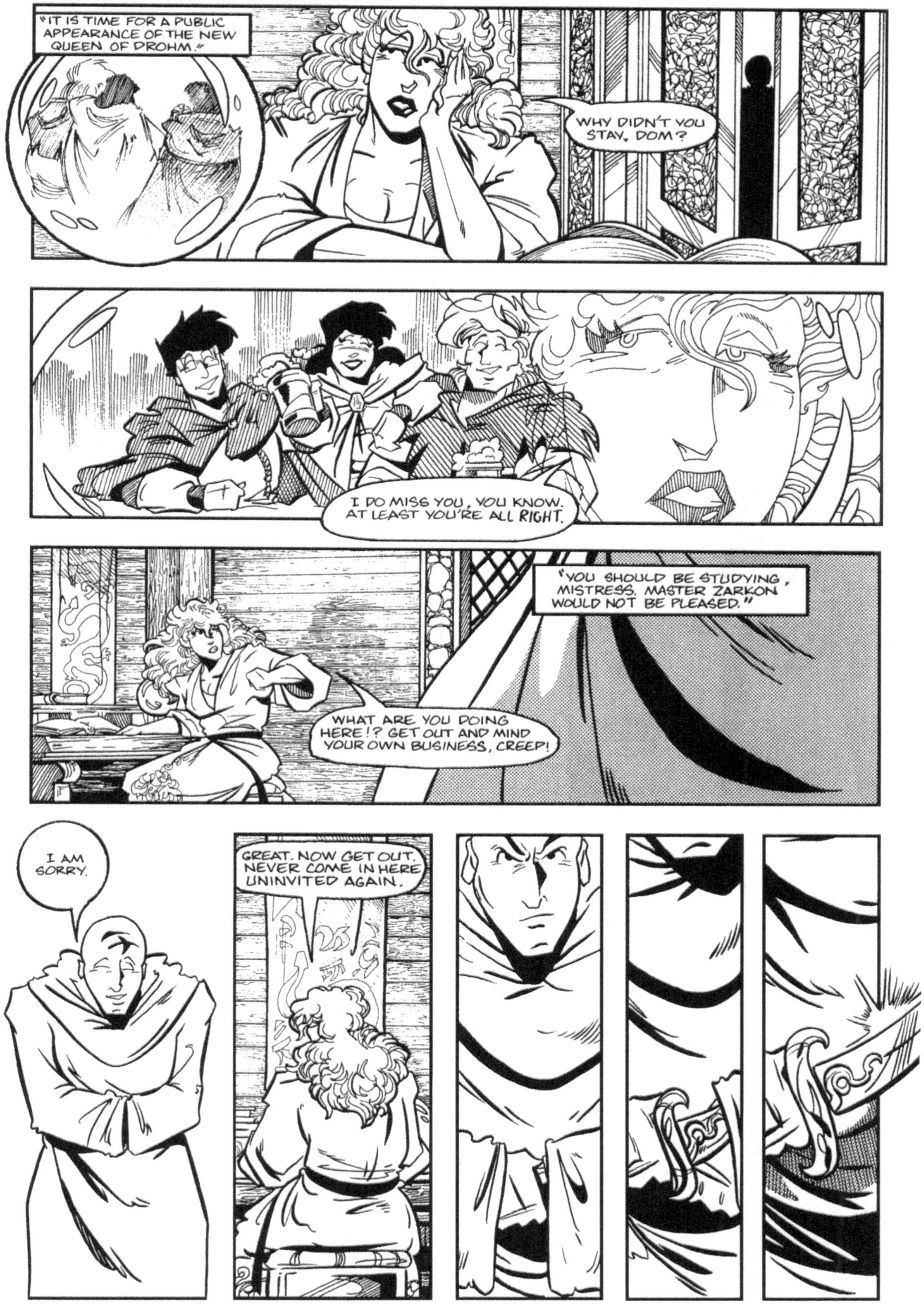
"IT IS TIME FOR A PUBLIC APPEARANCE OF THE NEW QUEEN OF DROHM."
WHY DIDN'T YOU STAY, DOM?
I DO MISS YOU, YOU KNOW. AT LEAST YOU'RE ALL RIGHT.
"YOU SHOULD BE STUDYING, MISTRESS. MASTER ZARKON WOULD NOT BE PLEASED."
WHAT ARE YOU DOING HERE!? GET OUT AND MIND YOUR OWN BUSINESS, CREEP!
I AM SORRY.
GREAT. NOW GET OUT. NEVER COME IN HERE UNINVITED AGAIN.

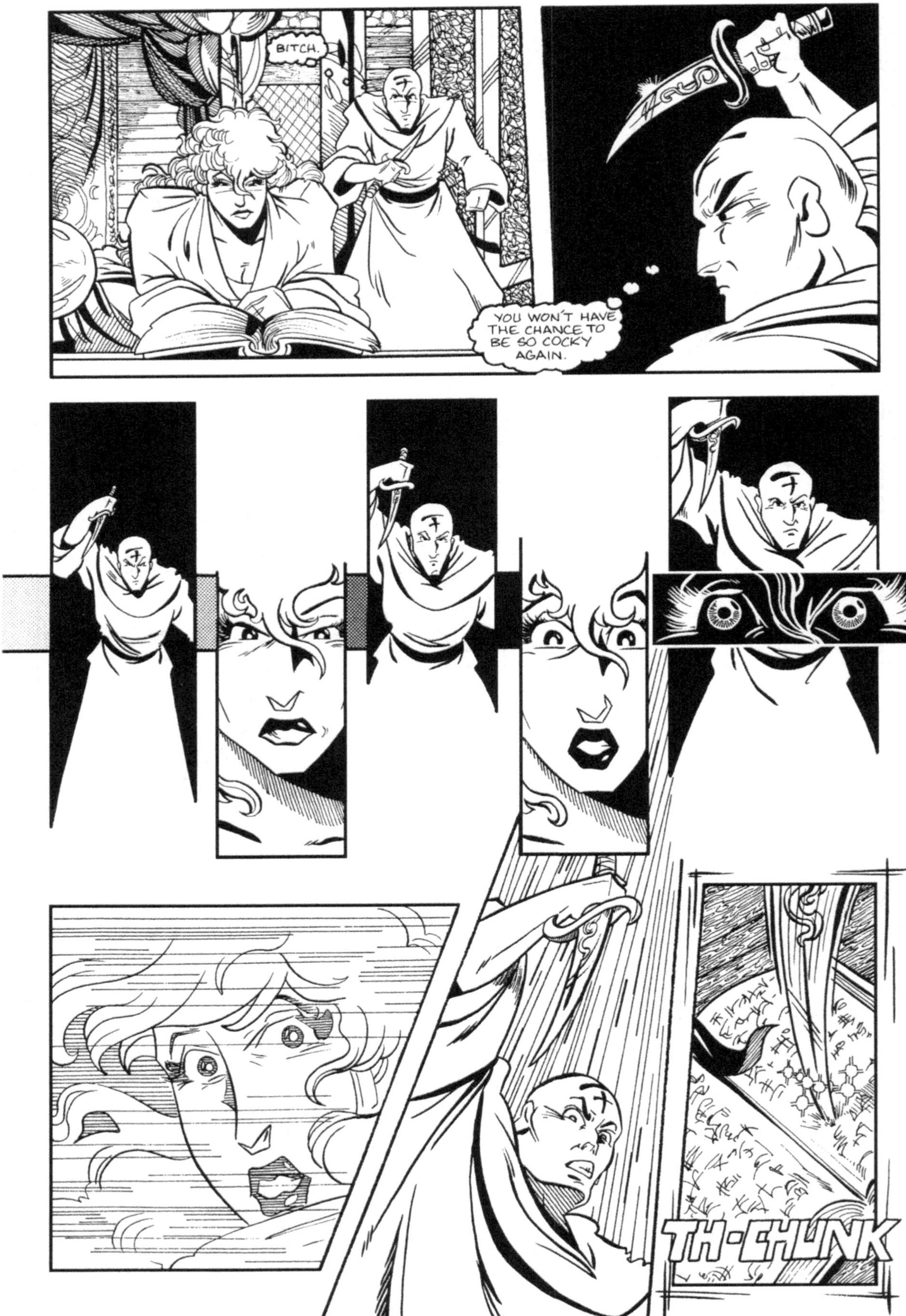
BITCH.
YOU WON'T HAVE THE CHANCE TO BE SO COCKY AGAIN.
TH-CHUNK

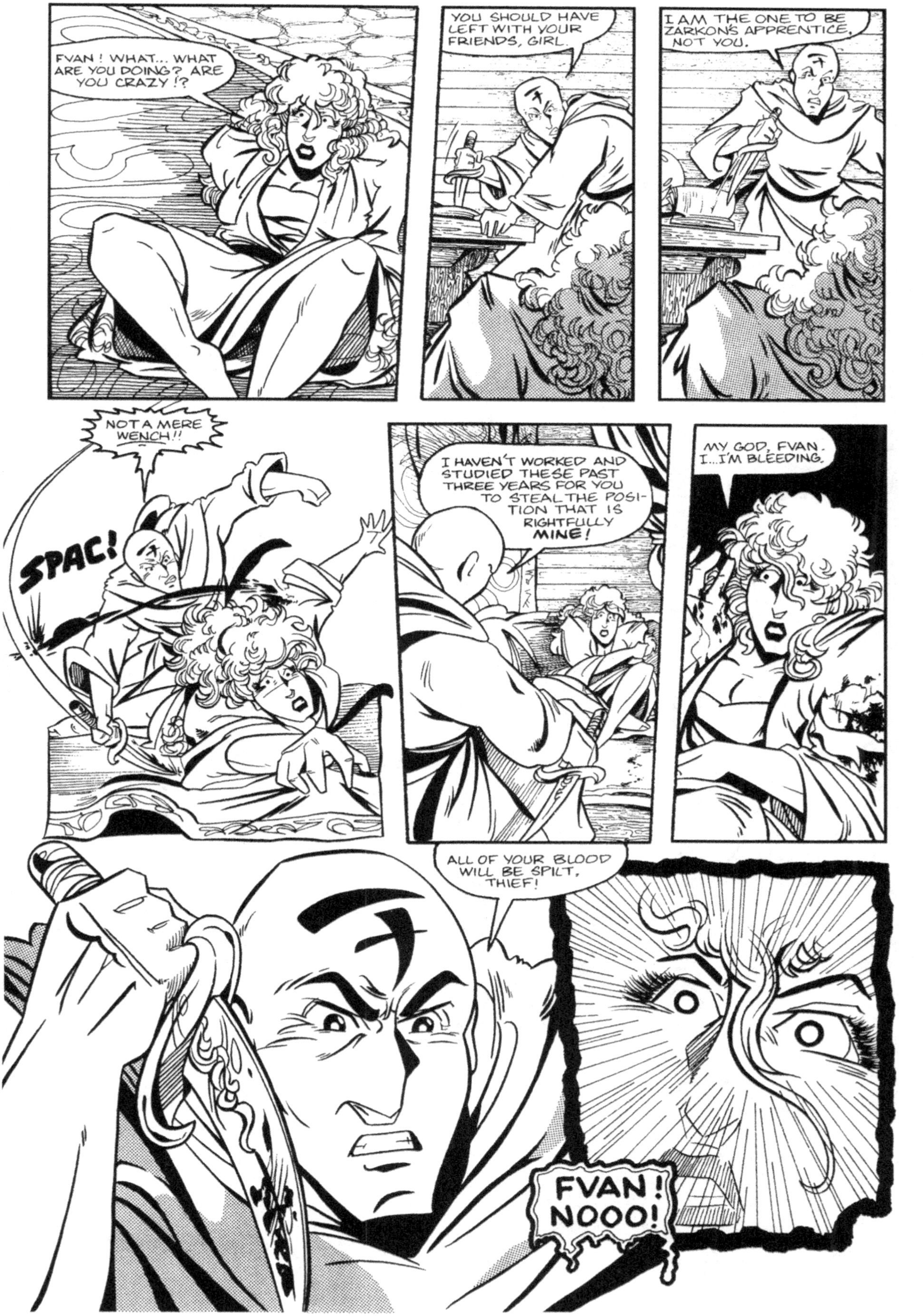
FVAN! WHAT... WHAT ARE YOU DOING? ARE YOU CRAZY!?
YOU SHOULD HAVE LEFT WITH YOUR FRIENDS, GIRL.
I AM THE ONE TO BE ZARKON'S APPRENTICE, NOT YOU.
NOT A MERE WENCH!!
SPAC!
I HAVEN'T WORKED AND STUDIED THESE PAST THREE YEARS FOR YOU TO STEAL THE POSITION THAT IS RIGHTFULLY MINE!
MY GOD, FVAN. I...I'M BLEEDING.
ALL OF YOUR BLOOD WILL BE SPILT, THIEF!
FVAN! NOOO!

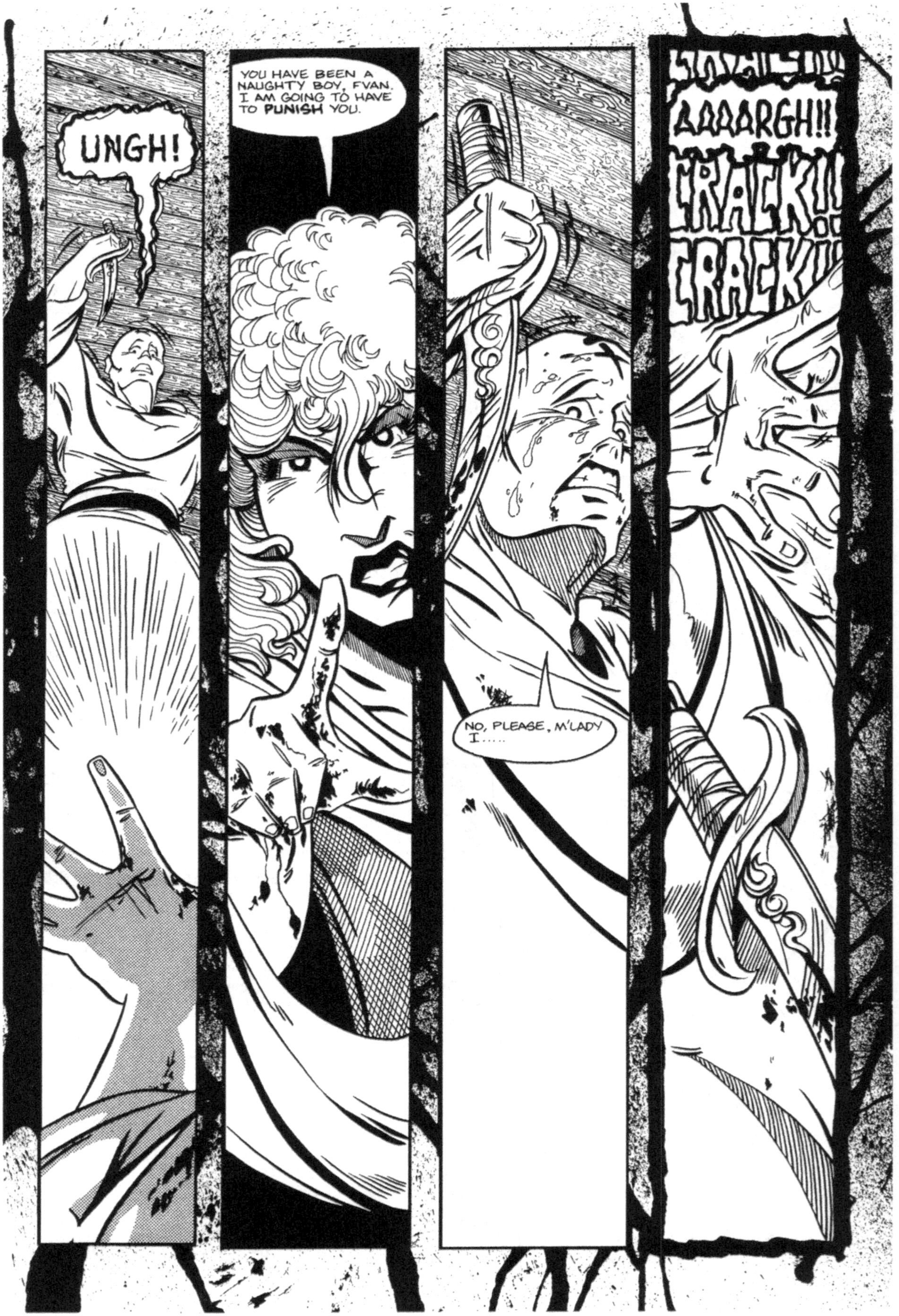
UNGH!
YOU HAVE BEEN A NAUGHTY BOY, FVAN. I AM GOING TO HAVE TO PUNISH YOU.
NO, PLEASE, M'LADY I.....
AAAARGH!!
CRACK!!
CRACK!!

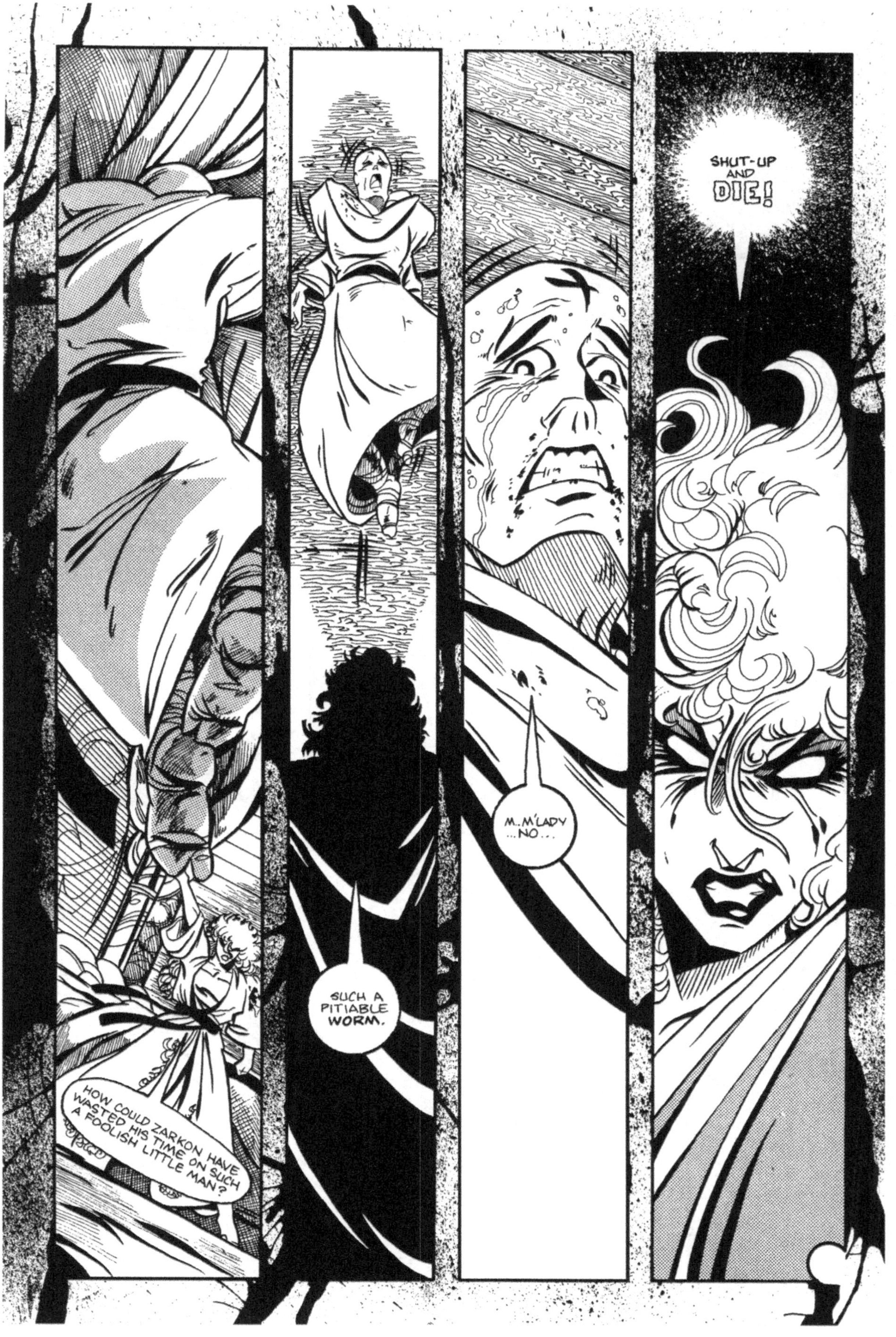
HOW COULD ZARKON HAVE WASTED HIS TIME ON SUCH A FOOLISH LITTLE MAN?
SUCH A PITIABLE WORM.
M..M'LADY ...NO...
SHUT-UP AND DIE!

DEEP WITHIN THE BOWELS OF CASTLE DARKOTH, THERE IS A CAVERN KNOWN TO BUT A VERY FEW OF THE DARK ONE'S FOLLOWERS. IT IS HERE THAT THE MYRIAD FORCES OF MAGIC IN AZOTH ARE MONITORED.

THE PERCEIVERS ARE CALM.

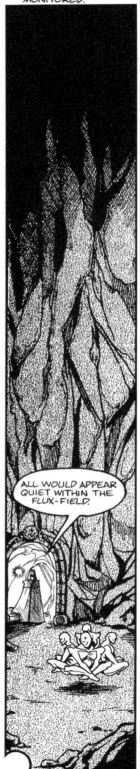

ALL WOULD APPEAR QUIET WITHIN THE FLUX-FIELD.

WHAT?!

AN ENERGY BURST WITHIN THE CASTLE WALLS!

MASTER ZARKON! THERE IS TROUBLE IN LADY SANDRA'S QUARTERS!

NO!

NOTHING MUST BEFALL MY NEW APPRENTICE.

TOOOM

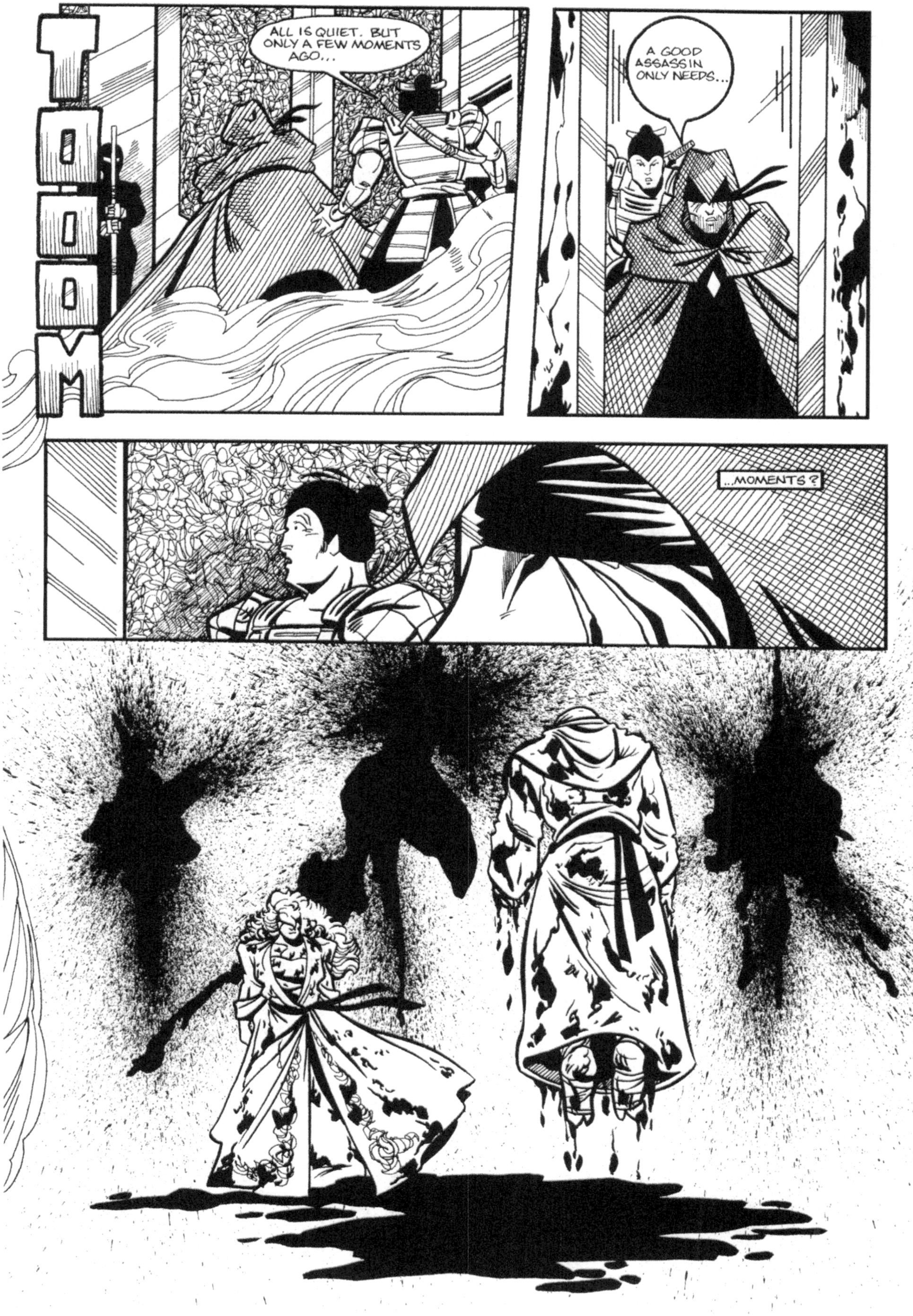

TOOOM
ALL IS QUIET. BUT ONLY A FEW MOMENTS AGO...
A GOOD ASSASSIN ONLY NEEDS...
...MOMENTS?

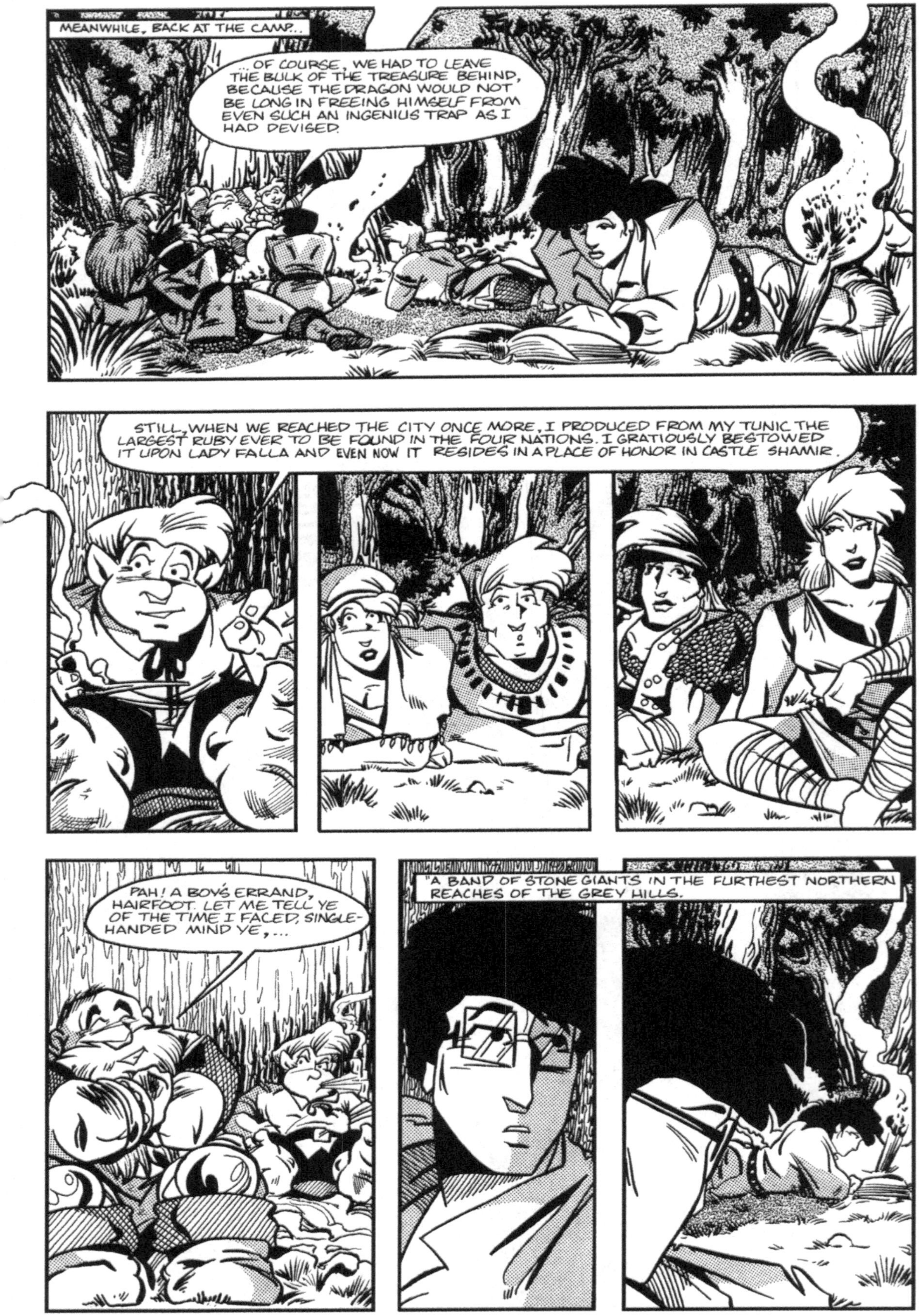

MEANWHILE, BACK AT THE CAMP...
...OF COURSE, WE HAD TO LEAVE THE BULK OF THE TREASURE BEHIND, BECAUSE THE DRAGON WOULD NOT BE LONG IN FREEING HIMSELF FROM EVEN SUCH AN INGENIUS TRAP AS I HAD DEVISED.
STILL, WHEN WE REACHED THE CITY ONCE MORE, I PRODUCED FROM MY TUNIC THE LARGEST RUBY EVER TO BE FOUND IN THE FOUR NATIONS. I GRATIOUSLY BESTOWED IT UPON LADY FALLA AND EVEN NOW IT RESIDES IN A PLACE OF HONOR IN CASTLE SHAMIR.
PAH! A BOY'S ERRAND, HAIRFOOT. LET ME TELL YE OF THE TIME I FACED, SINGLE-HANDED MIND YE,...
"A BAND OF STONE GIANTS IN THE FURTHEST NORTHERN REACHES OF THE GREY HILLS.

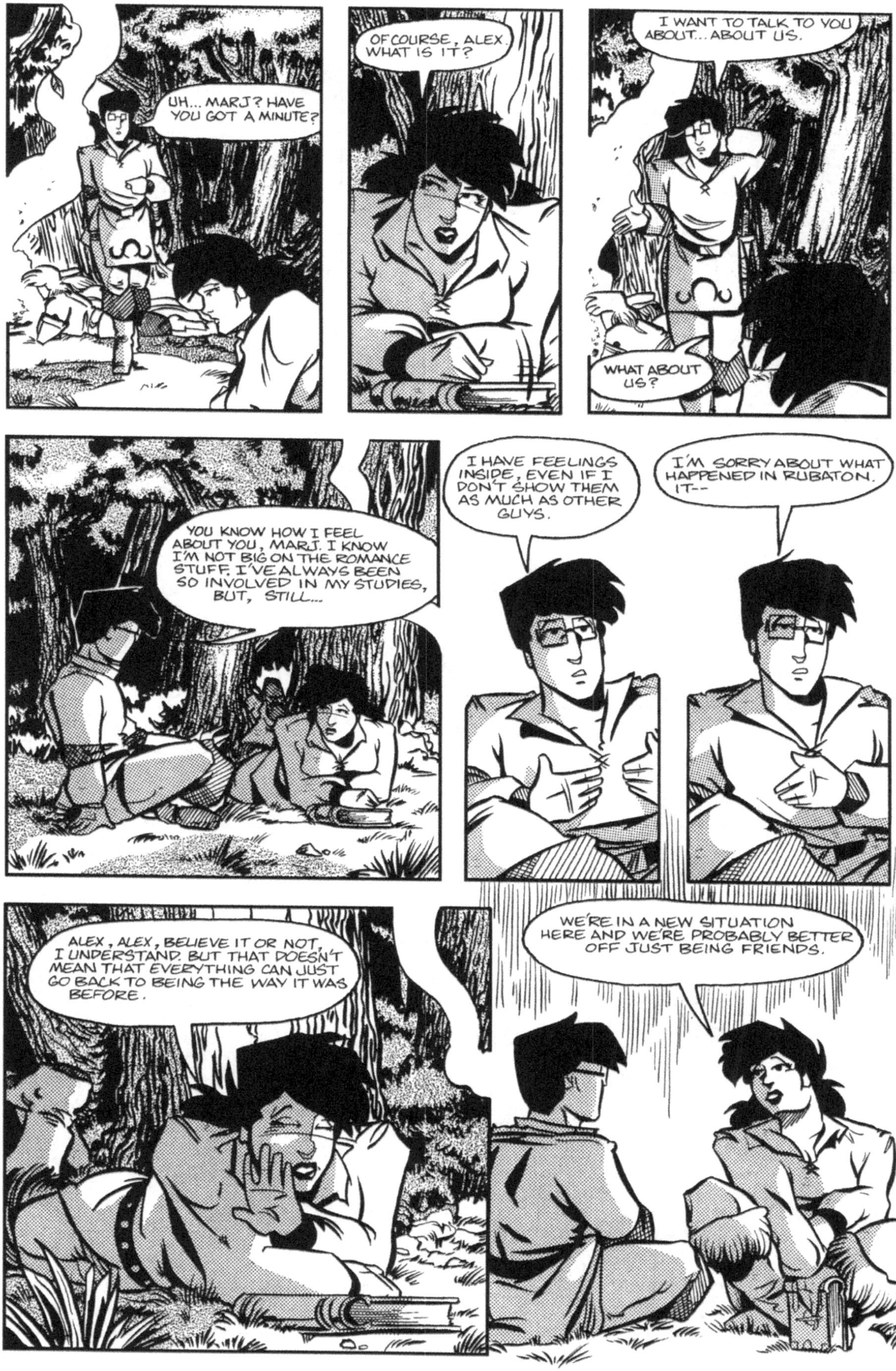
UH... MARJ? HAVE YOU GOT A MINUTE?
OF COURSE, ALEX. WHAT IS IT?
I WANT TO TALK TO YOU ABOUT... ABOUT US.
WHAT ABOUT US?
YOU KNOW HOW I FEEL ABOUT YOU, MARJ. I KNOW I'M NOT BIG ON THE ROMANCE STUFF. I'VE ALWAYS BEEN SO INVOLVED IN MY STUDIES, BUT, STILL...
I HAVE FEELINGS INSIDE, EVEN IF I DON'T SHOW THEM AS MUCH AS OTHER GUYS.
I'M SORRY ABOUT WHAT HAPPENED IN RUBATON. IT--
ALEX, ALEX, BELIEVE IT OR NOT, I UNDERSTAND. BUT THAT DOESN'T MEAN THAT EVERYTHING CAN JUST GO BACK TO BEING THE WAY IT WAS BEFORE.
WE'RE IN A NEW SITUATION HERE AND WE'RE PROBABLY BETTER OFF JUST BEING FRIENDS.

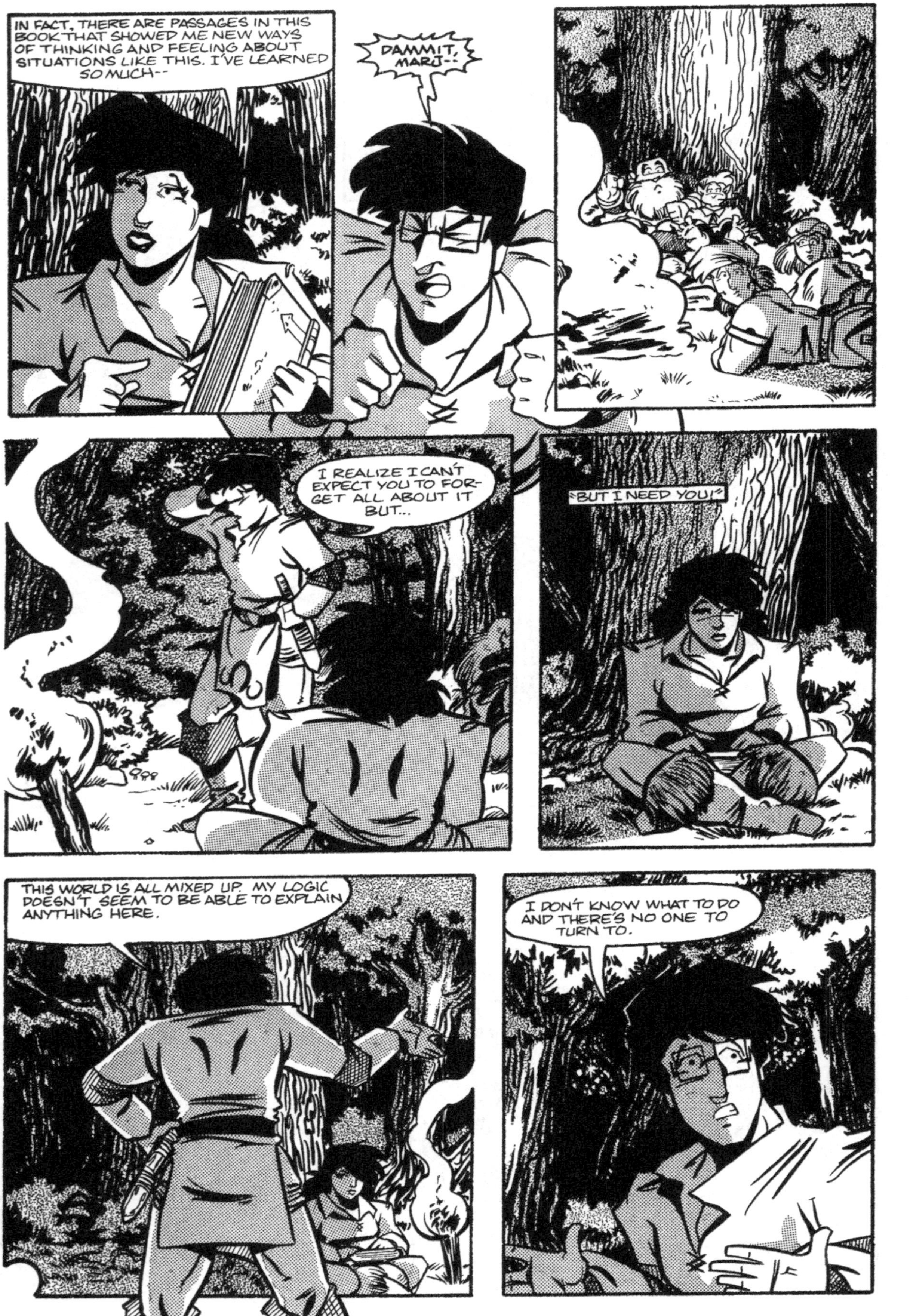
IN FACT, THERE ARE PASSAGES IN THIS BOOK THAT SHOWED ME NEW WAYS OF THINKING AND FEELING ABOUT SITUATIONS LIKE THIS. I'VE LEARNED SO MUCH--
DAMMIT, MARJ--
I REALIZE I CAN'T EXPECT YOU TO FOR-GET ALL ABOUT IT BUT...
"BUT I NEED YOU!"
THIS WORLD IS ALL MIXED UP. MY LOGIC DOESN'T SEEM TO BE ABLE TO EXPLAIN ANYTHING HERE.
I DON'T KNOW WHAT TO DO AND THERE'S NO ONE TO TURN TO.

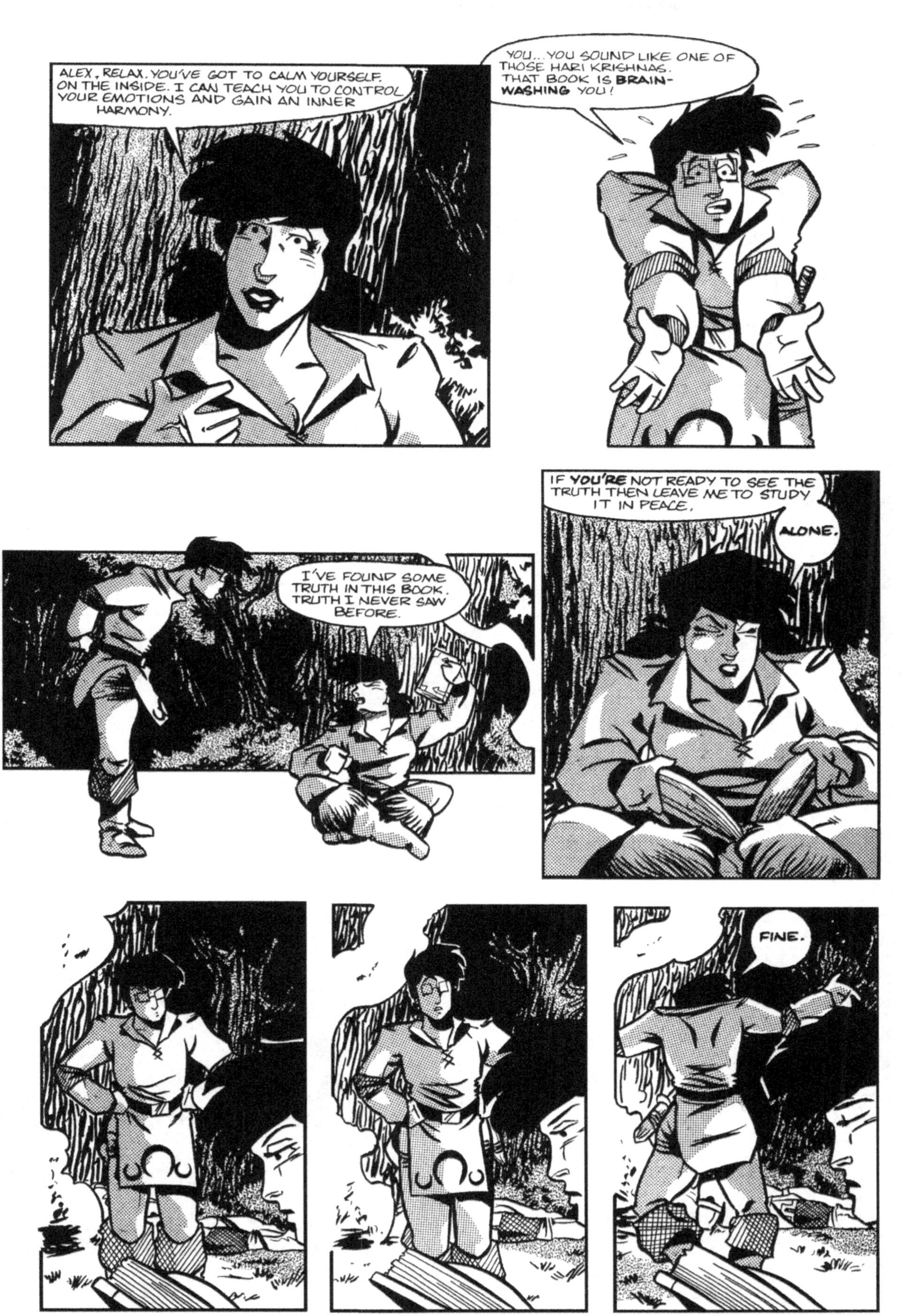
ALEX, RELAX. YOU'VE GOT TO CALM YOURSELF. ON THE INSIDE. I CAN TEACH YOU TO CONTROL YOUR EMOTIONS AND GAIN AN INNER HARMONY.
YOU... YOU SOUND LIKE ONE OF THOSE HARI KRISHNAS. THAT BOOK IS BRAIN-WASHING YOU!
I'VE FOUND SOME TRUTH IN THIS BOOK. TRUTH I NEVER SAW BEFORE.
IF YOU'RE NOT READY TO SEE THE TRUTH THEN LEAVE ME TO STUDY IT IN PEACE.
ALONE.
FINE.

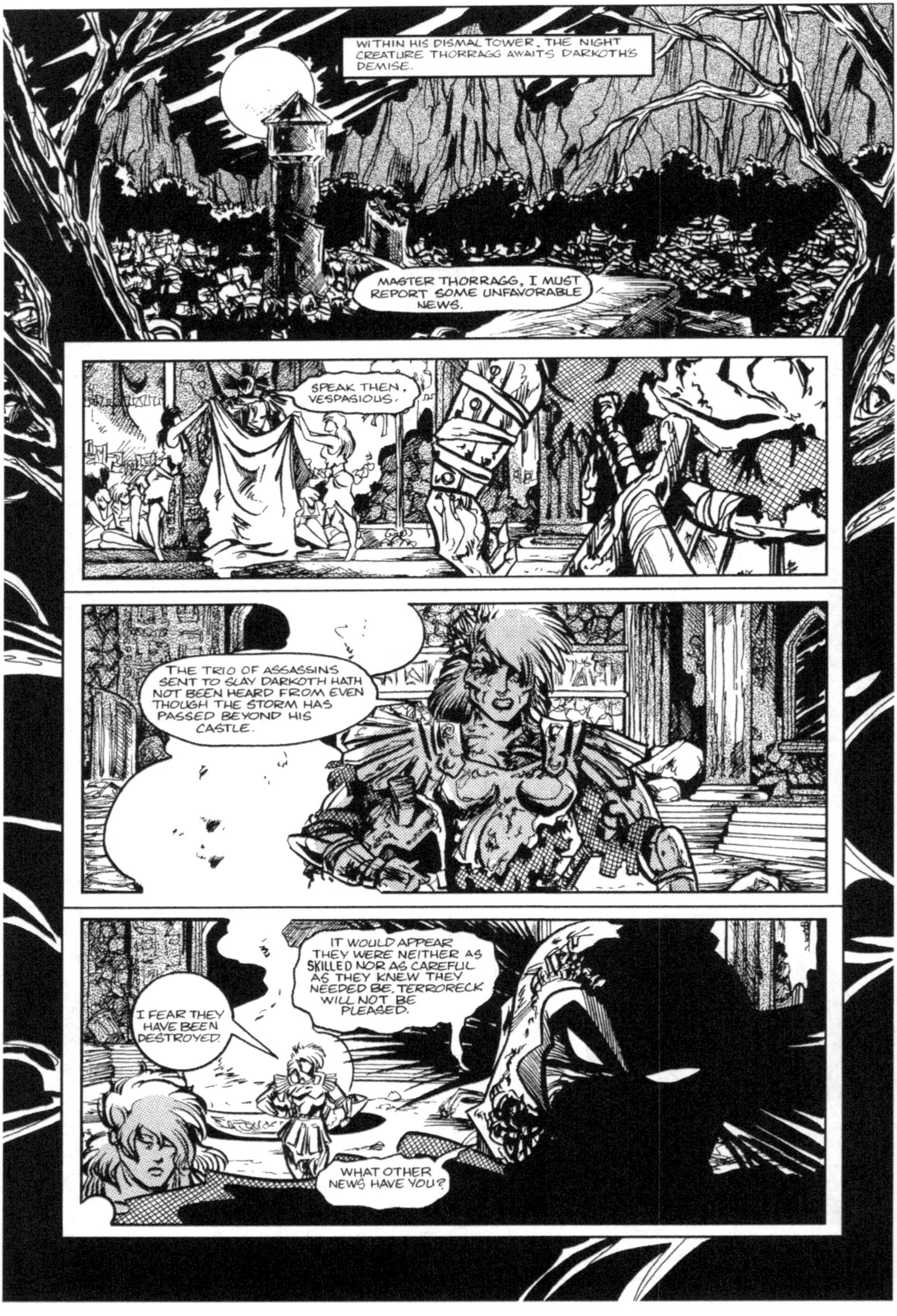
WITHIN HIS DISMAL TOWER, THE NIGHT CREATURE THORRAGG AWAITS DARKOTH'S DEMISE.
MASTER THORRAGG, I MUST REPORT SOME UNFAVORABLE NEWS.
SPEAK THEN, VESPASIOUS.
THE TRIO OF ASSASSINS SENT TO SLAY DARKOTH HATH NOT BEEN HEARD FROM EVEN THOUGH THE STORM HAS PASSED BEYOND HIS CASTLE.
I FEAR THEY HAVE BEEN DESTROYED.
IT WOULD APPEAR THEY WERE NEITHER AS SKILLED NOR AS CAREFUL AS THEY KNEW THEY NEEDED BE. TERRORECK WILL NOT BE PLEASED.
WHAT OTHER NEWS HAVE YOU?

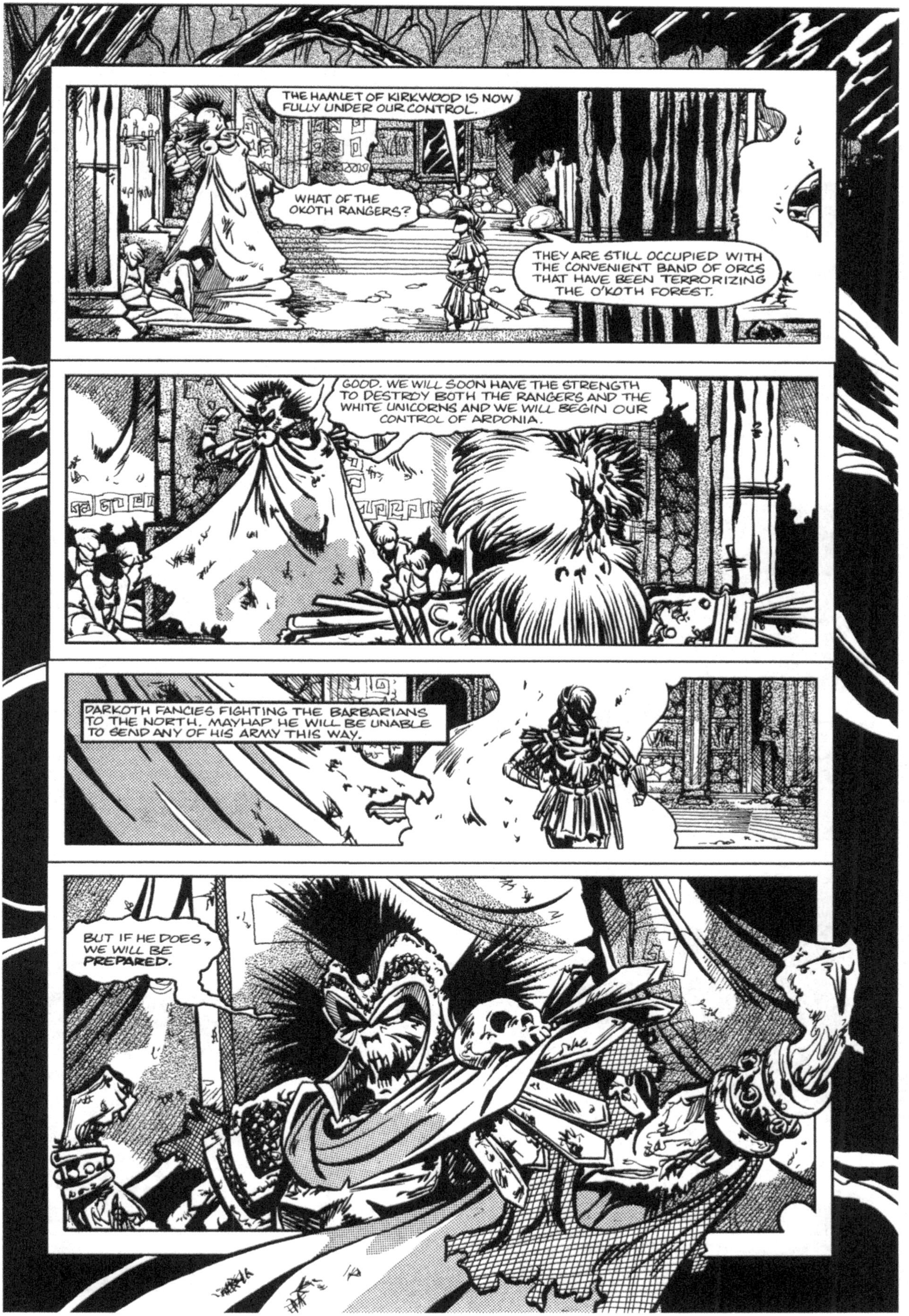
THE HAMLET OF KIRKWOOD IS NOW FULLY UNDER OUR CONTROL.
WHAT OF THE OKOTH RANGERS?
THEY ARE STILL OCCUPIED WITH THE CONVENIENT BAND OF ORCS THAT HAVE BEEN TERRORIZING THE O'KOTH FOREST.
GOOD. WE WILL SOON HAVE THE STRENGTH TO DESTROY BOTH THE RANGERS AND THE WHITE UNICORNS AND WE WILL BEGIN OUR CONTROL OF ARDONIA.
DARKOTH FANCIES FIGHTING THE BARBARIANS TO THE NORTH. MAYHAP HE WILL BE UNABLE TO SEND ANY OF HIS ARMY THIS WAY.
BUT IF HE DOES, WE WILL BE **PREPARED**.

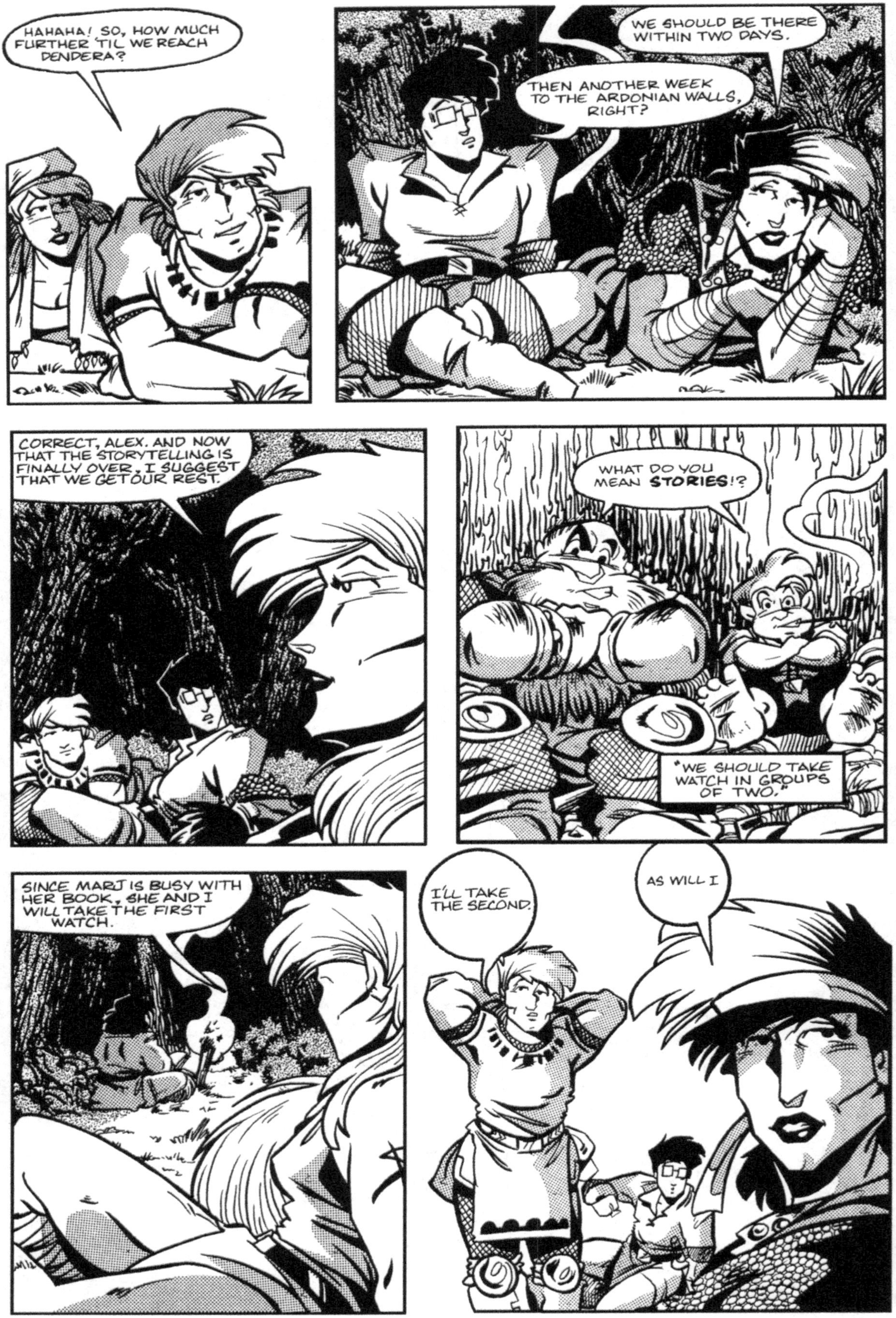

HAHAHA! SO, HOW MUCH FURTHER 'TIL WE REACH DENDERA?
WE SHOULD BE THERE WITHIN TWO DAYS.
THEN ANOTHER WEEK TO THE ARDONIAN WALLS, RIGHT?
CORRECT, ALEX. AND NOW THAT THE STORYTELLING IS FINALLY OVER, I SUGGEST THAT WE GET OUR REST.
WHAT DO YOU MEAN STORIES!?
"WE SHOULD TAKE WATCH IN GROUPS OF TWO."
SINCE MARJ IS BUSY WITH HER BOOK, SHE AND I WILL TAKE THE FIRST WATCH.
I'LL TAKE THE SECOND.
AS WILL I

I GUESS THAT LEAVES OL' GRUMPY AND I TO TAKE THE LAST.

WATCH WHO YER CALLIN' *OLD*.

WITHOUT OUR SUPPLIES THE NIGHT WILL BE RESTLESS.

PAH! 'TIS A BABY'S CRADLE COMPARED TO THE NIGHT I SPENT IN THE SWAMPS OF DARKNESS...

I GUESS THEY DON'T TRUST ME AFTER THE INCIDENT WITH THE BANDITS.* WHAT'S HAPPENED TO ME? I'M THE MOST USELESS MEMBER OF THE GROUP.

*ALEX FELL ASLEEP ON HIS LAST WATCH BACK IN ISSUE #2 --STU.

I'VE SURE TURNED INTO SOME 'GREAT MAGICIAN'. EVEN **MARI** IS MORE POWERFUL THAN I AM.

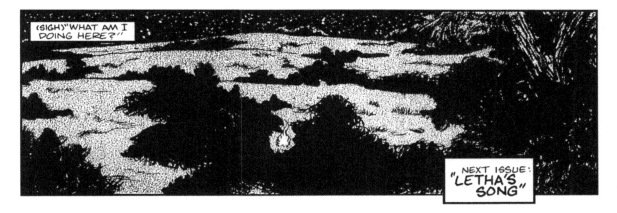

(SIGH) "WHAT AM I DOING HERE?"

NEXT ISSUE: "LETHA'S SONG"

LEGENDLORE

THE REALM - VOLUME ONE

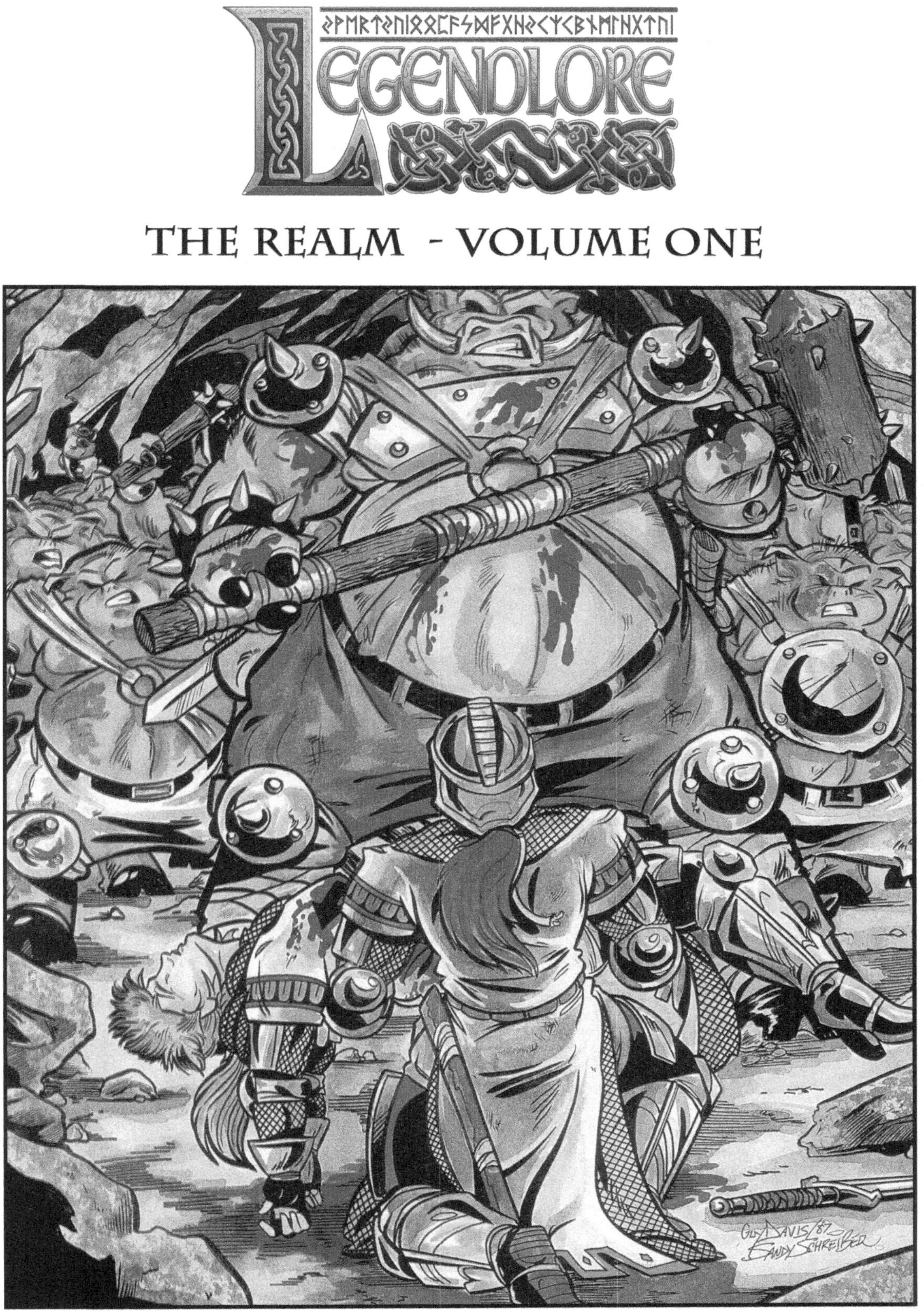

GUY DAVIS/87
SANDY SCHREIBER

ISSUE NINE

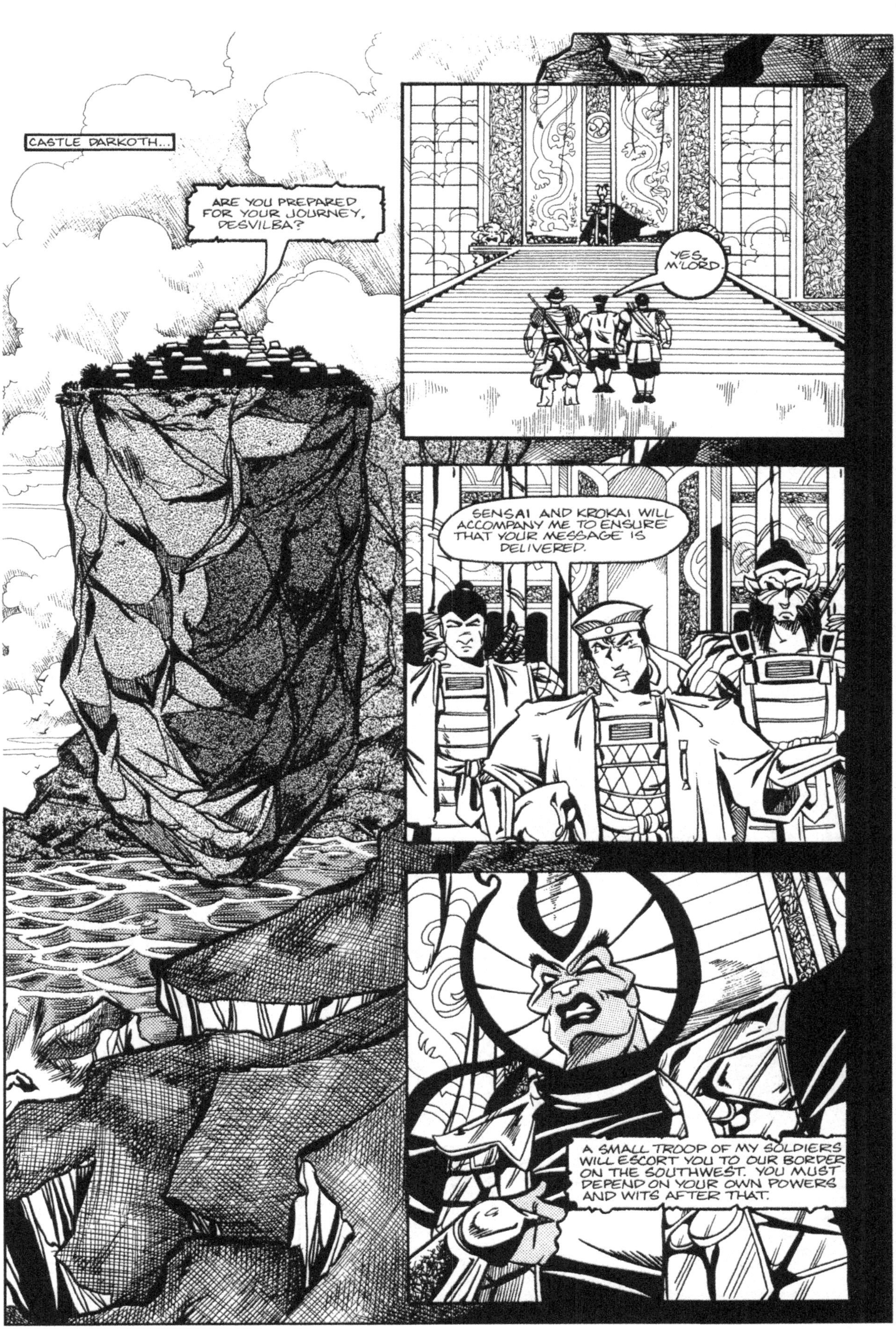
CASTLE DARKOTH...
ARE YOU PREPARED FOR YOUR JOURNEY, DESVILBA?
YES, M'LORD.
SENSAI AND KROKAI WILL ACCOMPANY ME TO ENSURE THAT YOUR MESSAGE IS DELIVERED.
A SMALL TROOP OF MY SOLDIERS WILL ESCORT YOU TO OUR BORDER ON THE SOUTHWEST. YOU MUST DEPEND ON YOUR OWN POWERS AND WITS AFTER THAT.

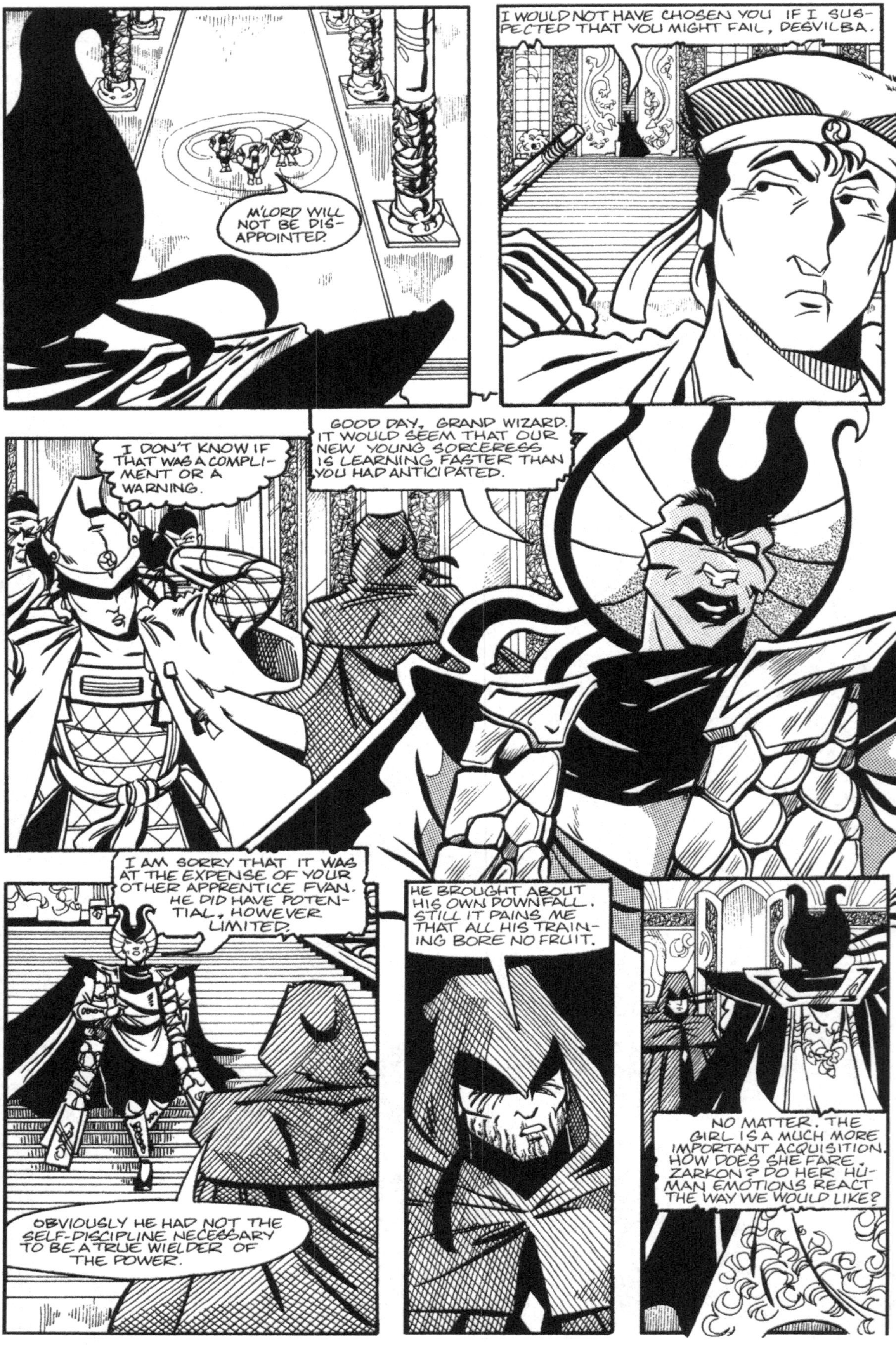
M'LORD WILL NOT BE DISAPPOINTED.
I WOULD NOT HAVE CHOSEN YOU IF I SUSPECTED THAT YOU MIGHT FAIL, DESVILBA.
I DON'T KNOW IF THAT WAS A COMPLIMENT OR A WARNING.
GOOD DAY, GRAND WIZARD. IT WOULD SEEM THAT OUR NEW YOUNG SORCERESS IS LEARNING FASTER THAN YOU HAD ANTICIPATED.
I AM SORRY THAT IT WAS AT THE EXPENSE OF YOUR OTHER APPRENTICE FVAN. HE DID HAVE POTENTIAL, HOWEVER LIMITED.
OBVIOUSLY HE HAD NOT THE SELF-DISCIPLINE NECESSARY TO BE A TRUE WIELDER OF THE POWER.
HE BROUGHT ABOUT HIS OWN DOWNFALL. STILL IT PAINS ME THAT ALL HIS TRAINING BORE NO FRUIT.
NO MATTER. THE GIRL IS A MUCH MORE IMPORTANT ACQUISITION. HOW DOES SHE FARE, ZARKON? DO HER HUMAN EMOTIONS REACT THE WAY WE WOULD LIKE?

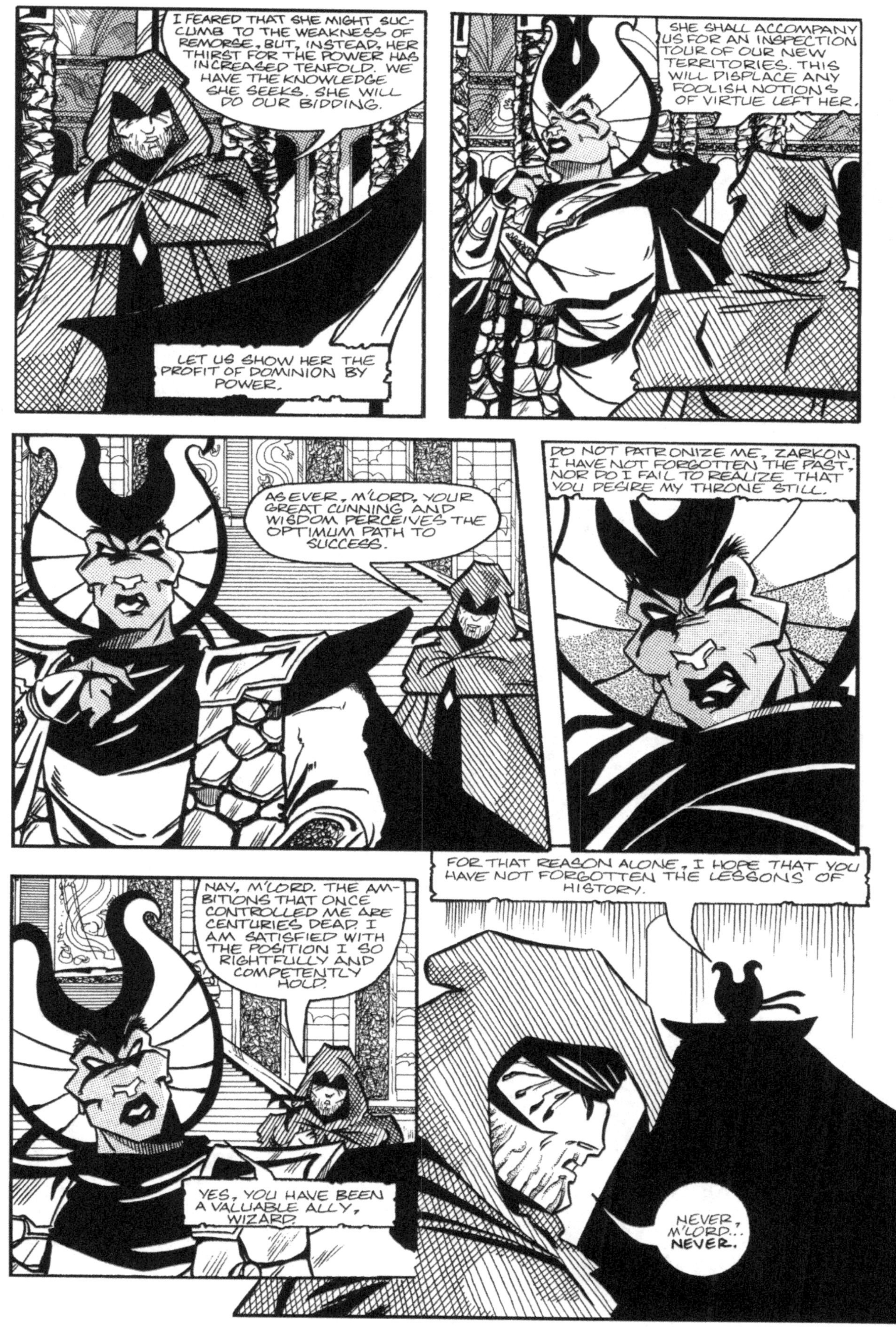
I FEARED THAT SHE MIGHT SUCCUMB TO THE WEAKNESS OF REMORSE, BUT, INSTEAD, HER THIRST FOR THE POWER HAS INCREASED TENFOLD. WE HAVE THE KNOWLEDGE SHE SEEKS. SHE WILL DO OUR BIDDING.
LET US SHOW HER THE PROFIT OF DOMINION BY POWER.
SHE SHALL ACCOMPANY US FOR AN INSPECTION TOUR OF OUR NEW TERRITORIES. THIS WILL DISPLACE ANY FOOLISH NOTIONS OF VIRTUE LEFT HER.
AS EVER, M'LORD, YOUR GREAT CUNNING AND WISDOM PERCEIVES THE OPTIMUM PATH TO SUCCESS.
DO NOT PATRONIZE ME, ZARKON. I HAVE NOT FORGOTTEN THE PAST, NOR DO I FAIL TO REALIZE THAT YOU DESIRE MY THRONE STILL.
FOR THAT REASON ALONE, I HOPE THAT YOU HAVE NOT FORGOTTEN THE LESSONS OF HISTORY.
NAY, M'LORD. THE AMBITIONS THAT ONCE CONTROLLED ME ARE CENTURIES DEAD. I AM SATISFIED WITH THE POSITION I SO RIGHTFULLY AND COMPETENTLY HOLD.
YES, YOU HAVE BEEN A VALUABLE ALLY, WIZARD.
NEVER, M'LORD... **NEVER.**

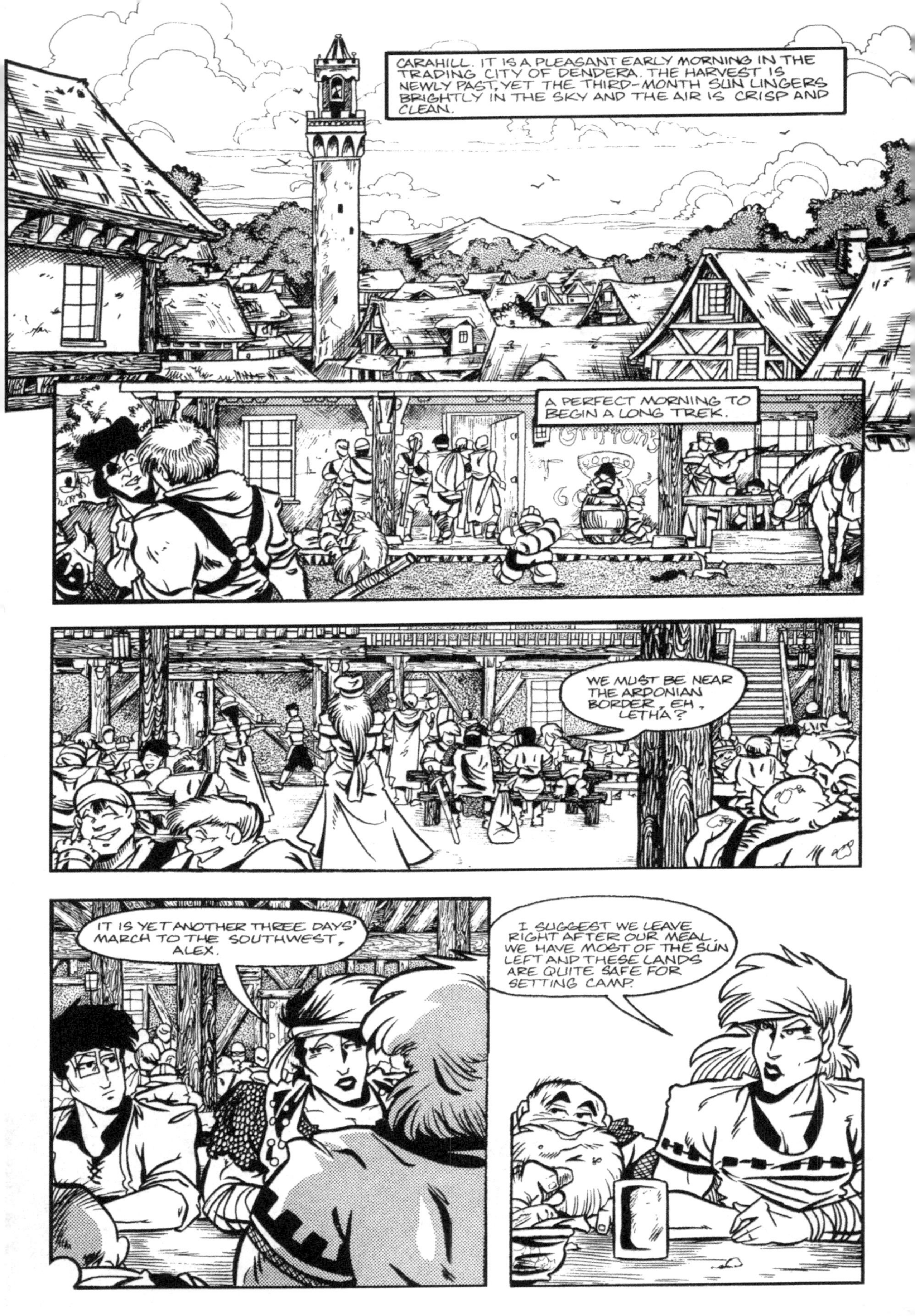
CARAHILL. IT IS A PLEASANT EARLY MORNING IN THE TRADING CITY OF DENDERA. THE HARVEST IS NEWLY PAST, YET THE THIRD-MONTH SUN LINGERS BRIGHTLY IN THE SKY AND THE AIR IS CRISP AND CLEAN.
A PERFECT MORNING TO BEGIN A LONG TREK.
WE MUST BE NEAR THE ARDONIAN BORDER, EH, LETHA?
IT IS YET ANOTHER THREE DAYS' MARCH TO THE SOUTHWEST, ALEX.
I SUGGEST WE LEAVE RIGHT AFTER OUR MEAL. WE HAVE MOST OF THE SUN LEFT AND THESE LANDS ARE QUITE SAFE FOR SETTING CAMP.

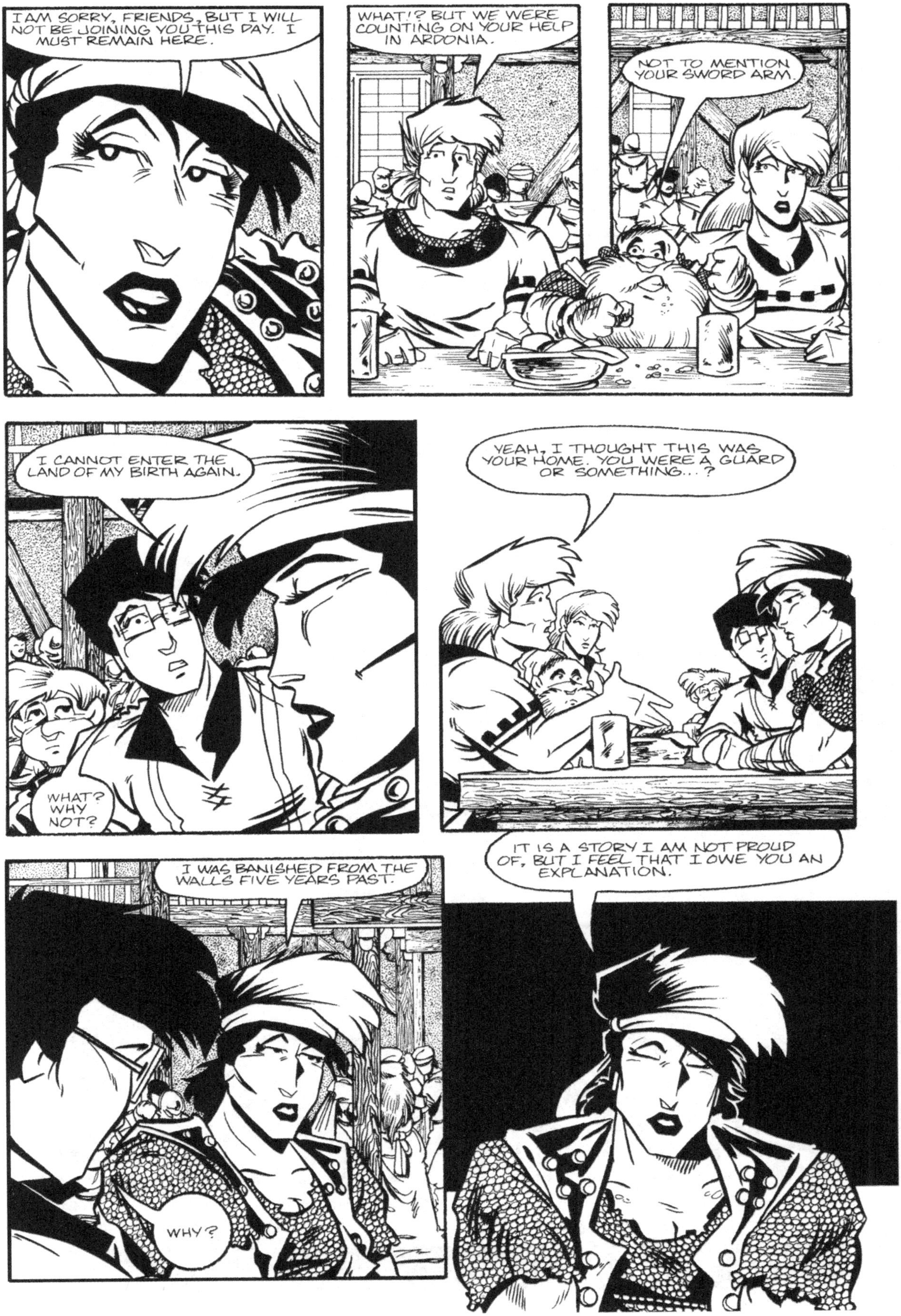
I AM SORRY, FRIENDS, BUT I WILL NOT BE JOINING YOU THIS DAY. I MUST REMAIN HERE.
WHAT!? BUT WE WERE COUNTING ON YOUR HELP IN ARDONIA.
NOT TO MENTION YOUR SWORD ARM.
I CANNOT ENTER THE LAND OF MY BIRTH AGAIN.
WHAT? WHY NOT?
YEAH, I THOUGHT THIS WAS YOUR HOME. YOU WERE A GUARD OR SOMETHING...?
I WAS BANISHED FROM THE WALLS FIVE YEARS PAST.
WHY?
IT IS A STORY I AM NOT PROUD OF, BUT I FEEL THAT I OWE YOU AN EXPLANATION.

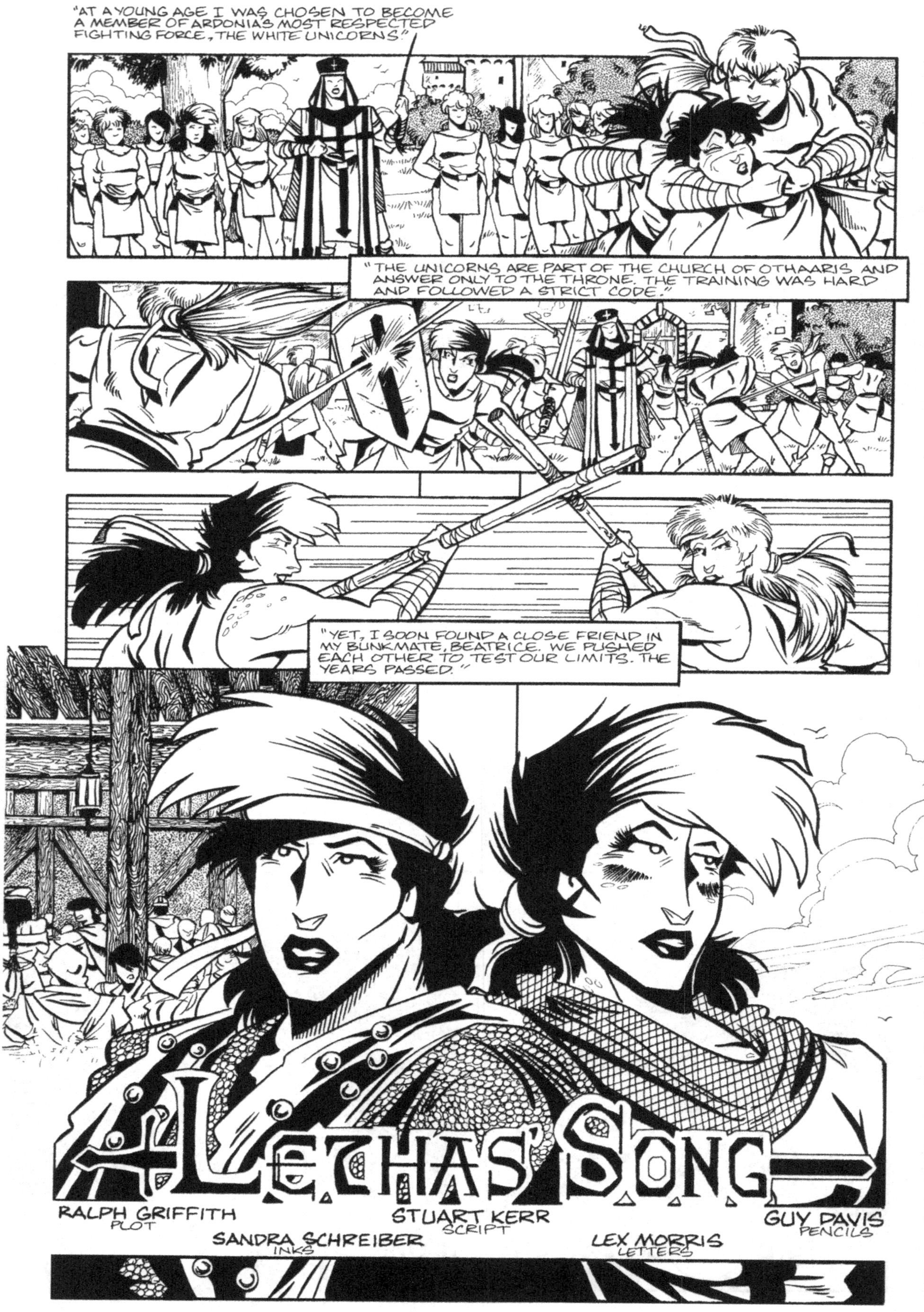
"AT A YOUNG AGE I WAS CHOSEN TO BECOME A MEMBER OF ARDONIA'S MOST RESPECTED FIGHTING FORCE, THE WHITE UNICORNS."
"THE UNICORNS ARE PART OF THE CHURCH OF OTHAARIS AND ANSWER ONLY TO THE THRONE. THE TRAINING WAS HARD AND FOLLOWED A STRICT CODE."
"YET, I SOON FOUND A CLOSE FRIEND IN MY BUNKMATE, BEATRICE. WE PUSHED EACH OTHER TO TEST OUR LIMITS. THE YEARS PASSED."
LETHA'S SONG
RALPH GRIFFITH PLOT
SANDRA SCHREIBER INKS
STUART KERR SCRIPT
LEX MORRIS LETTERS
GUY DAVIS PENCILS

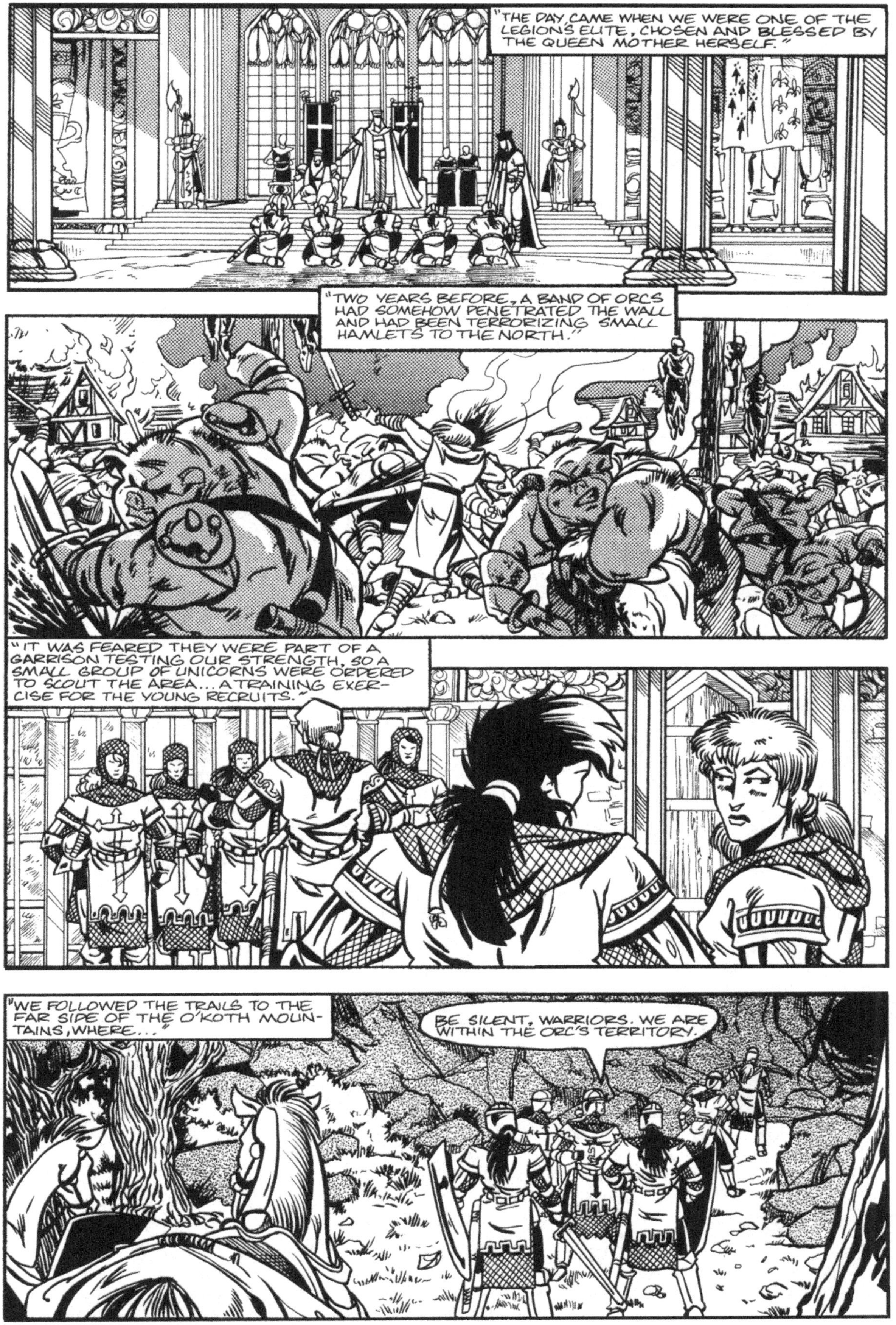
"THE DAY CAME WHEN WE WERE ONE OF THE LEGION'S ELITE, CHOSEN AND BLESSED BY THE QUEEN MOTHER HERSELF."
"TWO YEARS BEFORE, A BAND OF ORCS HAD SOMEHOW PENETRATED THE WALL AND HAD BEEN TERRORIZING SMALL HAMLETS TO THE NORTH."
"IT WAS FEARED THEY WERE PART OF A GARRISON TESTING OUR STRENGTH, SO A SMALL GROUP OF UNICORNS WERE ORDERED TO SCOUT THE AREA... A TRAINING EXERCISE FOR THE YOUNG RECRUITS."
"WE FOLLOWED THE TRAILS TO THE FAR SIDE OF THE O'KOTH MOUNTAINS, WHERE..."
BE SILENT, WARRIORS. WE ARE WITHIN THE ORC'S TERRITORY.

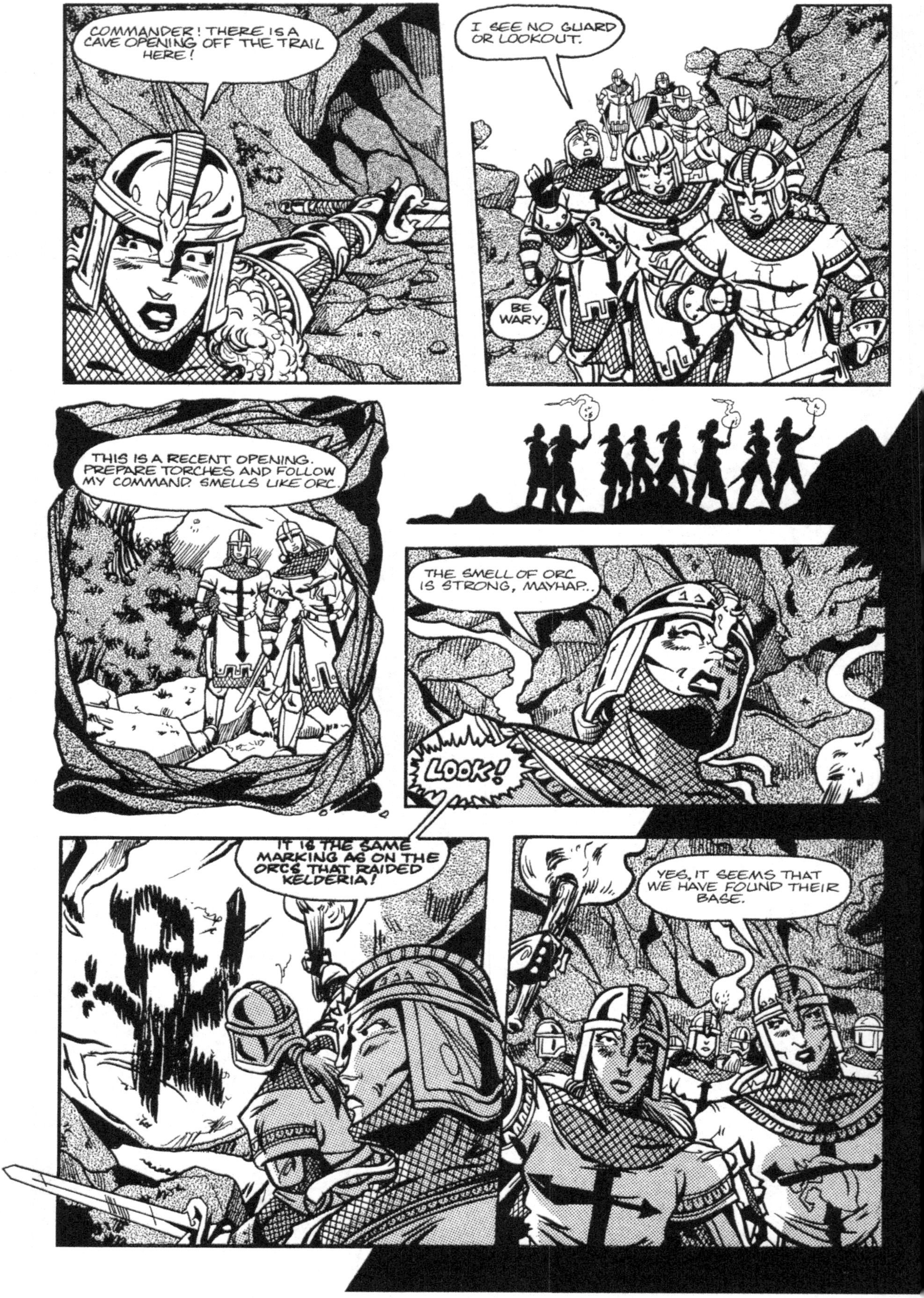
COMMANDER! THERE IS A CAVE OPENING OFF THE TRAIL HERE!
I SEE NO GUARD OR LOOKOUT.
BE WARY.
THIS IS A RECENT OPENING. PREPARE TORCHES AND FOLLOW MY COMMAND. SMELLS LIKE ORC.
THE SMELL OF ORC IS STRONG, MAYHAP...
LOOK!
IT IS THE SAME MARKING AS ON THE ORCS THAT RAIDED KELDERIA!
YES, IT SEEMS THAT WE HAVE FOUND THEIR BASE.

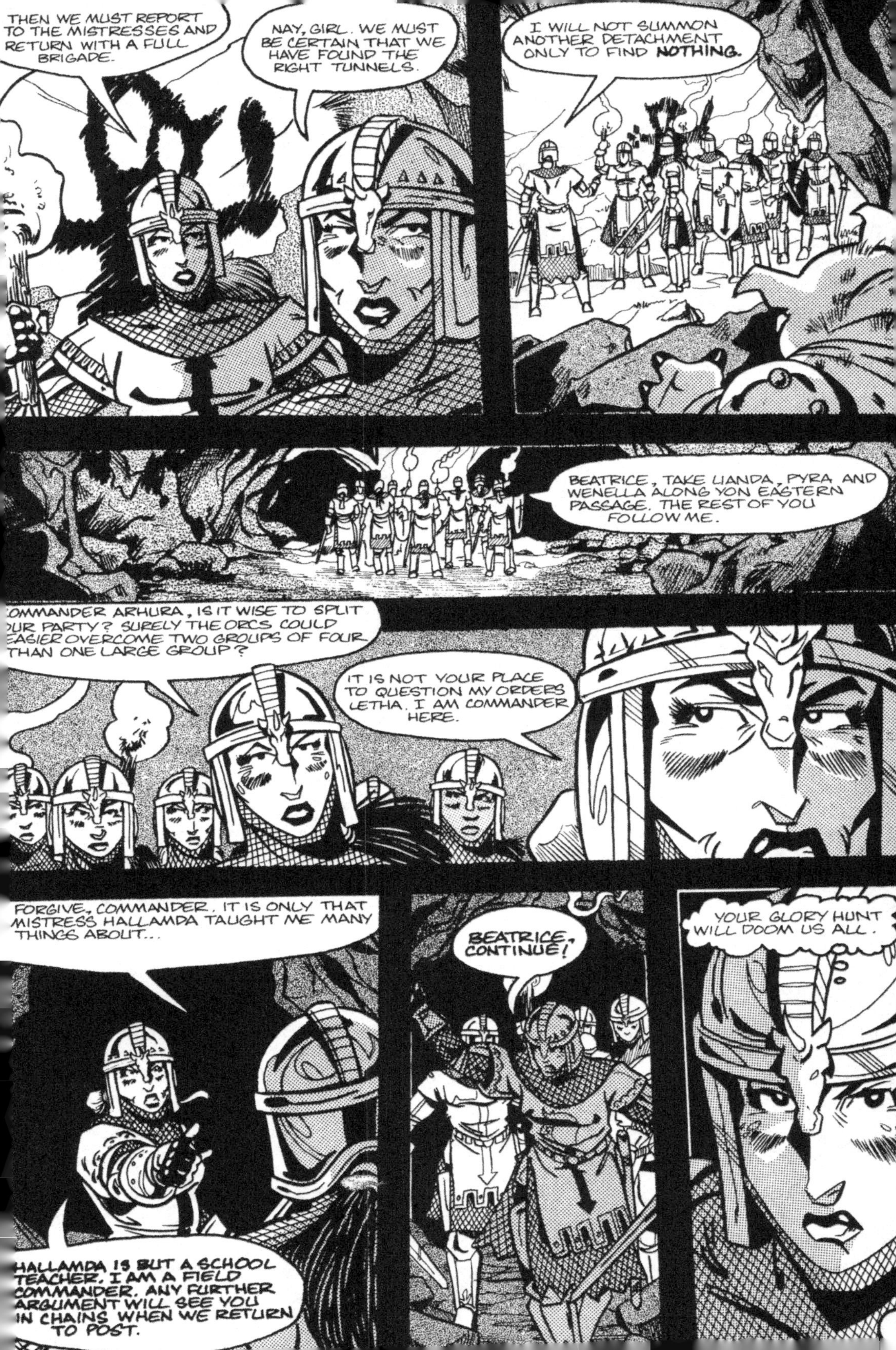

THEN WE MUST REPORT TO THE MISTRESSES AND RETURN WITH A FULL BRIGADE.
NAY, GIRL. WE MUST BE CERTAIN THAT WE HAVE FOUND THE RIGHT TUNNELS.
I WILL NOT SUMMON ANOTHER DETACHMENT ONLY TO FIND NOTHING.
BEATRICE, TAKE LIANDA, PYRA AND WENELLA ALONG YON EASTERN PASSAGE. THE REST OF YOU FOLLOW ME.
COMMANDER ARHURA, IS IT WISE TO SPLIT YOUR PARTY? SURELY THE ORCS COULD EASIER OVERCOME TWO GROUPS OF FOUR THAN ONE LARGE GROUP?
IT IS NOT YOUR PLACE TO QUESTION MY ORDERS LETHA. I AM COMMANDER HERE.
FORGIVE, COMMANDER. IT IS ONLY THAT MISTRESS HALLAMDA TAUGHT ME MANY THINGS ABOUT...
HALLAMDA IS BUT A SCHOOL TEACHER. I AM A FIELD COMMANDER. ANY FURTHER ARGUMENT WILL SEE YOU IN CHAINS WHEN WE RETURN TO POST.
BEATRICE, CONTINUE!
YOUR GLORY HUNT WILL DOOM US ALL.

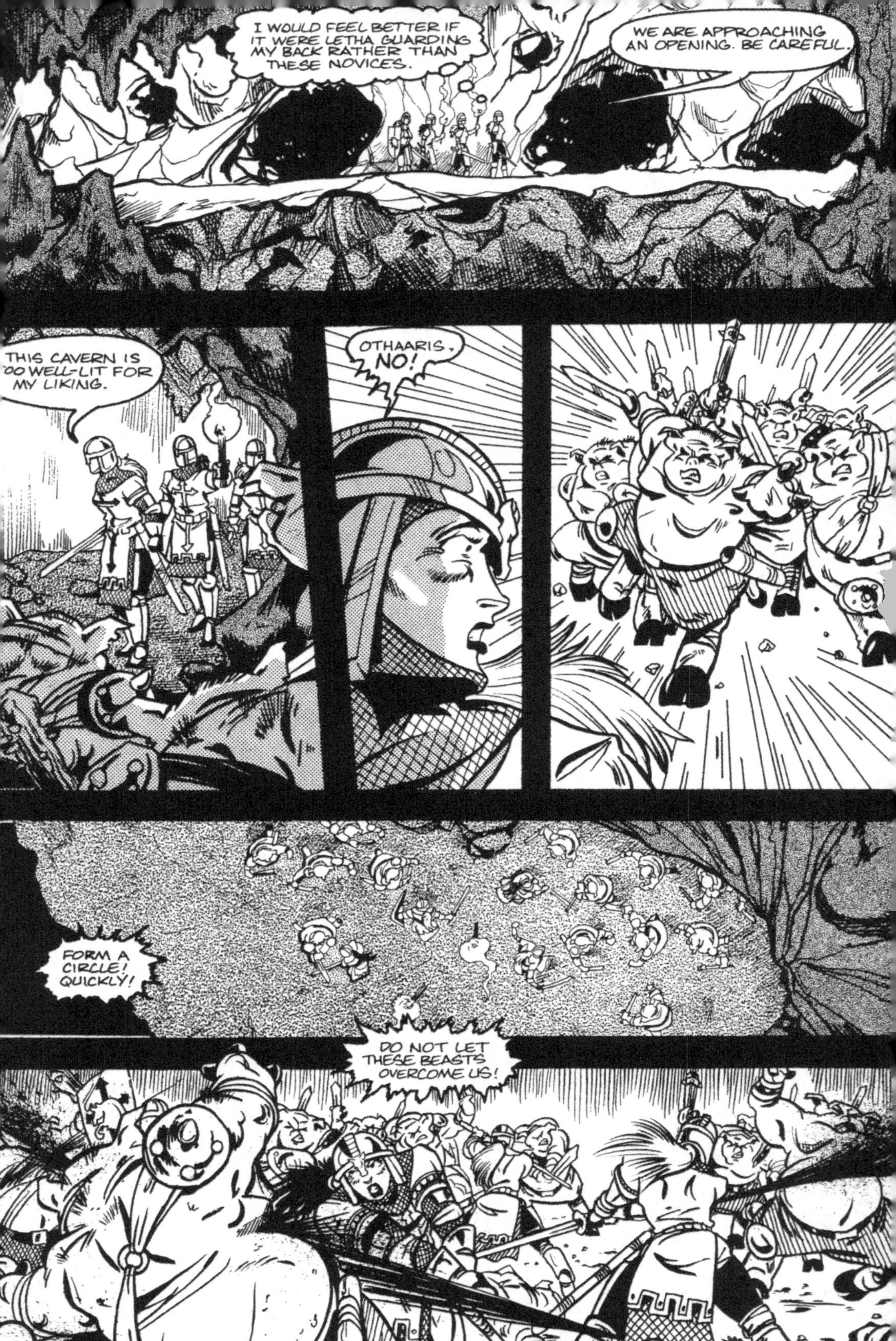

I WOULD FEEL BETTER IF IT WERE LETHA GUARDING MY BACK RATHER THAN THESE NOVICES.
WE ARE APPROACHING AN OPENING. BE CAREFUL.
THIS CAVERN IS TOO WELL-LIT FOR MY LIKING.
OTHAARIS, NO!
FORM A CIRCLE! QUICKLY!
DO NOT LET THESE BEASTS OVERCOME US!

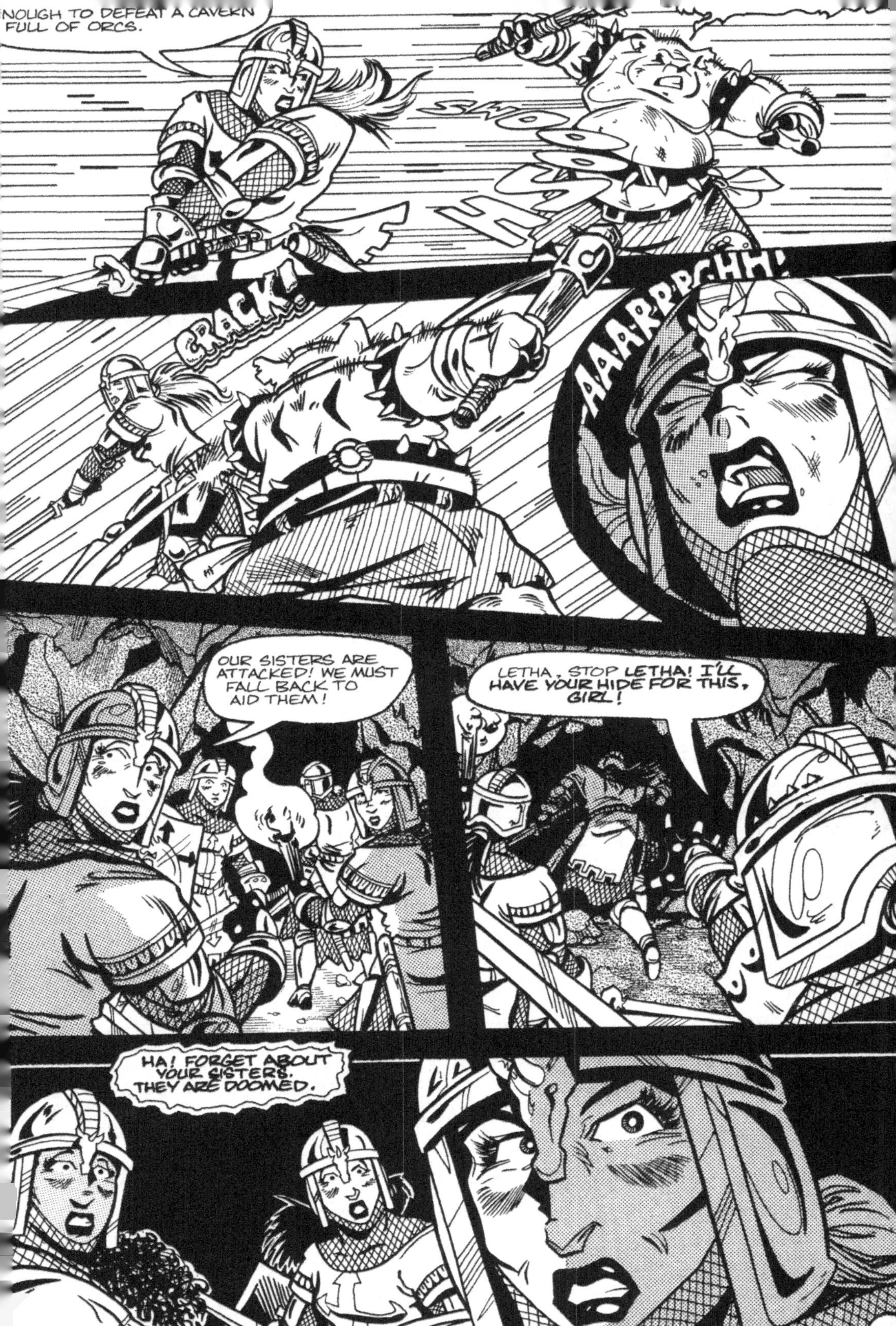
NOUGH TO DEFEAT A CAVERN FULL OF ORCS.
SWOOSH
CRACK!
AAARRGHH!
OUR SISTERS ARE ATTACKED! WE MUST FALL BACK TO AID THEM!
LETHA, STOP LETHA! I'LL HAVE YOUR HIDE FOR THIS, GIRL!
HA! FORGET ABOUT YOUR SISTERS. THEY ARE DOOMED.

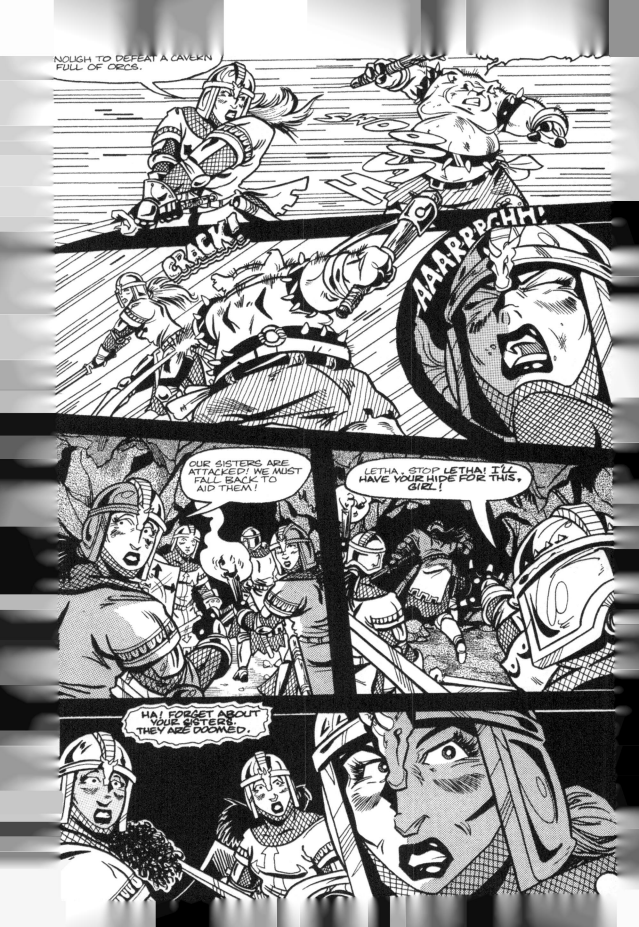

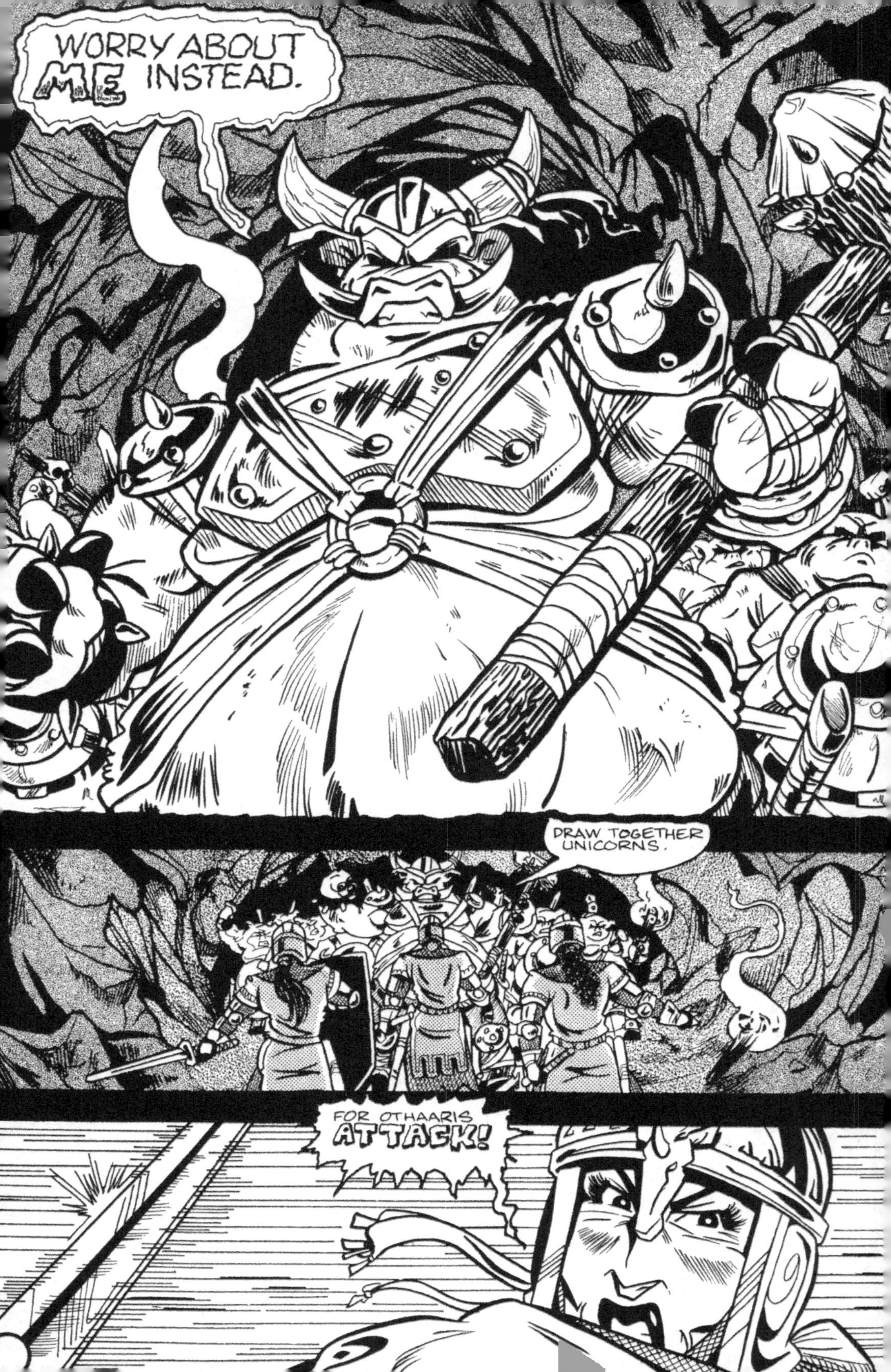
WORRY ABOUT ME INSTEAD.
DRAW TOGETHER UNICORNS.
FOR OTHAARIS ATTACK!

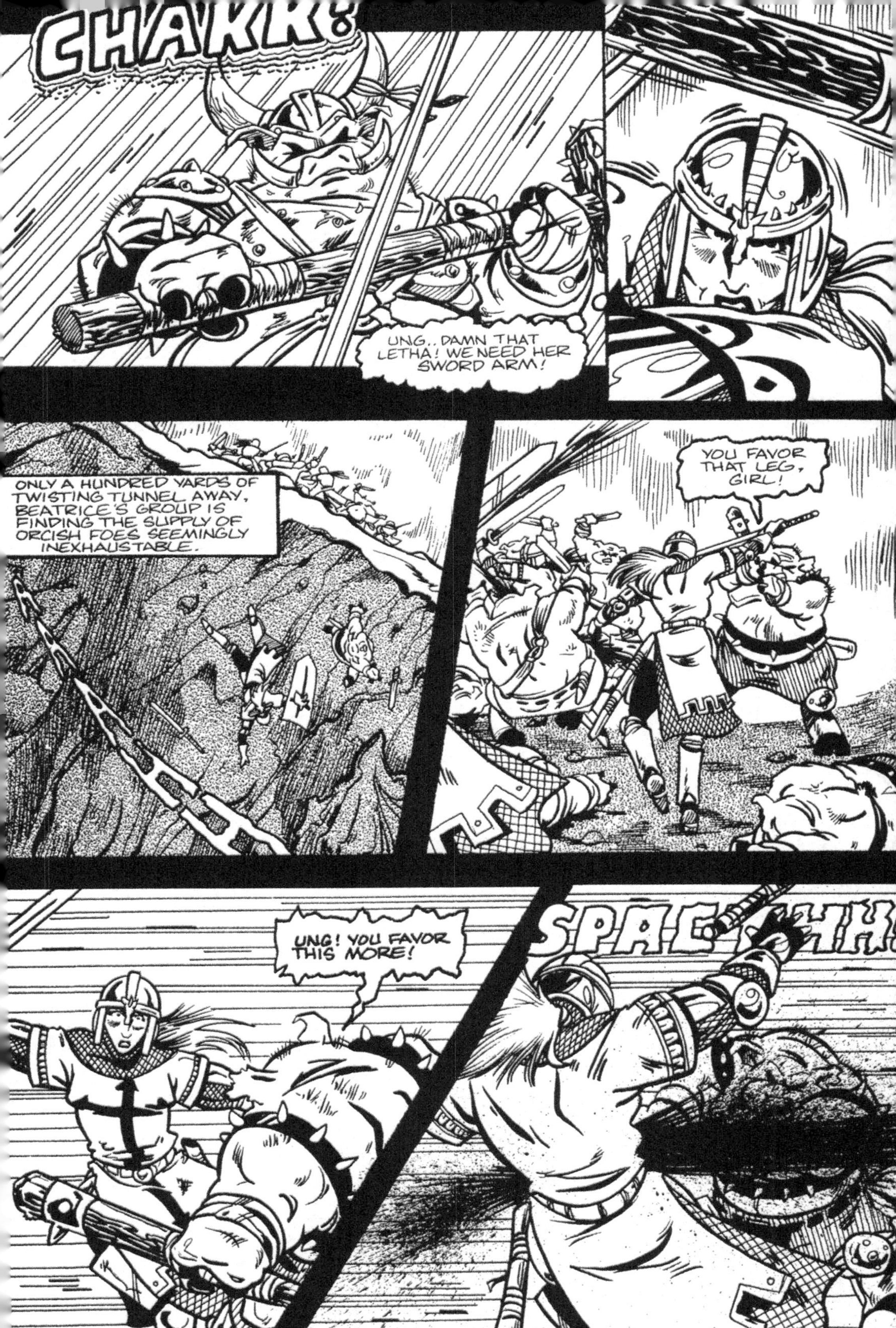
CHAKK!
UNG.. DAMN THAT LETHA! WE NEED HER SWORD ARM!
ONLY A HUNDRED YARDS OF TWISTING TUNNEL AWAY, BEATRICE'S GROUP IS FINDING THE SUPPLY OF ORCISH FOES SEEMINGLY INEXHAUSTABLE.
YOU FAVOR THAT LEG, GIRL!
UNG! YOU FAVOR THIS MORE!

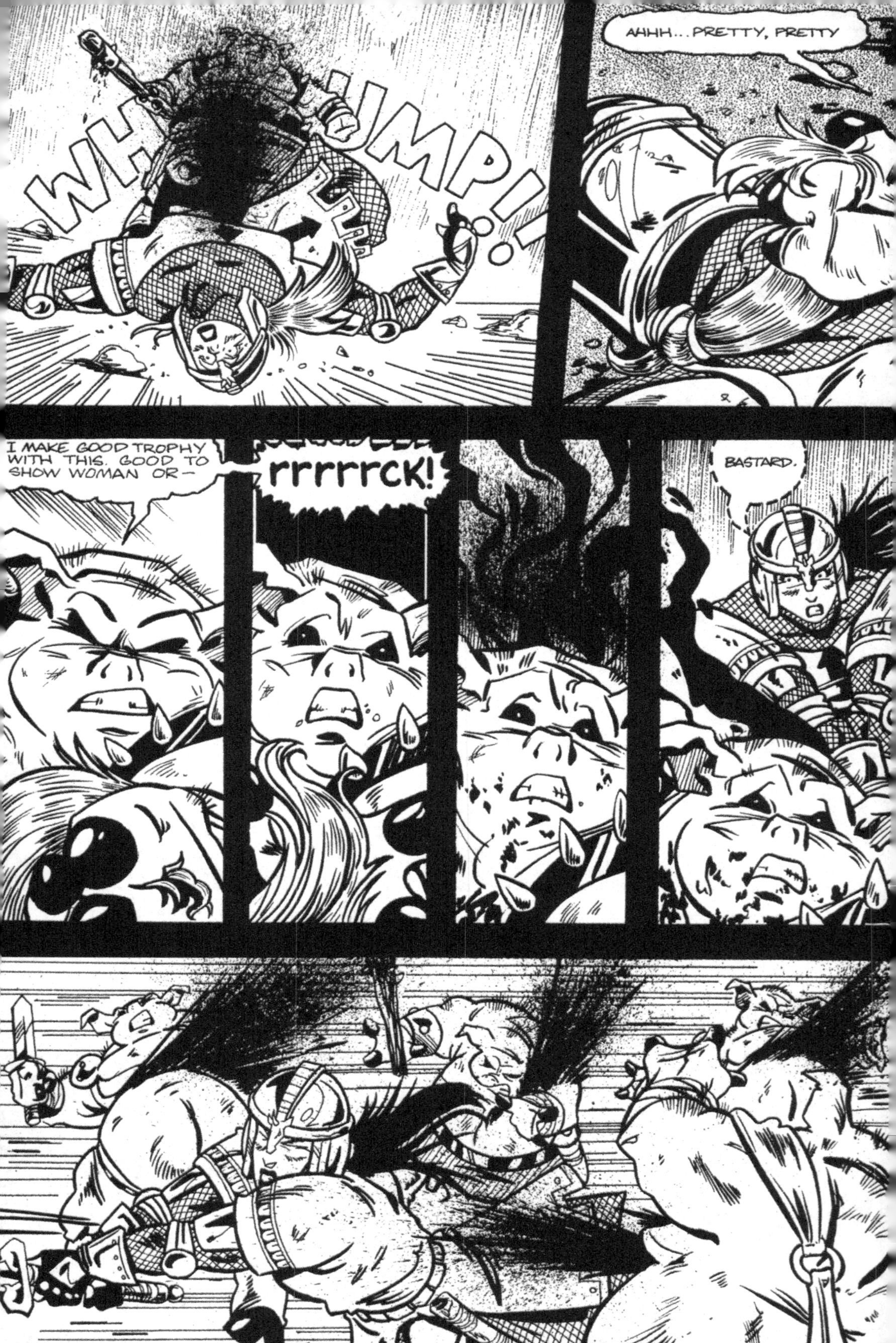
WHUMP!!
AHHH... PRETTY, PRETTY
I MAKE GOOD TROPHY WITH THIS. GOOD TO SHOW WOMAN OR—
rrrrrck!
BASTARD.

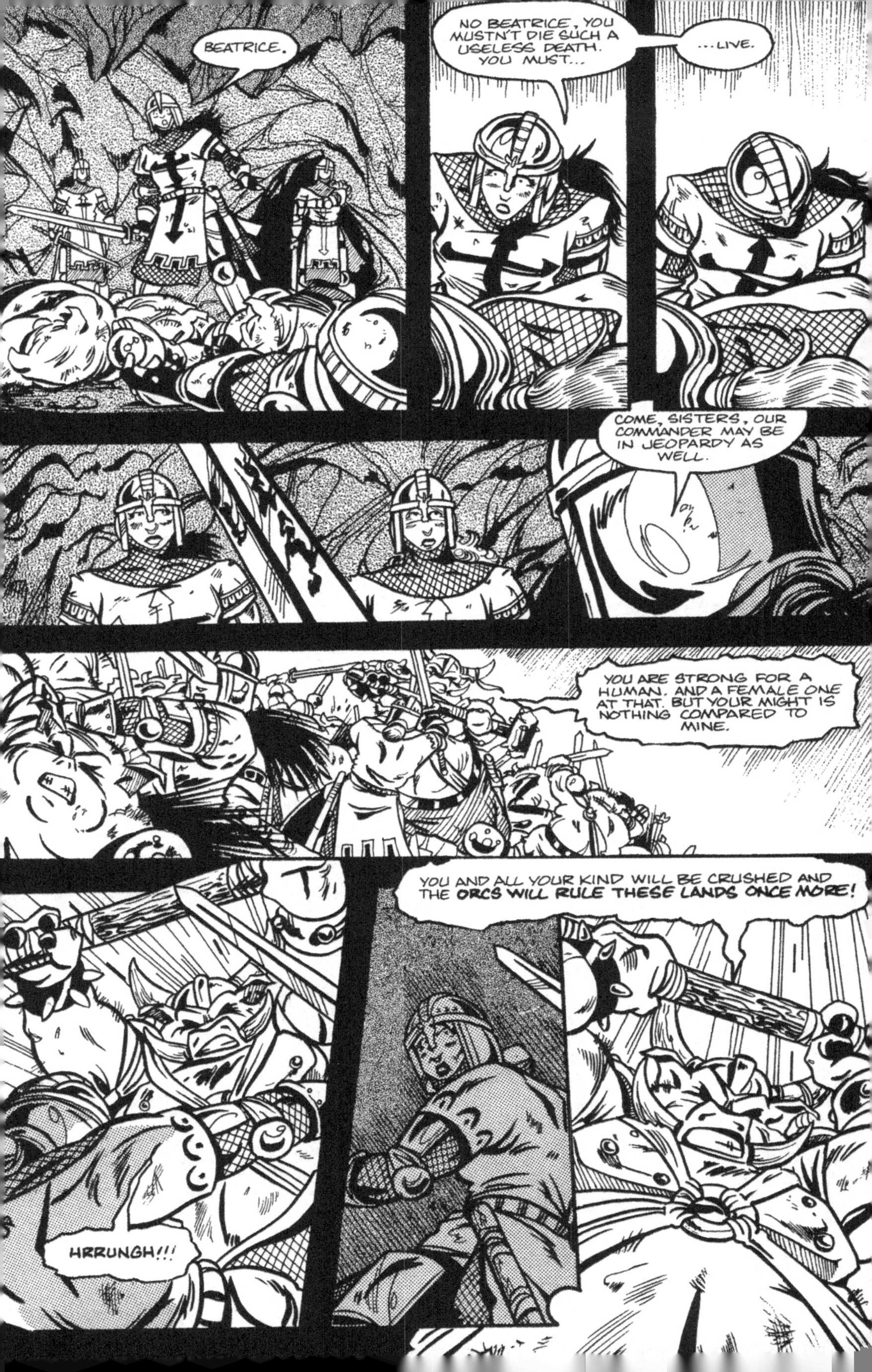

BEATRICE.
NO BEATRICE, YOU MUSTN'T DIE SUCH A USELESS DEATH. YOU MUST...
...LIVE.
COME, SISTERS, OUR COMMANDER MAY BE IN JEOPARDY AS WELL.
YOU ARE STRONG FOR A HUMAN. AND A FEMALE ONE AT THAT. BUT YOUR MIGHT IS NOTHING COMPARED TO MINE.
YOU AND ALL YOUR KIND WILL BE CRUSHED AND THE ORCS WILL RULE THESE LANDS ONCE MORE!
HRRUNGH!!!

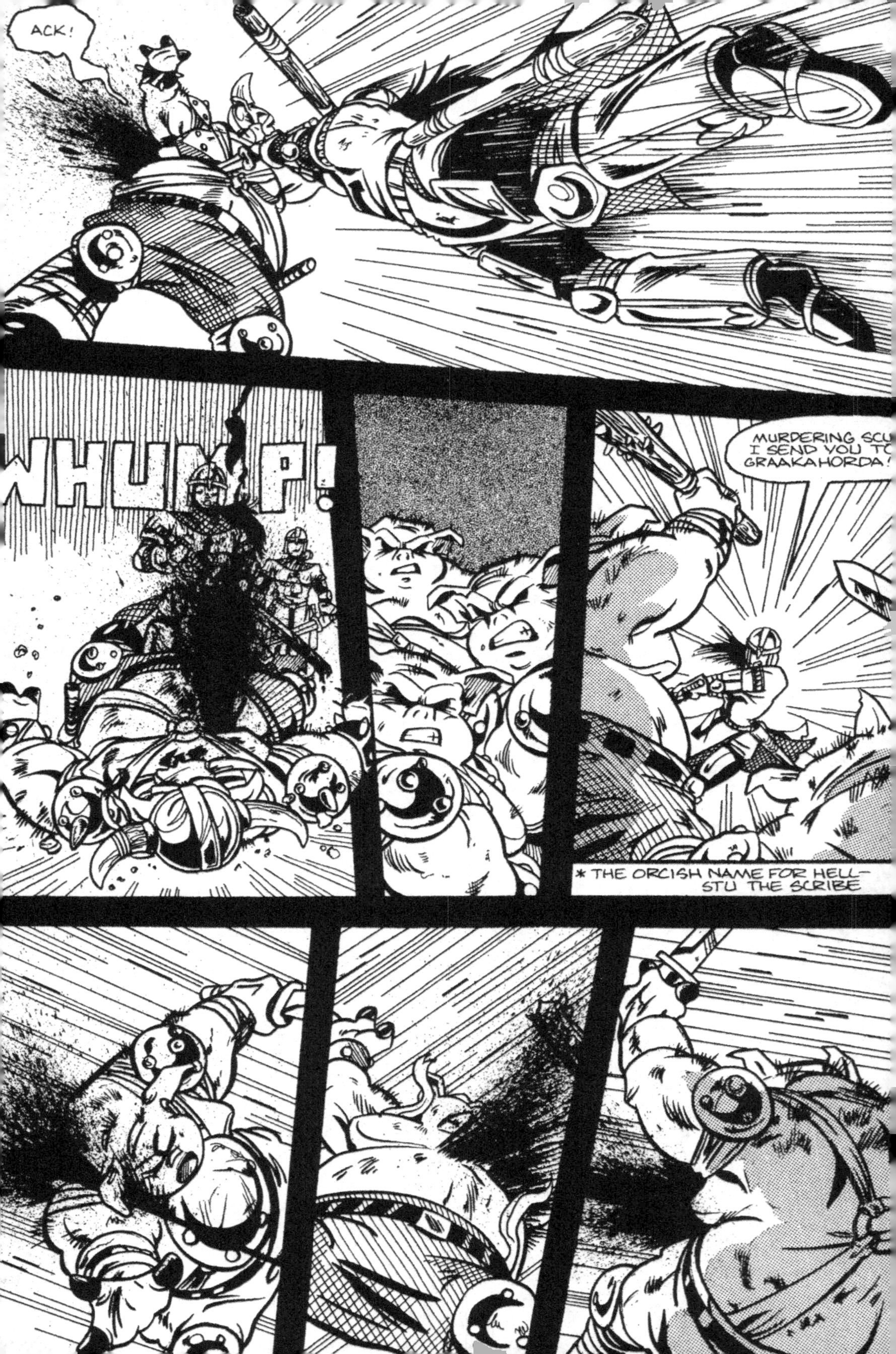
ACK!
WHUMP!
MURDERING SCU
I SEND YOU TO
GRAAKAHORDA!
* THE ORCISH NAME FOR HELL—
STU THE SCRIBE

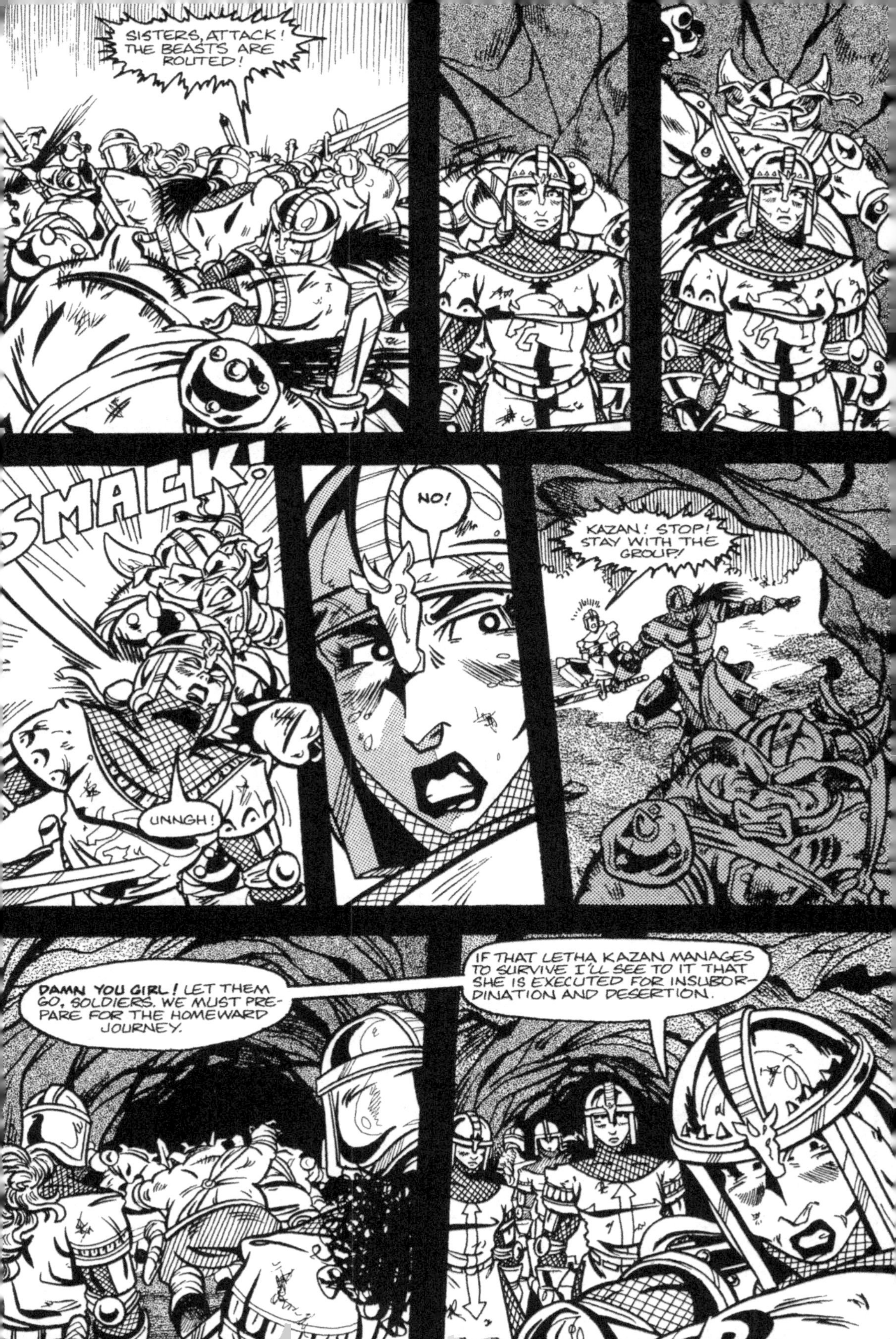

SISTERS, ATTACK! THE BEASTS ARE ROUTED!
SMACK!
NO!
UNNGH!
KAZAN! STOP! STAY WITH THE GROUP!
DAMN YOU GIRL! LET THEM GO, SOLDIERS. WE MUST PREPARE FOR THE HOMEWARD JOURNEY.
IF THAT LETHA KAZAN MANAGES TO SURVIVE I'LL SEE TO IT THAT SHE IS EXECUTED FOR INSUBORDINATION AND DESERTION.

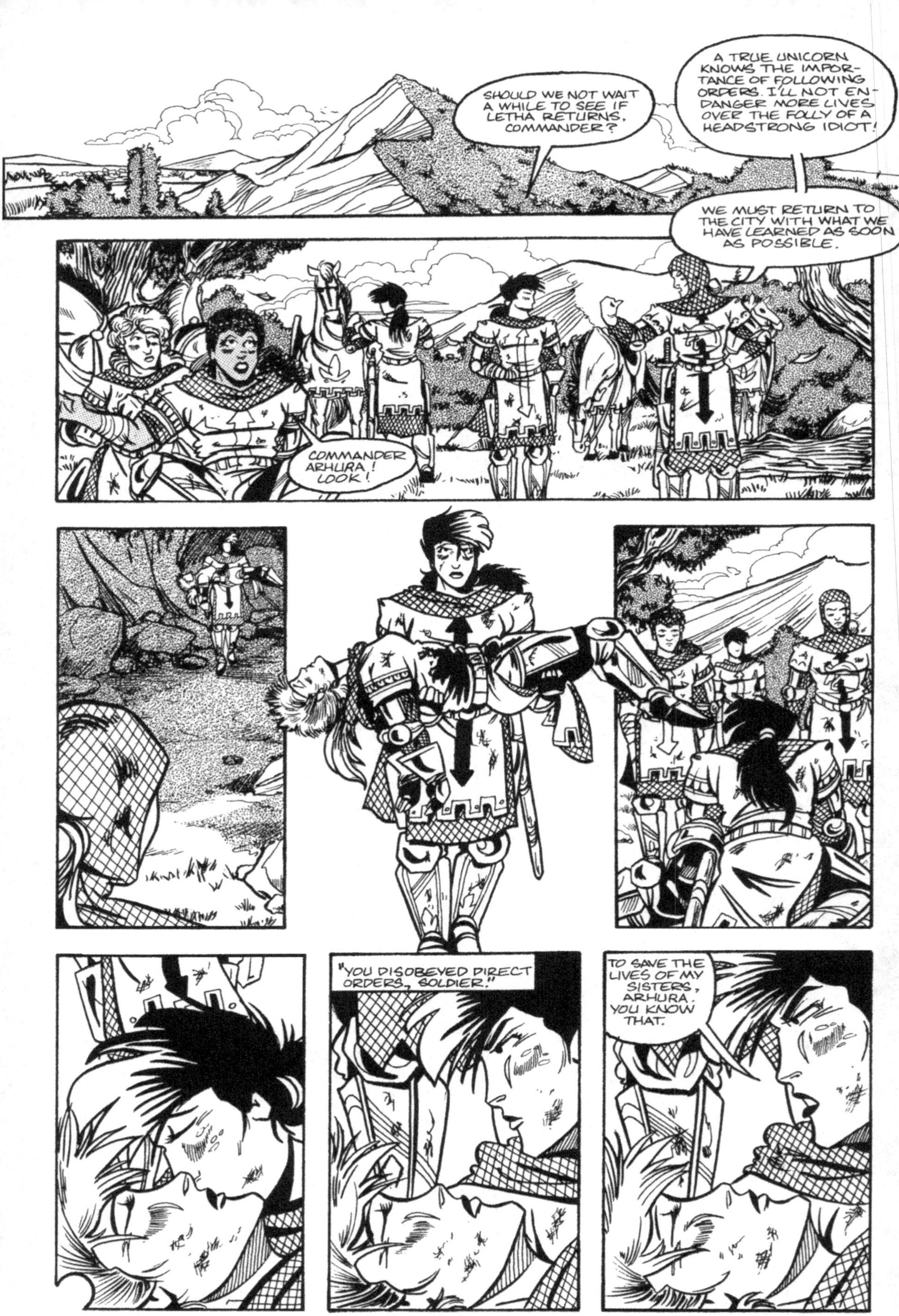
SHOULD WE NOT WAIT A WHILE TO SEE IF LETHA RETURNS, COMMANDER?
A TRUE UNICORN KNOWS THE IMPORTANCE OF FOLLOWING ORDERS. I'LL NOT ENDANGER MORE LIVES OVER THE FOLLY OF A HEADSTRONG IDIOT!
WE MUST RETURN TO THE CITY WITH WHAT WE HAVE LEARNED AS SOON AS POSSIBLE.
COMMANDER ARHURA! LOOK!
"YOU DISOBEYED DIRECT ORDERS, SOLDIER."
TO SAVE THE LIVES OF MY SISTERS, ARHURA. YOU KNOW THAT.

I KNOW NOTHING BUT THAT ONE OF MY ELITE TRAINING SQUAD IS DEAD ALONG WITH ONE COMBAT VETERAN. I THINK THE TOLL WOULD HAVE BEEN LESS IF YOU HAD OBEYED ME.

WHAT!? YOU ARE INSANE!

TWO OF THE FALLEN WERE IN THE GROUP I WENT TO JOIN!

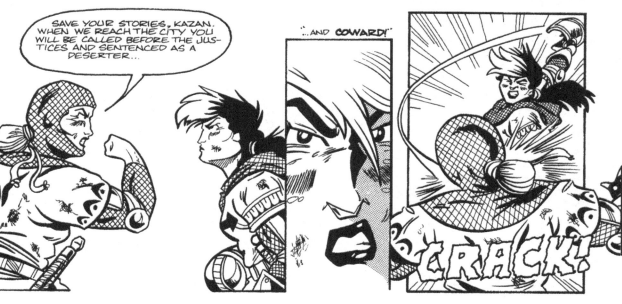

SAVE YOUR STORIES, KAZAN. WHEN WE REACH THE CITY YOU WILL BE CALLED BEFORE THE JUSTICES AND SENTENCED AS A DESERTER...

"...AND **COWARD!**"

CRACK!

HA! YOU CRY COWARD TO COVER FOR THE IDIOCY OF YOUR DECISIONS! I WILL GLADLY PAY THE PENALTY FOR THIS!

LETHA, YOU DON'T KNOW WHAT YOU'RE DOING!

I WILL SEE YOU HUNG FOR THIS...

HUNG!

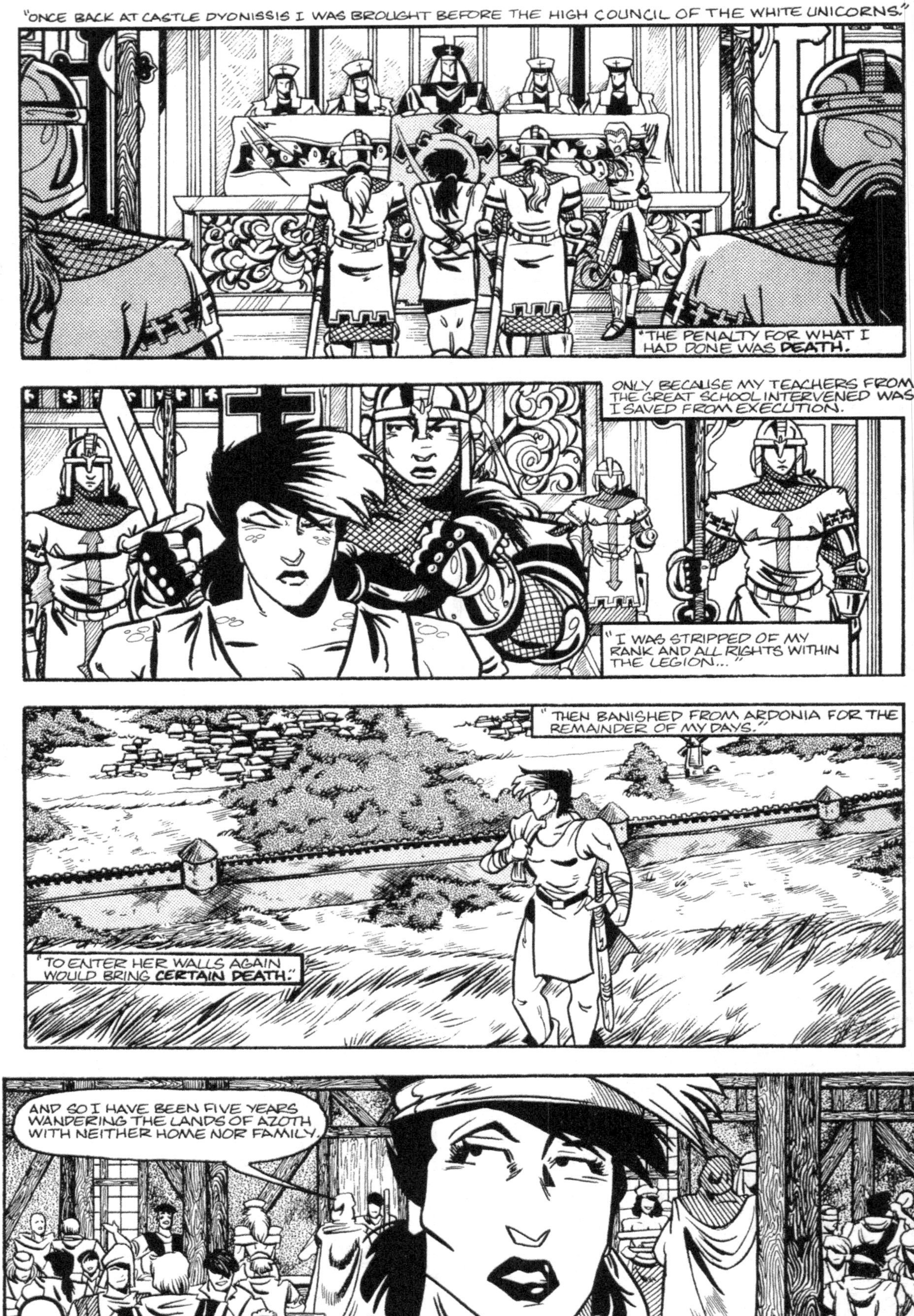
"ONCE BACK AT CASTLE DYONISSIS I WAS BROUGHT BEFORE THE HIGH COUNCIL OF THE WHITE UNICORNS."
"THE PENALTY FOR WHAT I HAD DONE WAS **DEATH.**
ONLY BECAUSE MY TEACHERS FROM THE GREAT SCHOOL INTERVENED WAS I SAVED FROM EXECUTION.
"I WAS STRIPPED OF MY RANK AND ALL RIGHTS WITHIN THE LEGION..."
"THEN BANISHED FROM ARDONIA FOR THE REMAINDER OF MY DAYS."
"TO ENTER HER WALLS AGAIN WOULD BRING **CERTAIN DEATH**."
AND SO I HAVE BEEN FIVE YEARS WANDERING THE LANDS OF AZOTH WITH NEITHER HOME NOR FAMILY.

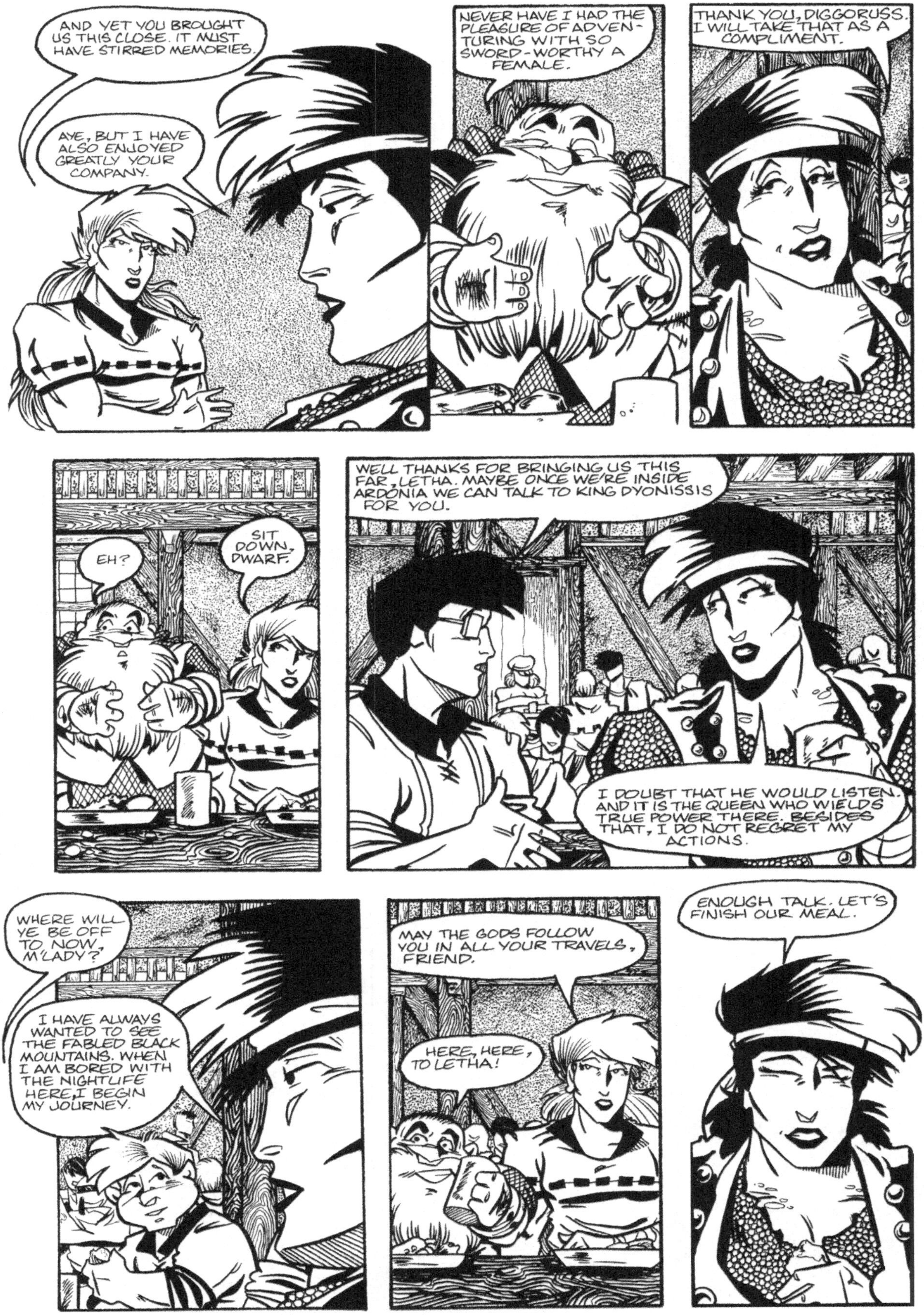
AND YET YOU BROUGHT US THIS CLOSE. IT MUST HAVE STIRRED MEMORIES.
AYE, BUT I HAVE ALSO ENJOYED GREATLY YOUR COMPANY.
NEVER HAVE I HAD THE PLEASURE OF ADVENTURING WITH SO SWORD-WORTHY A FEMALE.
THANK YOU, DIGGORUSS. I WILL TAKE THAT AS A COMPLIMENT.
EH?
SIT DOWN, DWARF.
WELL THANKS FOR BRINGING US THIS FAR, LETHA. MAYBE ONCE WE'RE INSIDE ARDONIA WE CAN TALK TO KING DYONISSIS FOR YOU.
I DOUBT THAT HE WOULD LISTEN. AND IT IS THE QUEEN WHO WIELDS TRUE POWER THERE. BESIDES THAT, I DO NOT REGRET MY ACTIONS.
WHERE WILL YE BE OFF TO NOW, M'LADY?
I HAVE ALWAYS WANTED TO SEE THE FABLED BLACK MOUNTAINS. WHEN I AM BORED WITH THE NIGHTLIFE HERE, I BEGIN MY JOURNEY.
MAY THE GODS FOLLOW YOU IN ALL YOUR TRAVELS, FRIEND.
HERE, HERE, TO LETHA!
ENOUGH TALK. LET'S FINISH OUR MEAL.

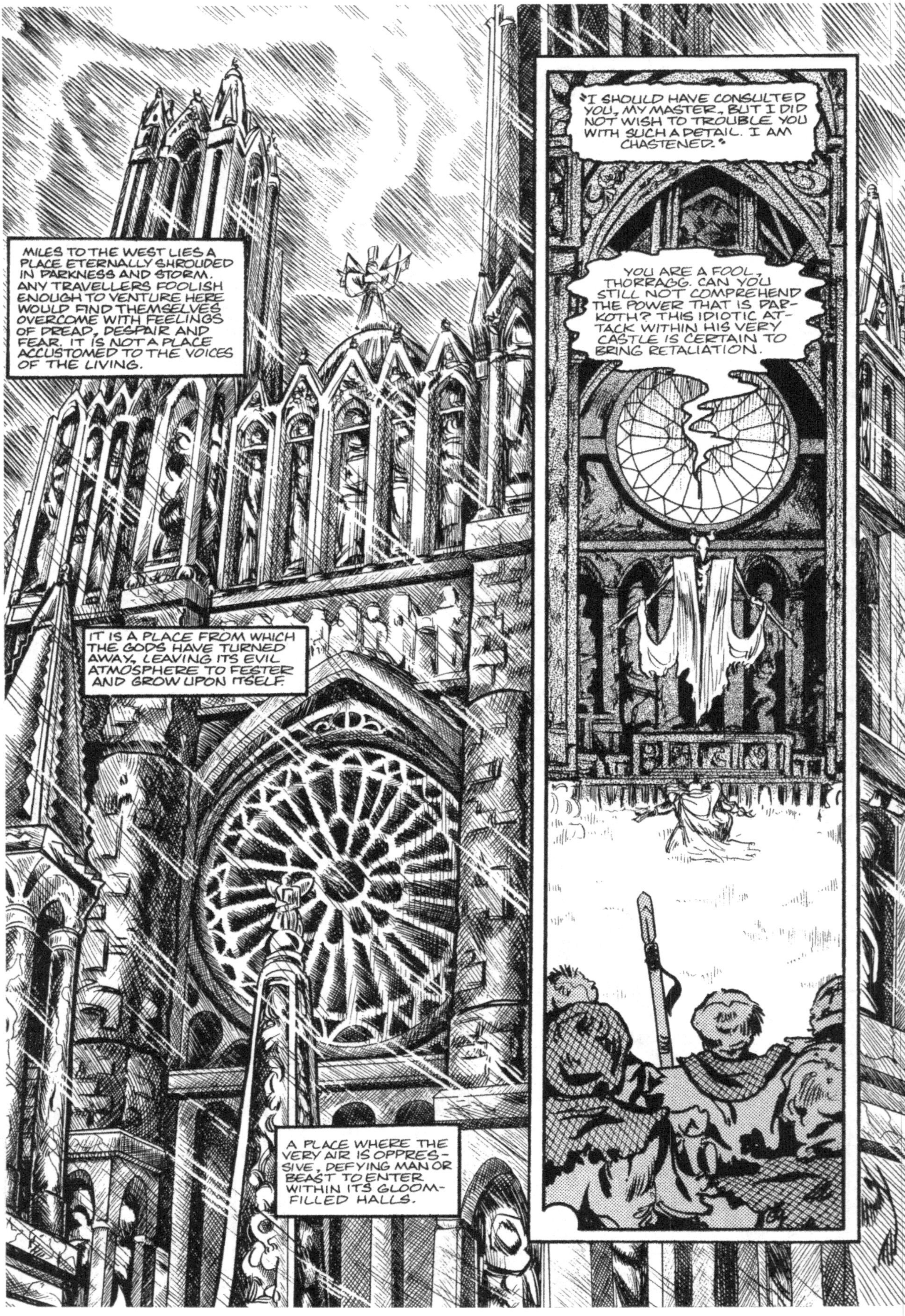
MILES TO THE WEST LIES A PLACE ETERNALLY SHROUDED IN DARKNESS AND STORM. ANY TRAVELLERS FOOLISH ENOUGH TO VENTURE HERE WOULD FIND THEMSELVES OVERCOME WITH FEELINGS OF DREAD, DESPAIR AND FEAR. IT IS NOT A PLACE ACCUSTOMED TO THE VOICES OF THE LIVING.
IT IS A PLACE FROM WHICH THE GODS HAVE TURNED AWAY, LEAVING ITS EVIL ATMOSPHERE TO FESTER AND GROW UPON ITSELF.
A PLACE WHERE THE VERY AIR IS OPPRESSIVE, DEFYING MAN OR BEAST TO ENTER WITHIN ITS GLOOM-FILLED HALLS.
"I SHOULD HAVE CONSULTED YOU, MY MASTER, BUT I DID NOT WISH TO TROUBLE YOU WITH SUCH A DETAIL. I AM CHASTENED."
YOU ARE A FOOL, THORRAGG. CAN YOU STILL NOT COMPREHEND THE POWER THAT IS DARKOTH? THIS IDIOTIC ATTACK WITHIN HIS VERY CASTLE IS CERTAIN TO BRING RETALIATION.

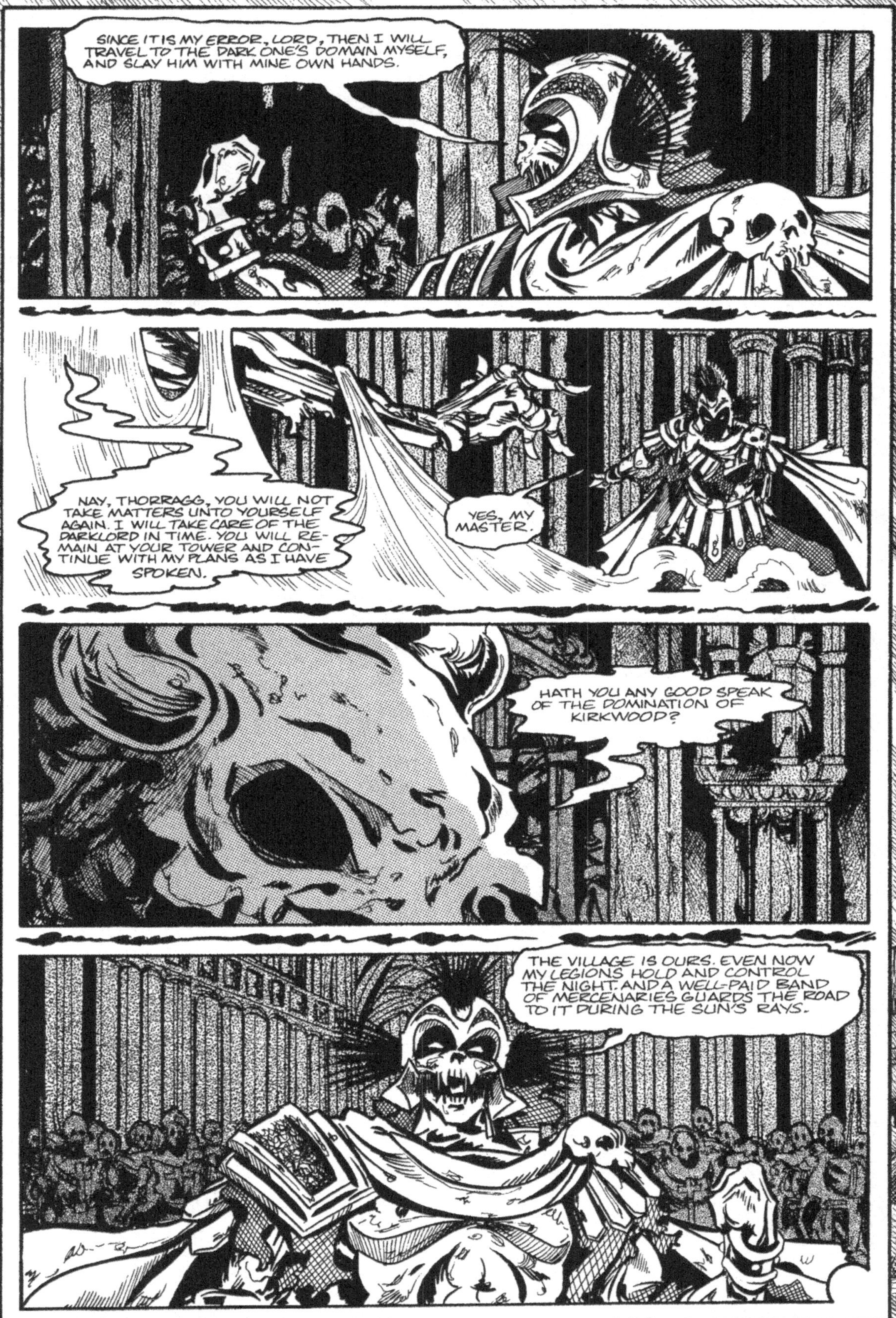
SINCE IT IS MY ERROR, LORD, THEN I WILL TRAVEL TO THE DARK ONE'S DOMAIN MYSELF, AND SLAY HIM WITH MINE OWN HANDS.
NAY, THORRAGG, YOU WILL NOT TAKE MATTERS UNTO YOURSELF AGAIN. I WILL TAKE CARE OF THE DARKLORD IN TIME. YOU WILL RE-MAIN AT YOUR TOWER AND CON-TINUE WITH MY PLANS AS I HAVE SPOKEN.
YES, MY MASTER.
HATH YOU ANY GOOD SPEAK OF THE DOMINATION OF KIRKWOOD?
THE VILLAGE IS OURS. EVEN NOW MY LEGIONS HOLD AND CONTROL THE NIGHT. AND A WELL-PAID BAND OF MERCENARIES GUARDS THE ROAD TO IT DURING THE SUN'S RAYS.

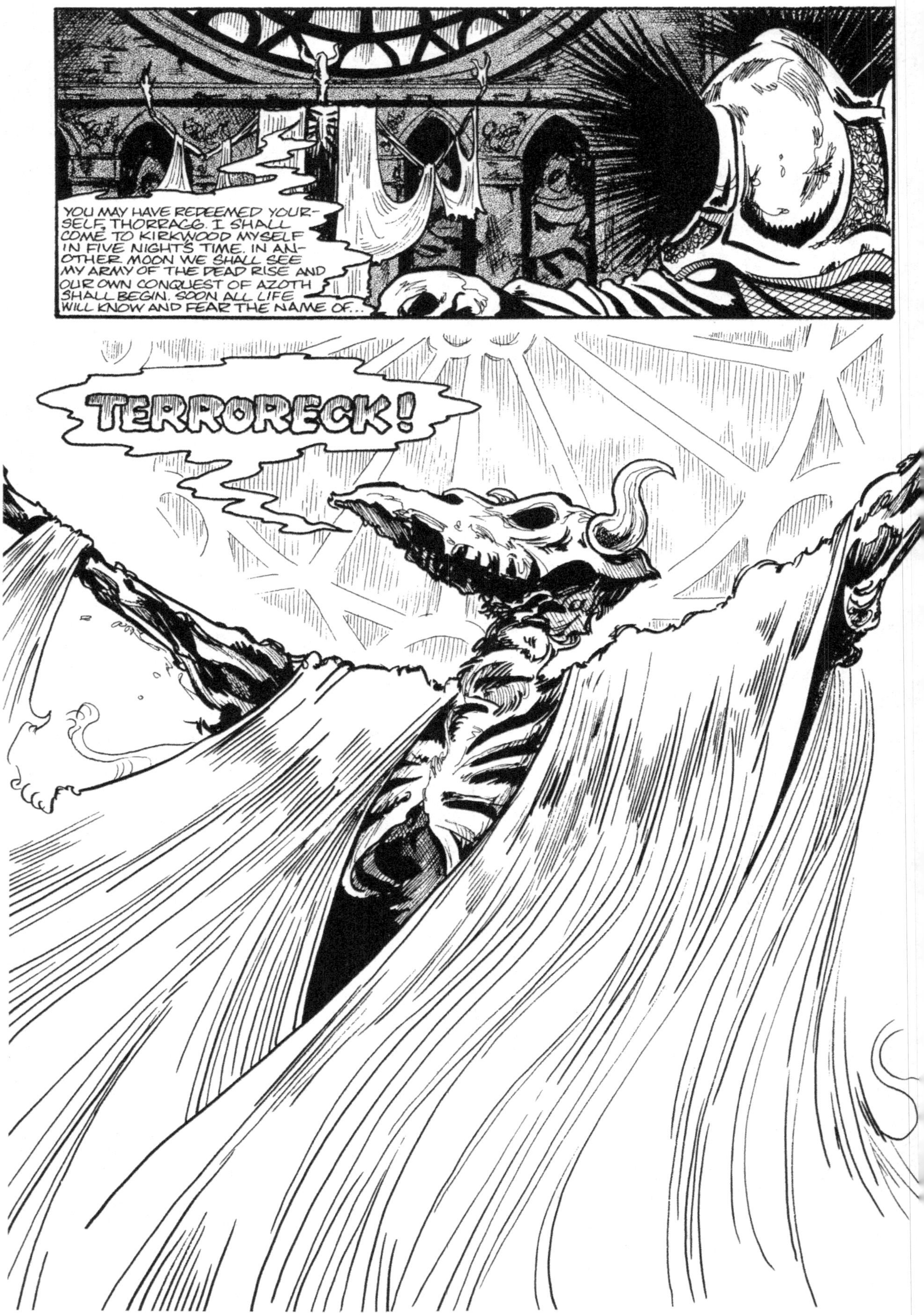
YOU MAY HAVE REDEEMED YOURSELF, THORRAGG. I SHALL COME TO KIRKWOOD MYSELF IN FIVE NIGHT'S TIME. IN ANOTHER MOON WE SHALL SEE MY ARMY OF THE DEAD RISE AND OUR OWN CONQUEST OF AZOTH SHALL BEGIN. SOON ALL LIFE WILL KNOW AND FEAR THE NAME OF...
TERRORECK!

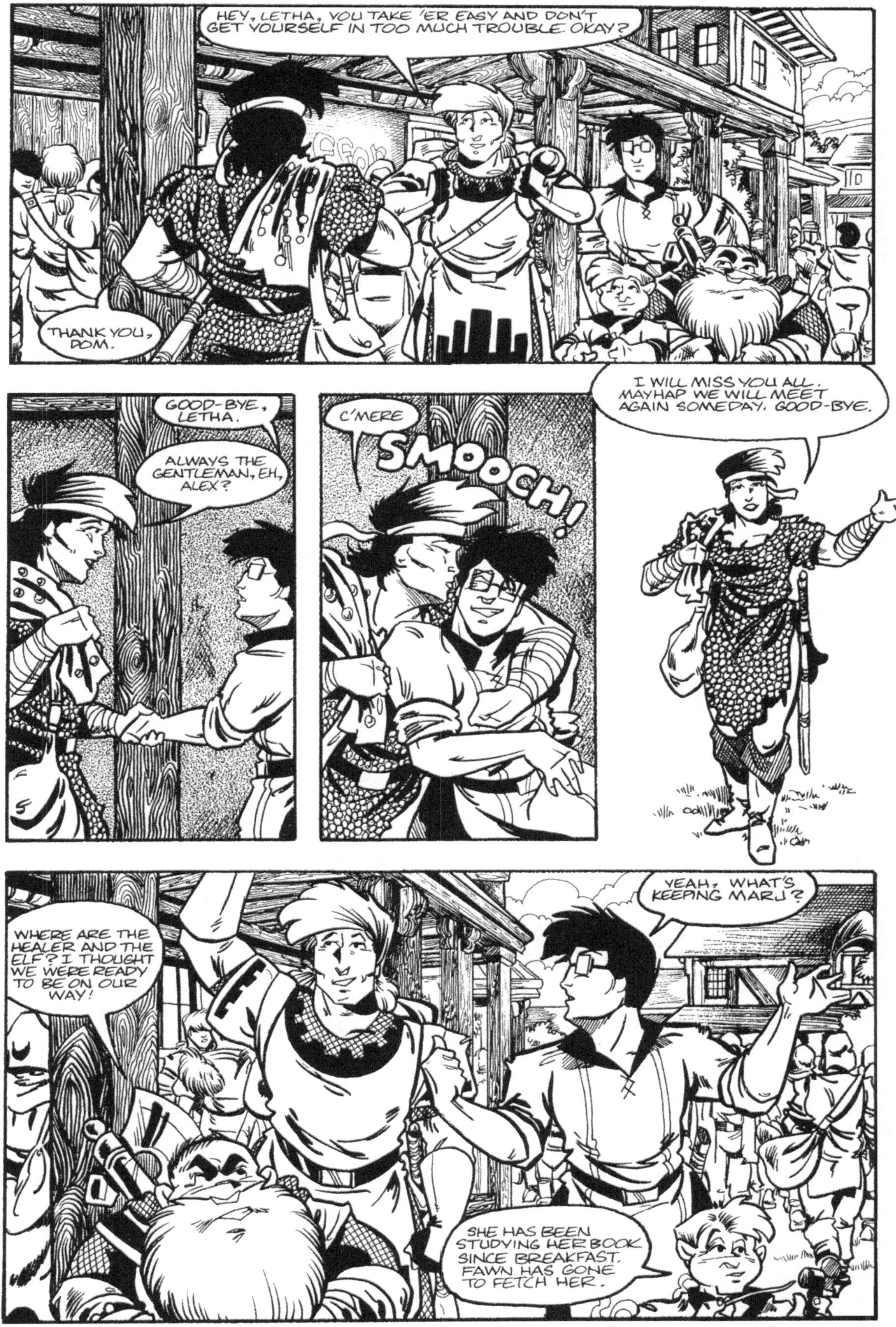
HEY, LETHA, YOU TAKE 'ER EASY AND DON'T GET YOURSELF IN TOO MUCH TROUBLE. OKAY?
THANK YOU, DOM.
GOOD-BYE, LETHA.
ALWAYS THE GENTLEMAN, EH, ALEX?
C'MERE
SMOOCH!
I WILL MISS YOU ALL. MAYHAP WE WILL MEET AGAIN SOMEDAY. GOOD-BYE.
WHERE ARE THE HEALER AND THE ELF? I THOUGHT WE WERE READY TO BE ON OUR WAY!
YEAH, WHAT'S KEEPING MARJ?
SHE HAS BEEN STUDYING HER BOOK SINCE BREAKFAST. FAWN HAS GONE TO FETCH HER.

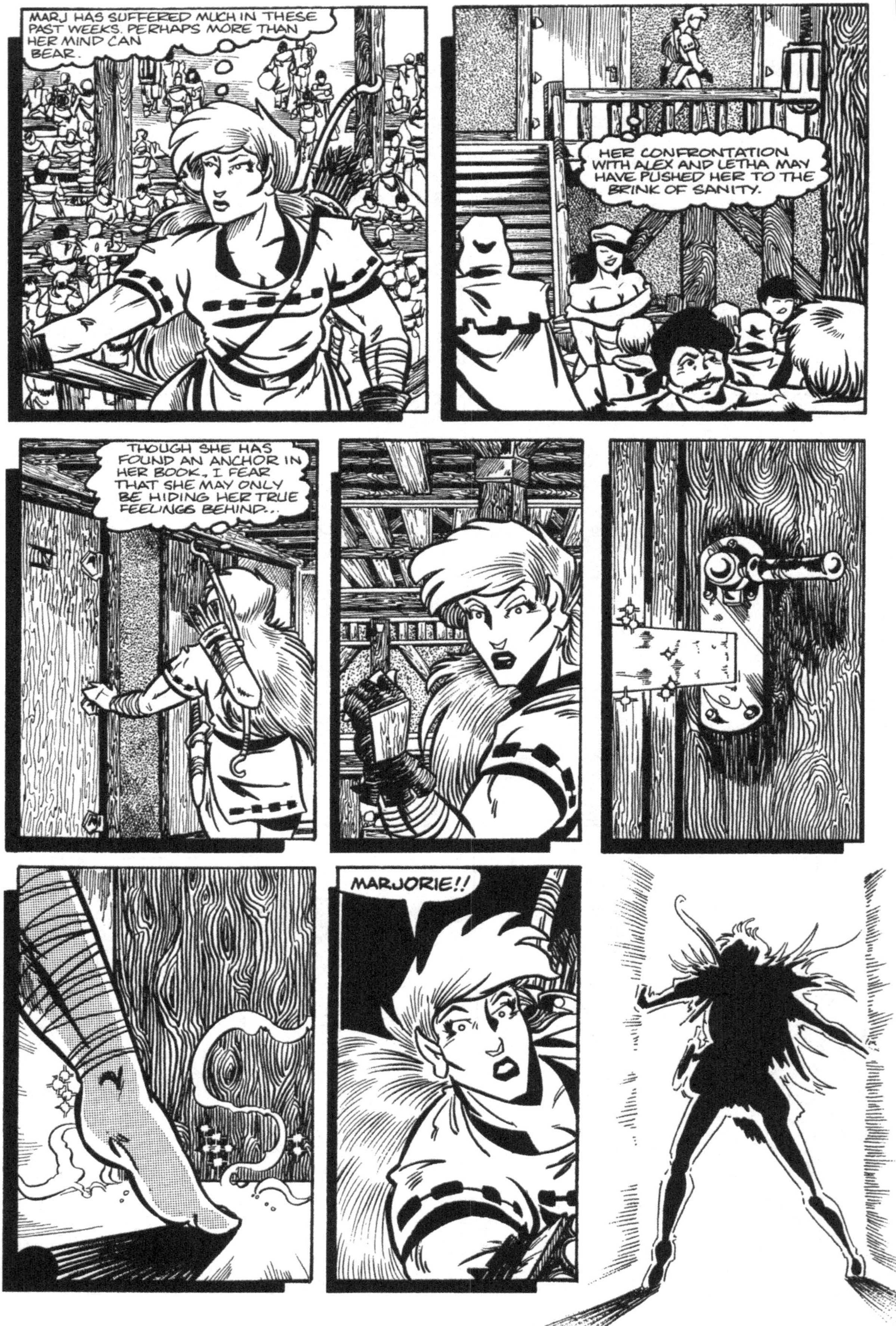
MARJ HAS SUFFERED MUCH IN THESE PAST WEEKS. PERHAPS MORE THAN HER MIND CAN BEAR.
HER CONFRONTATION WITH ALEX AND LETHA MAY HAVE PUSHED HER TO THE BRINK OF SANITY.
THOUGH SHE HAS FOUND AN ANCHOR IN HER BOOK, I FEAR THAT SHE MAY ONLY BE HIDING HER TRUE FEELINGS BEHIND...
MARJORIE!!

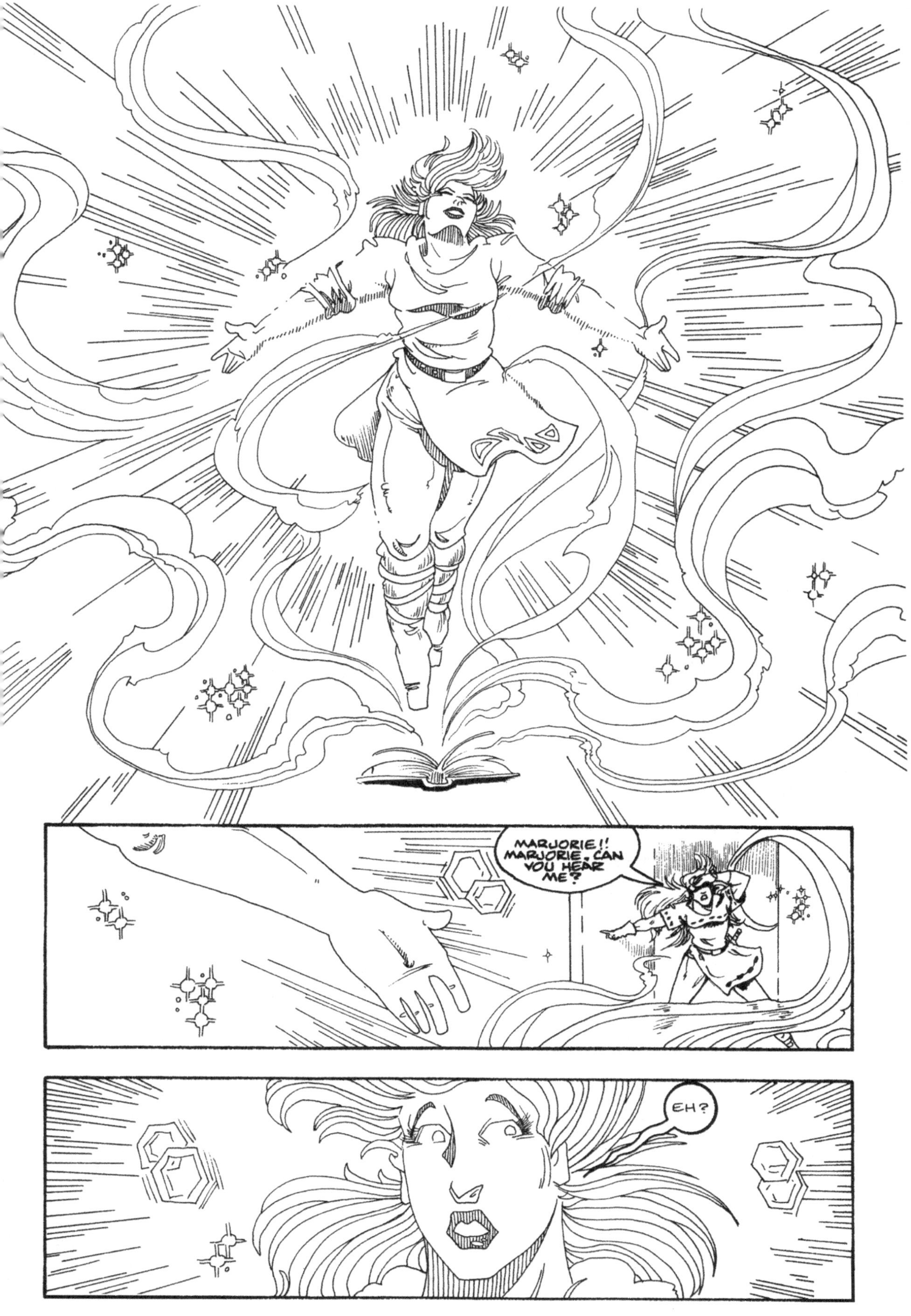
MARJORIE!! MARJORIE, CAN YOU HEAR ME?
EH?

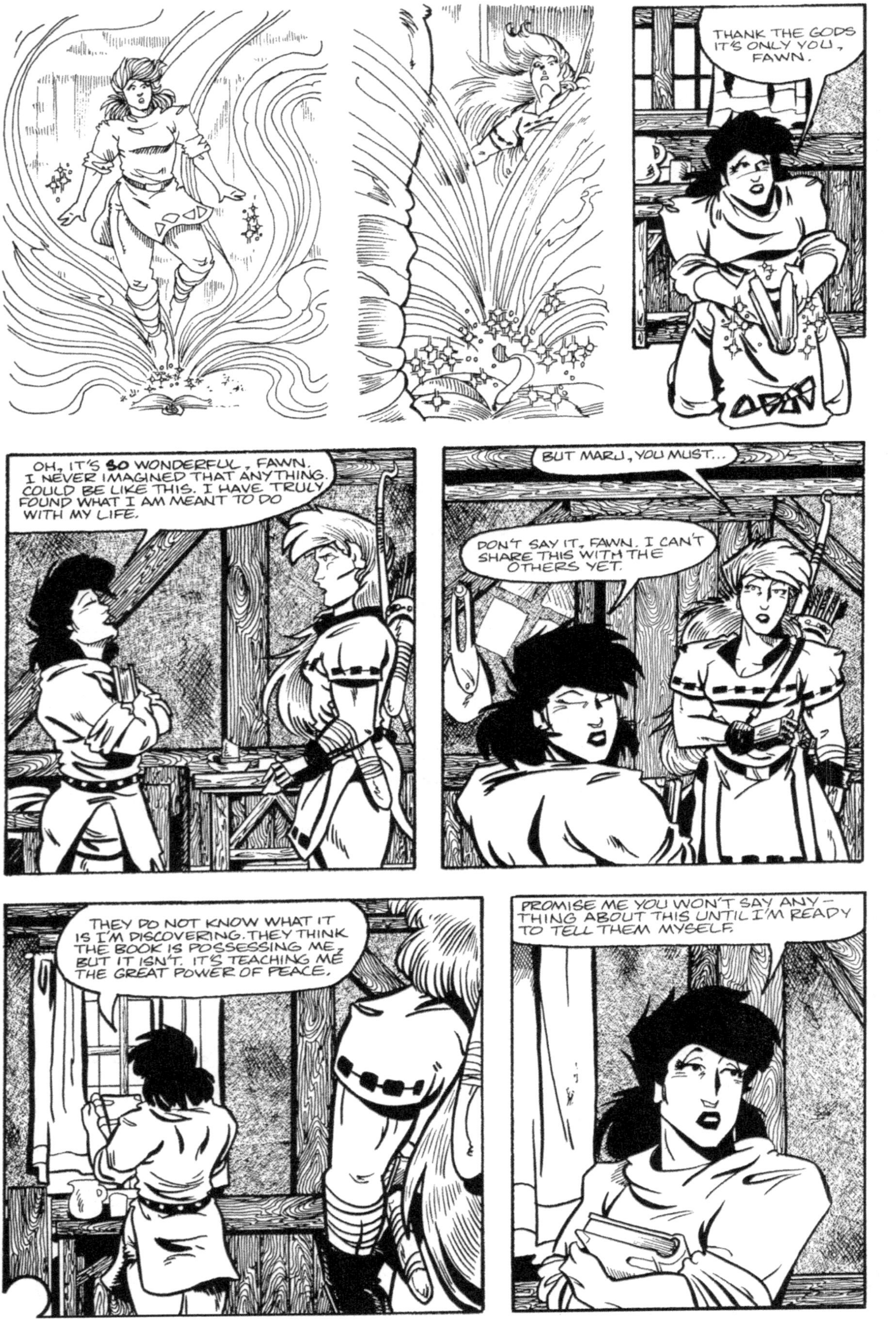
THANK THE GODS IT'S ONLY YOU, FAWN.
OH, IT'S SO WONDERFUL, FAWN. I NEVER IMAGINED THAT ANYTHING COULD BE LIKE THIS. I HAVE TRULY FOUND WHAT I AM MEANT TO DO WITH MY LIFE.
BUT MARU, YOU MUST...
DON'T SAY IT, FAWN. I CAN'T SHARE THIS WITH THE OTHERS YET.
THEY DO NOT KNOW WHAT IT IS I'M DISCOVERING. THEY THINK THE BOOK IS POSSESSING ME, BUT IT ISN'T. IT'S TEACHING ME THE GREAT POWER OF PEACE.
PROMISE ME YOU WON'T SAY ANY-THING ABOUT THIS UNTIL I'M READY TO TELL THEM MYSELF.

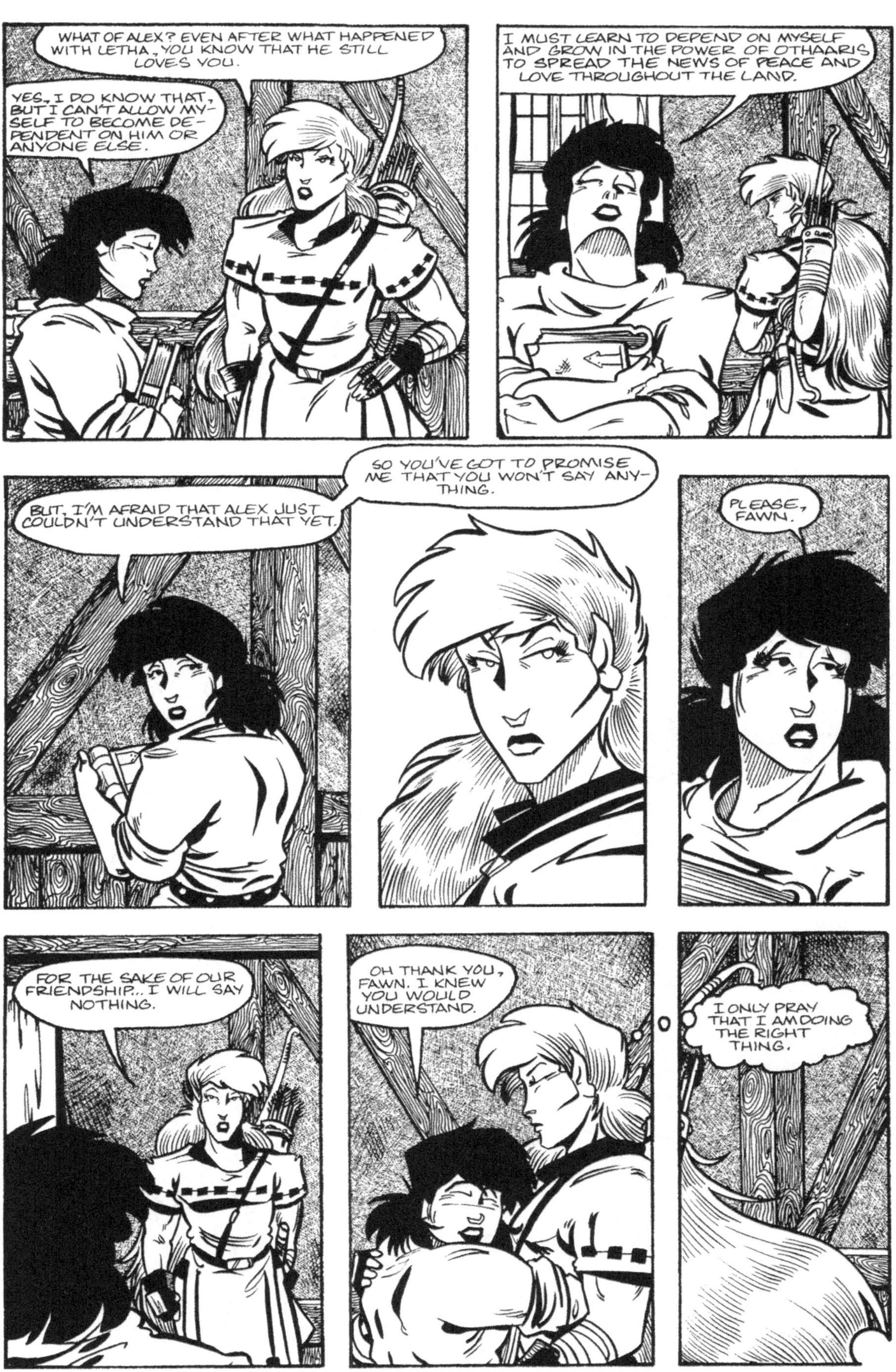
WHAT OF ALEX? EVEN AFTER WHAT HAPPENED WITH LETHA, YOU KNOW THAT HE STILL LOVES YOU.
YES, I DO KNOW THAT, BUT I CAN'T ALLOW MY-SELF TO BECOME DE-PENDENT ON HIM OR ANYONE ELSE.
I MUST LEARN TO DEPEND ON MYSELF AND GROW IN THE POWER OF OTHAARIS TO SPREAD THE NEWS OF PEACE AND LOVE THROUGHOUT THE LAND.
BUT, I'M AFRAID THAT ALEX JUST COULDN'T UNDERSTAND THAT YET.
SO YOU'VE GOT TO PROMISE ME THAT YOU WON'T SAY ANY-THING.
PLEASE, FAWN.
FOR THE SAKE OF OUR FRIENDSHIP... I WILL SAY NOTHING.
OH THANK YOU, FAWN. I KNEW YOU WOULD UNDERSTAND.
I ONLY PRAY THAT I AM DOING THE RIGHT THING.

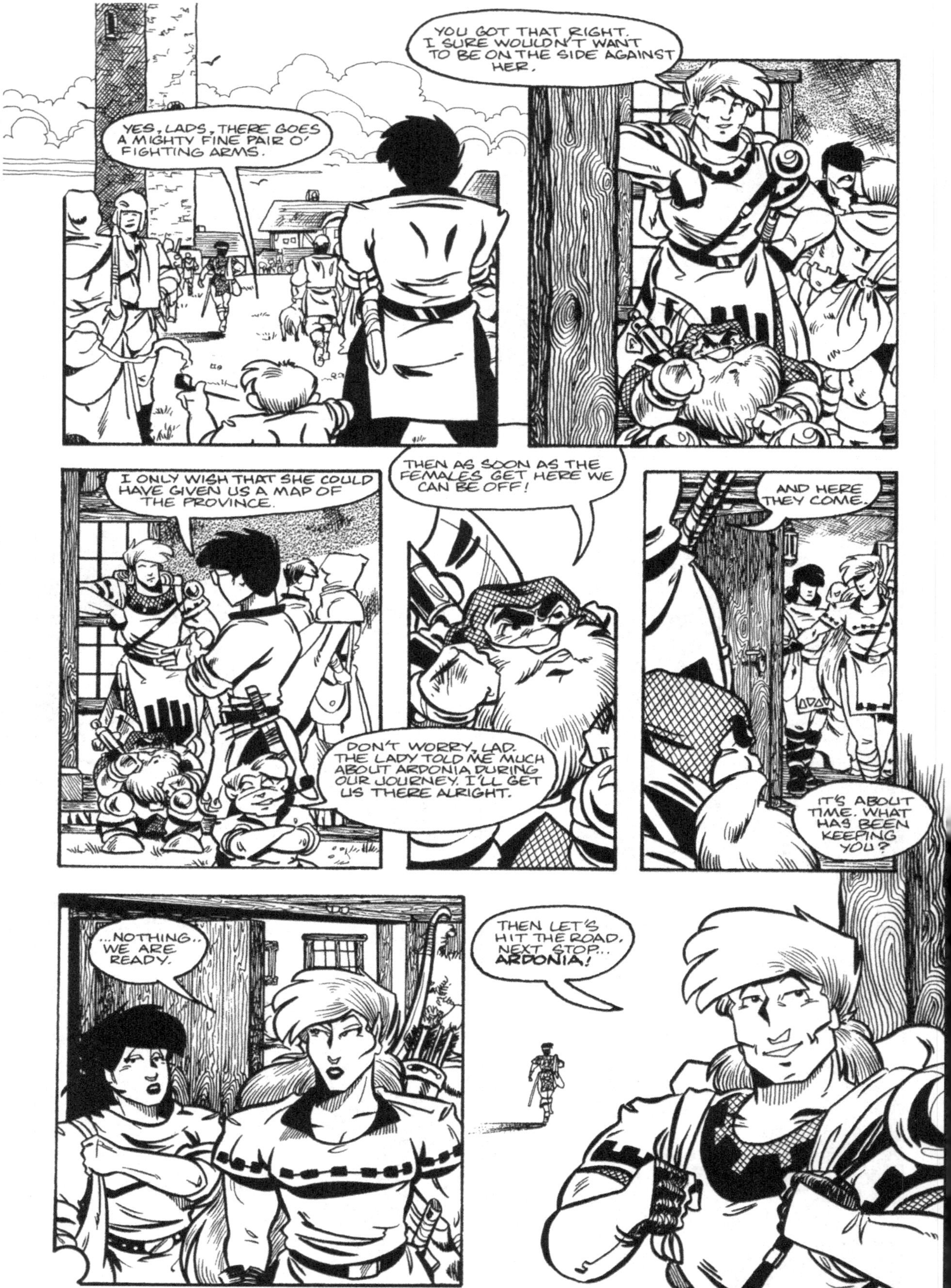
YES, LADS, THERE GOES A MIGHTY FINE PAIR O' FIGHTING ARMS.
YOU GOT THAT RIGHT. I SURE WOULDN'T WANT TO BE ON THE SIDE AGAINST HER.
I ONLY WISH THAT SHE COULD HAVE GIVEN US A MAP OF THE PROVINCE.
DON'T WORRY, LAD. THE LADY TOLD ME MUCH ABOUT ARDONIA DURING OUR JOURNEY. I'LL GET US THERE ALRIGHT.
THEN AS SOON AS THE FEMALES GET HERE WE CAN BE OFF!
AND HERE THEY COME.
IT'S ABOUT TIME. WHAT HAS BEEN KEEPING YOU?
...NOTHING.. WE ARE READY.
THEN LET'S HIT THE ROAD. NEXT STOP... **ARDONIA!**

NEXT ISSUE:

HAIL TO OUR QUEEN

LEGENDLORE

THE REALM - VOLUME ONE

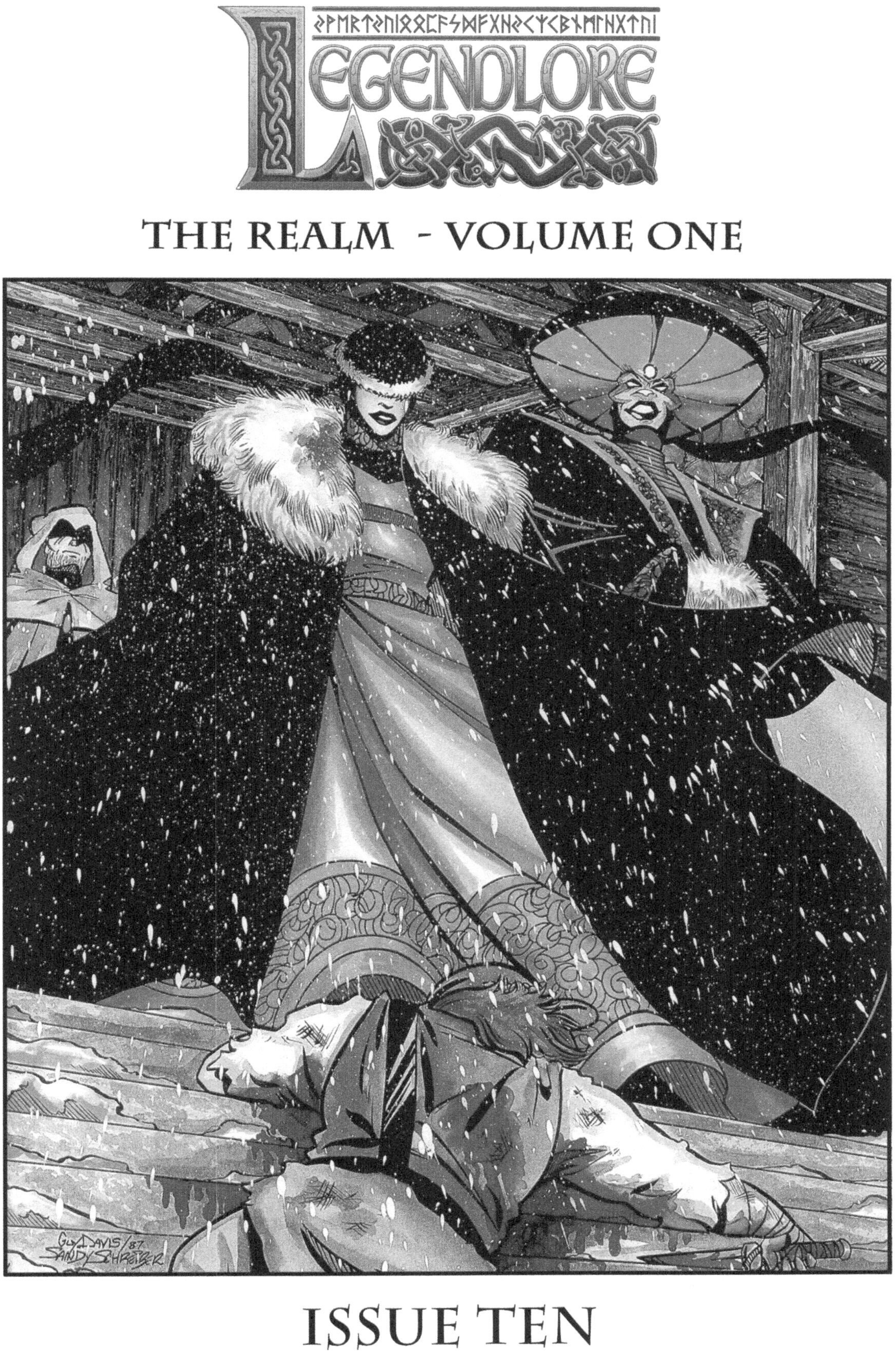
GUY DAVIS/'87
SANDY SCHREIBER

ISSUE TEN

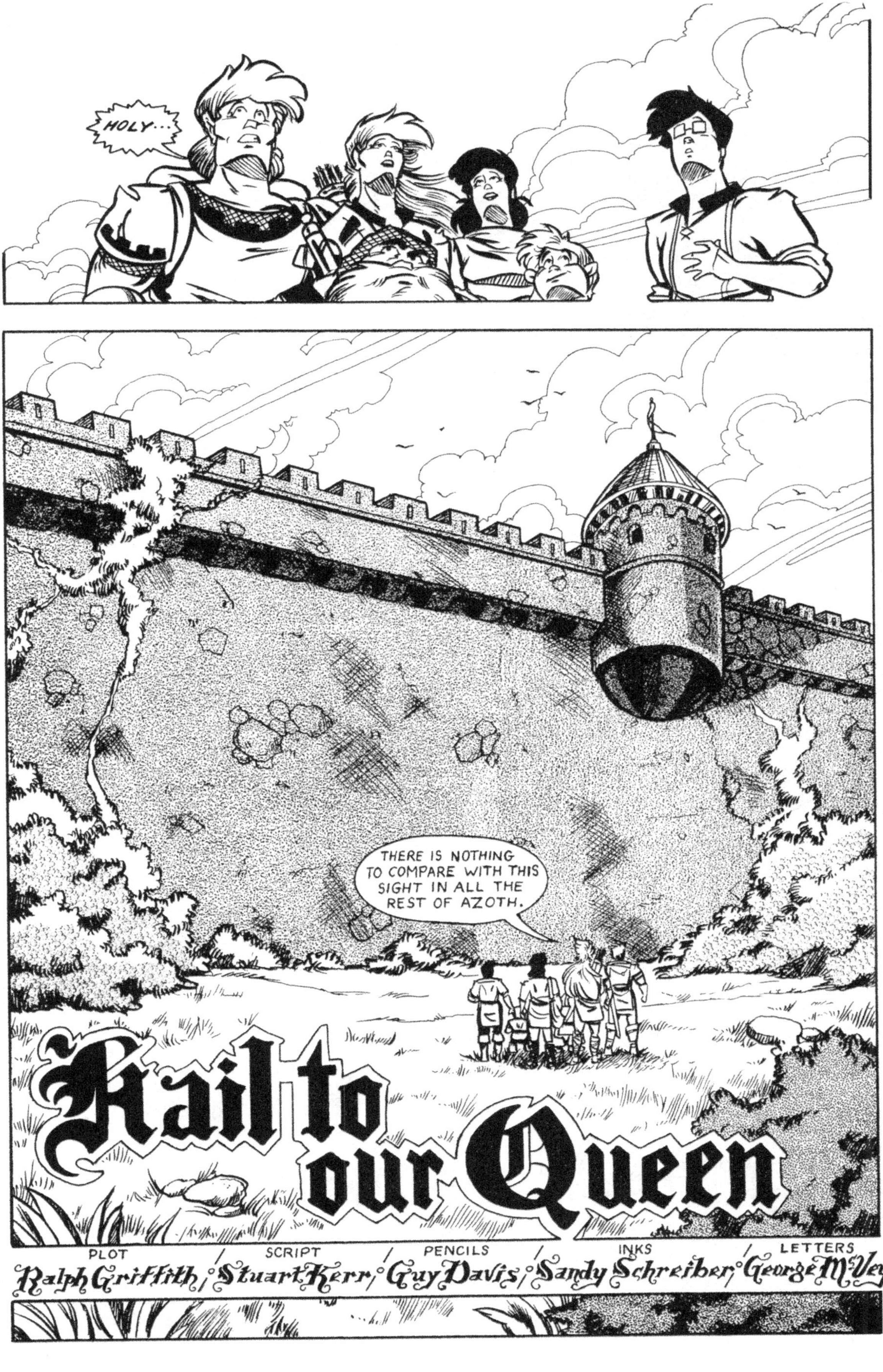
HOLY...
THERE IS NOTHING TO COMPARE WITH THIS SIGHT IN ALL THE REST OF AZOTH.
Hail to our Queen
PLOT Ralph Griffith / SCRIPT Stuart Kerr / PENCILS Guy Davis / INKS Sandy Schreiber / LETTERS George McVey

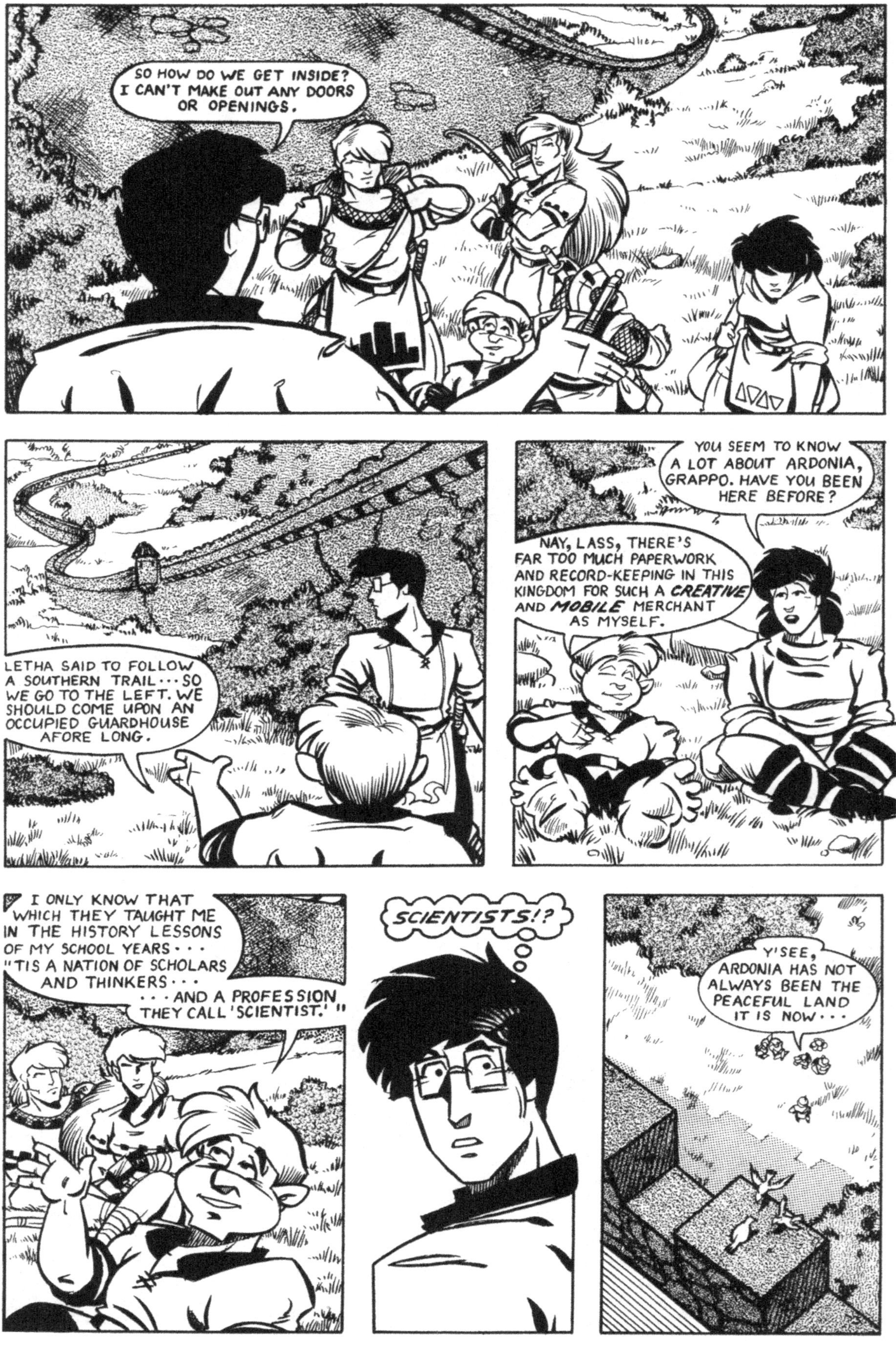
SO HOW DO WE GET INSIDE? I CAN'T MAKE OUT ANY DOORS OR OPENINGS.
LETHA SAID TO FOLLOW A SOUTHERN TRAIL··· SO WE GO TO THE LEFT. WE SHOULD COME UPON AN OCCUPIED GUARDHOUSE AFORE LONG.
YOU SEEM TO KNOW A LOT ABOUT ARDONIA, GRAPPO. HAVE YOU BEEN HERE BEFORE?
NAY, LASS, THERE'S FAR TOO MUCH PAPERWORK AND RECORD-KEEPING IN THIS KINGDOM FOR SUCH A CREATIVE AND MOBILE MERCHANT AS MYSELF.
I ONLY KNOW THAT WHICH THEY TAUGHT ME IN THE HISTORY LESSONS OF MY SCHOOL YEARS··· "TIS A NATION OF SCHOLARS AND THINKERS··· ···AND A PROFESSION THEY CALL 'SCIENTIST.'"
SCIENTISTS!?
Y'SEE, ARDONIA HAS NOT ALWAYS BEEN THE PEACEFUL LAND IT IS NOW···

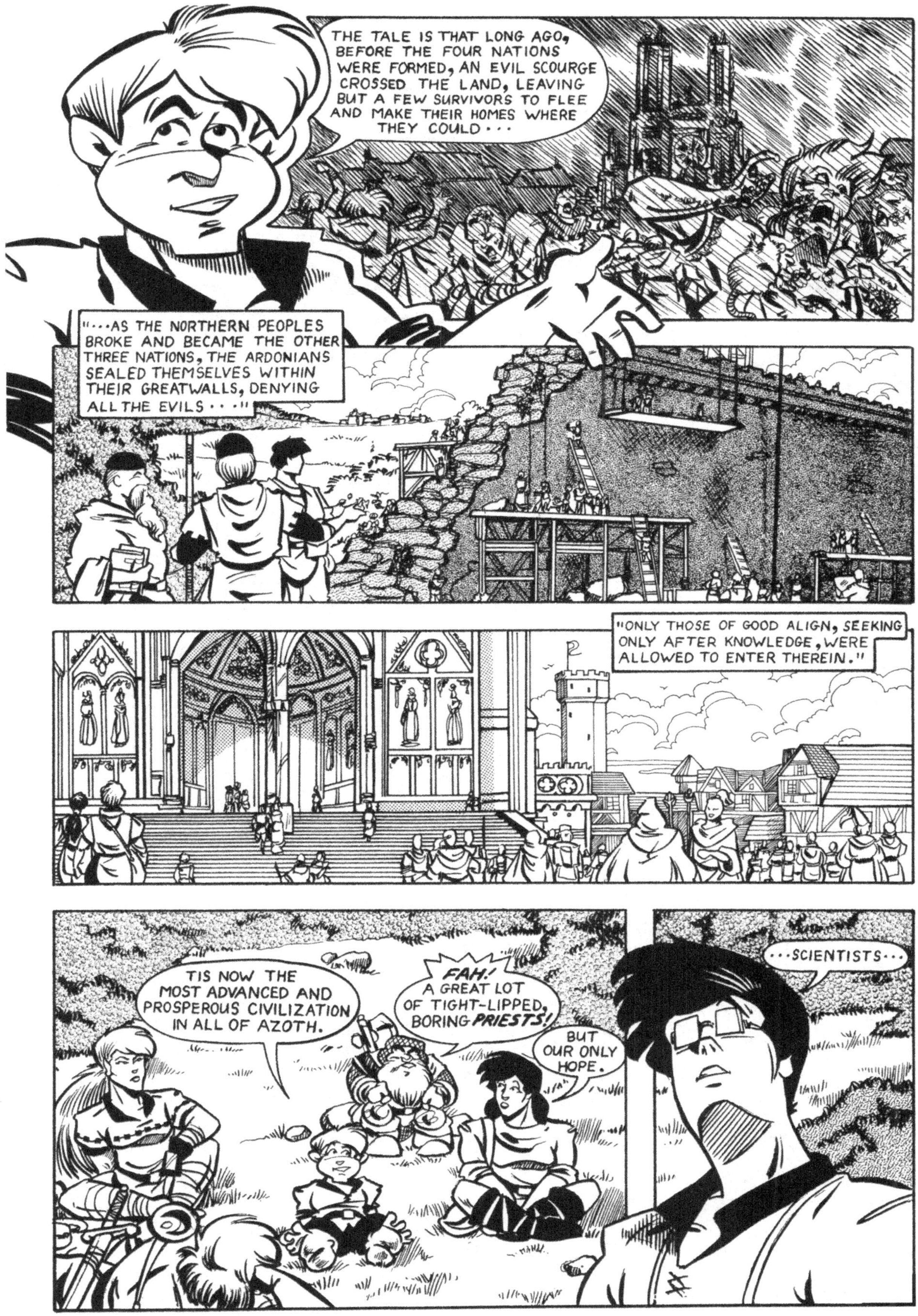
THE TALE IS THAT LONG AGO, BEFORE THE FOUR NATIONS WERE FORMED, AN EVIL SCOURGE CROSSED THE LAND, LEAVING BUT A FEW SURVIVORS TO FLEE AND MAKE THEIR HOMES WHERE THEY COULD...
"...AS THE NORTHERN PEOPLES BROKE AND BECAME THE OTHER THREE NATIONS, THE ARDONIANS SEALED THEMSELVES WITHIN THEIR GREATWALLS, DENYING ALL THE EVILS..."
"ONLY THOSE OF GOOD ALIGN, SEEKING ONLY AFTER KNOWLEDGE, WERE ALLOWED TO ENTER THEREIN."
TIS NOW THE MOST ADVANCED AND PROSPEROUS CIVILIZATION IN ALL OF AZOTH.
FAH! A GREAT LOT OF TIGHT-LIPPED, BORING PRIESTS!
BUT OUR ONLY HOPE.
...SCIENTISTS...

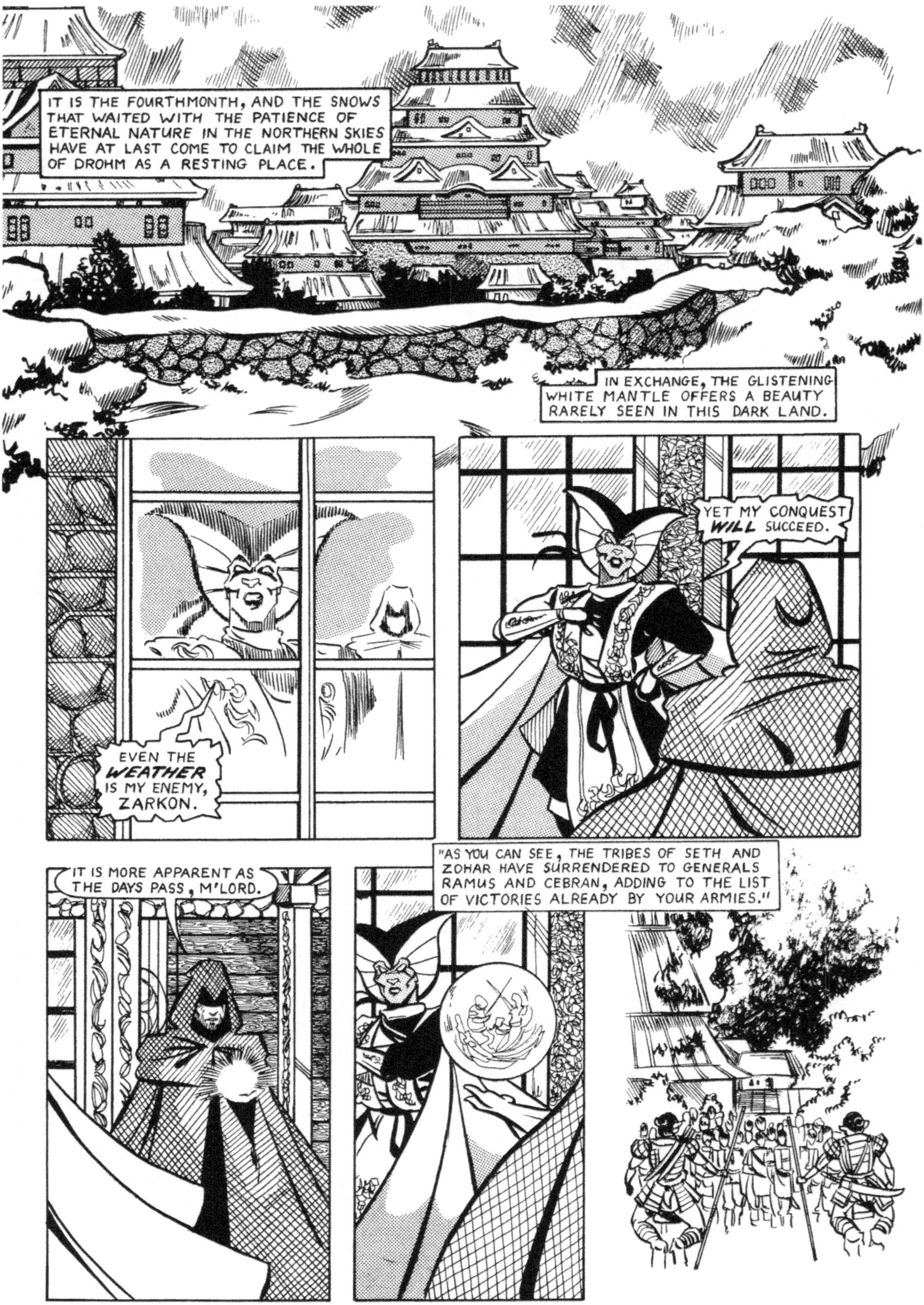
IT IS THE FOURTHMONTH, AND THE SNOWS THAT WAITED WITH THE PATIENCE OF ETERNAL NATURE IN THE NORTHERN SKIES HAVE AT LAST COME TO CLAIM THE WHOLE OF DROHM AS A RESTING PLACE.
IN EXCHANGE, THE GLISTENING WHITE MANTLE OFFERS A BEAUTY RARELY SEEN IN THIS DARK LAND.
EVEN THE WEATHER IS MY ENEMY, ZARKON.
YET MY CONQUEST WILL SUCCEED.
IT IS MORE APPARENT AS THE DAYS PASS, M'LORD.
"AS YOU CAN SEE, THE TRIBES OF SETH AND ZOHAR HAVE SURRENDERED TO GENERALS RAMUS AND CEBRAN, ADDING TO THE LIST OF VICTORIES ALREADY BY YOUR ARMIES."

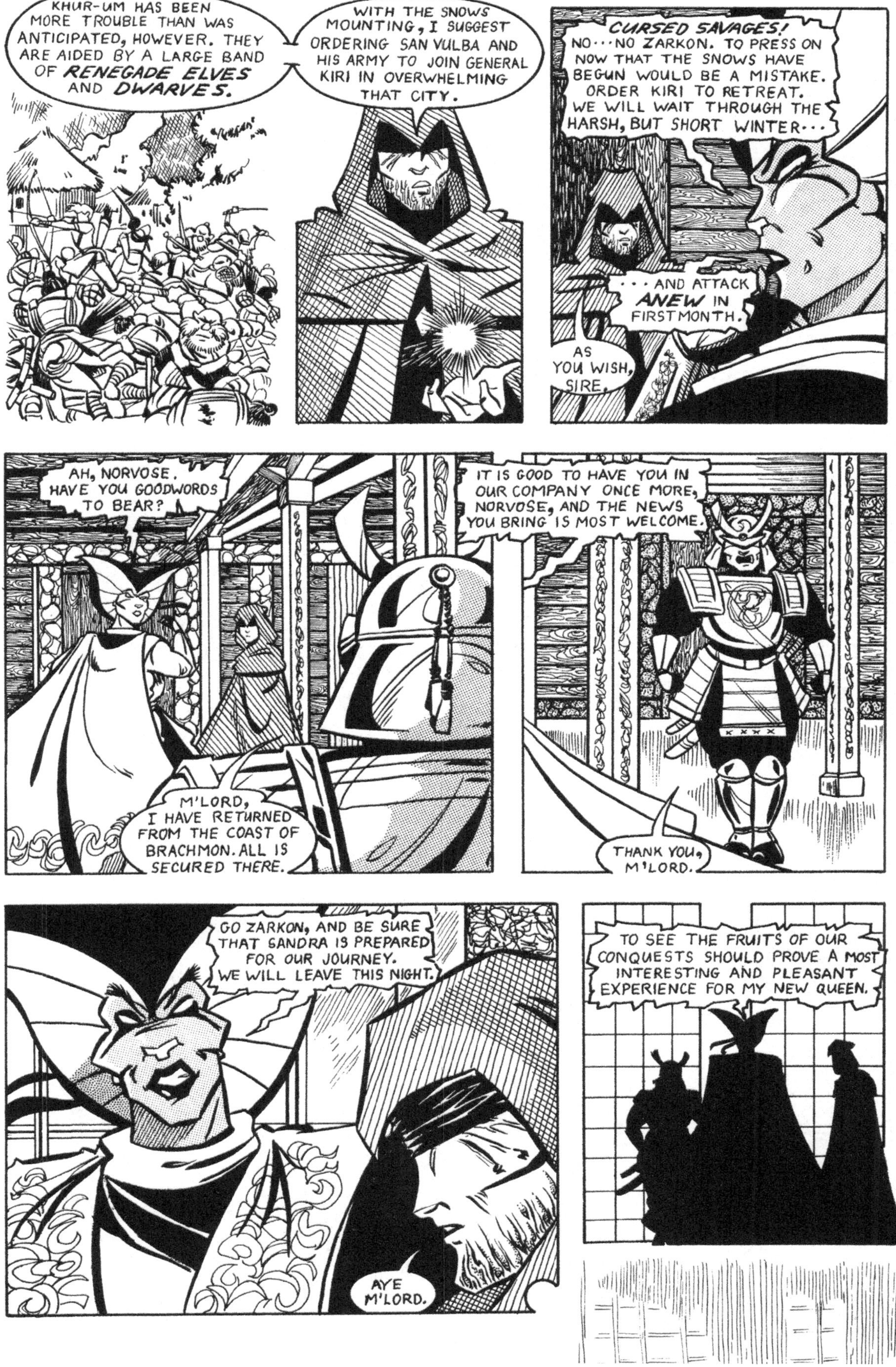
KHUR-UM HAS BEEN MORE TROUBLE THAN WAS ANTICIPATED, HOWEVER. THEY ARE AIDED BY A LARGE BAND OF RENEGADE ELVES AND DWARVES.
WITH THE SNOWS MOUNTING, I SUGGEST ORDERING SAN VULBA AND HIS ARMY TO JOIN GENERAL KIRI IN OVERWHELMING THAT CITY.
CURSED SAVAGES! NO··· NO ZARKON. TO PRESS ON NOW THAT THE SNOWS HAVE BEGUN WOULD BE A MISTAKE. ORDER KIRI TO RETREAT. WE WILL WAIT THROUGH THE HARSH, BUT SHORT WINTER···
···AND ATTACK ANEW IN FIRSTMONTH.
AS YOU WISH, SIRE.
AH, NORVOSE. HAVE YOU GOODWORDS TO BEAR?
M'LORD, I HAVE RETURNED FROM THE COAST OF BRACHMON. ALL IS SECURED THERE.
IT IS GOOD TO HAVE YOU IN OUR COMPANY ONCE MORE, NORVOSE, AND THE NEWS YOU BRING IS MOST WELCOME.
THANK YOU, M'LORD.
GO ZARKON, AND BE SURE THAT SANDRA IS PREPARED FOR OUR JOURNEY. WE WILL LEAVE THIS NIGHT.
AYE M'LORD.
TO SEE THE FRUITS OF OUR CONQUESTS SHOULD PROVE A MOST INTERESTING AND PLEASANT EXPERIENCE FOR MY NEW QUEEN.

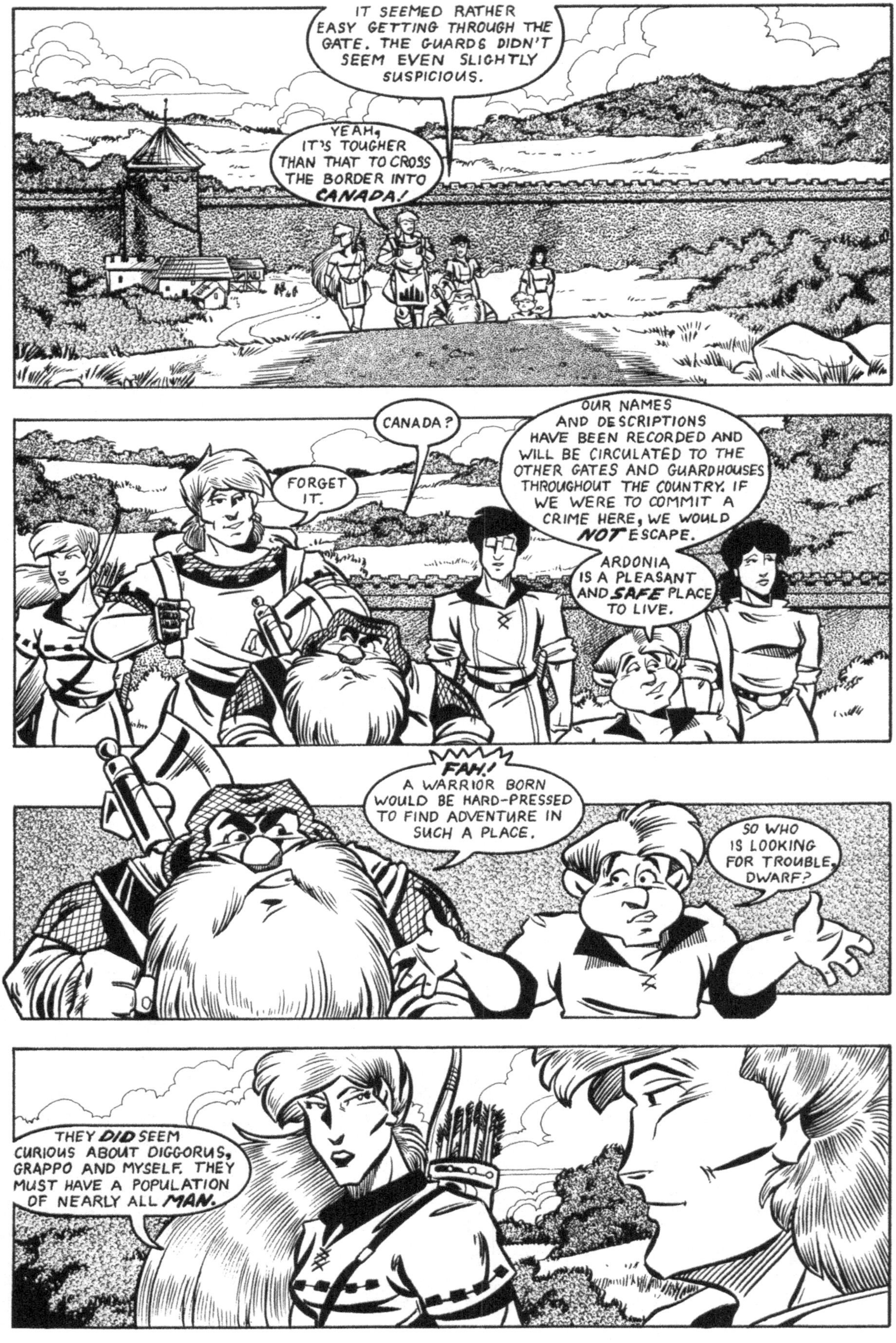
IT SEEMED RATHER EASY GETTING THROUGH THE GATE. THE GUARDS DIDN'T SEEM EVEN SLIGHTLY SUSPICIOUS.
YEAH, IT'S TOUGHER THAN THAT TO CROSS THE BORDER INTO CANADA!
CANADA?
FORGET IT.
OUR NAMES AND DESCRIPTIONS HAVE BEEN RECORDED AND WILL BE CIRCULATED TO THE OTHER GATES AND GUARDHOUSES THROUGHOUT THE COUNTRY. IF WE WERE TO COMMIT A CRIME HERE, WE WOULD NOT ESCAPE.
ARDONIA IS A PLEASANT AND SAFE PLACE TO LIVE.
FAH! A WARRIOR BORN WOULD BE HARD-PRESSED TO FIND ADVENTURE IN SUCH A PLACE.
SO WHO IS LOOKING FOR TROUBLE, DWARF?
THEY DID SEEM CURIOUS ABOUT DIGGORUS, GRAPPO AND MYSELF. THEY MUST HAVE A POPULATION OF NEARLY ALL MAN.

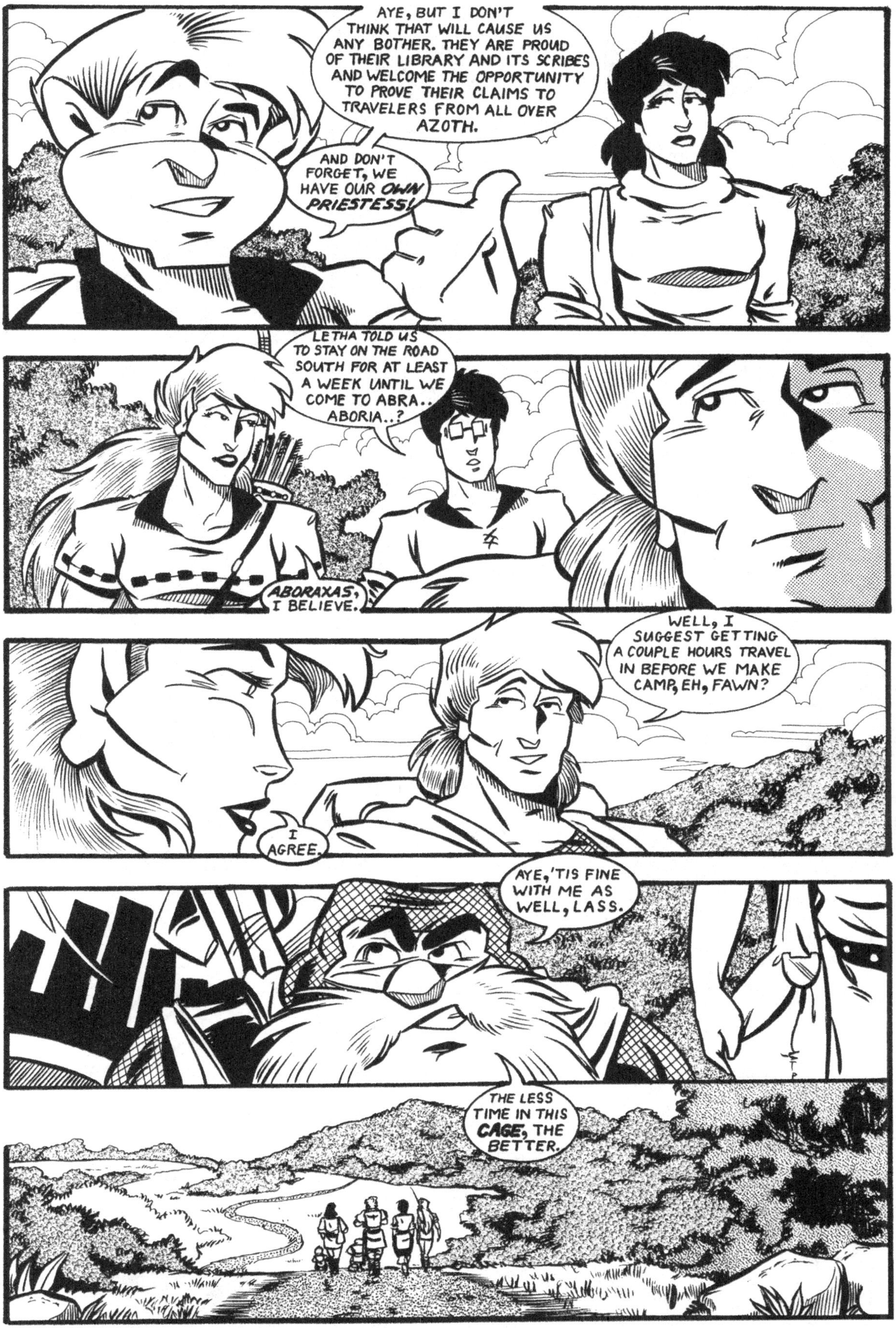
AYE, BUT I DON'T THINK THAT WILL CAUSE US ANY BOTHER. THEY ARE PROUD OF THEIR LIBRARY AND ITS SCRIBES AND WELCOME THE OPPORTUNITY TO PROVE THEIR CLAIMS TO TRAVELERS FROM ALL OVER AZOTH.
AND DON'T FORGET, WE HAVE OUR *OWN PRIESTESS!*
LETHA TOLD US TO STAY ON THE ROAD SOUTH FOR AT LEAST A WEEK UNTIL WE COME TO ABRA.. ABORIA..?
ABORAXAS, I BELIEVE.
WELL, I SUGGEST GETTING A COUPLE HOURS TRAVEL IN BEFORE WE MAKE CAMP, EH, FAWN?
I AGREE.
AYE, 'TIS FINE WITH ME AS WELL, LASS.
THE LESS TIME IN THIS *CAGE*, THE BETTER.

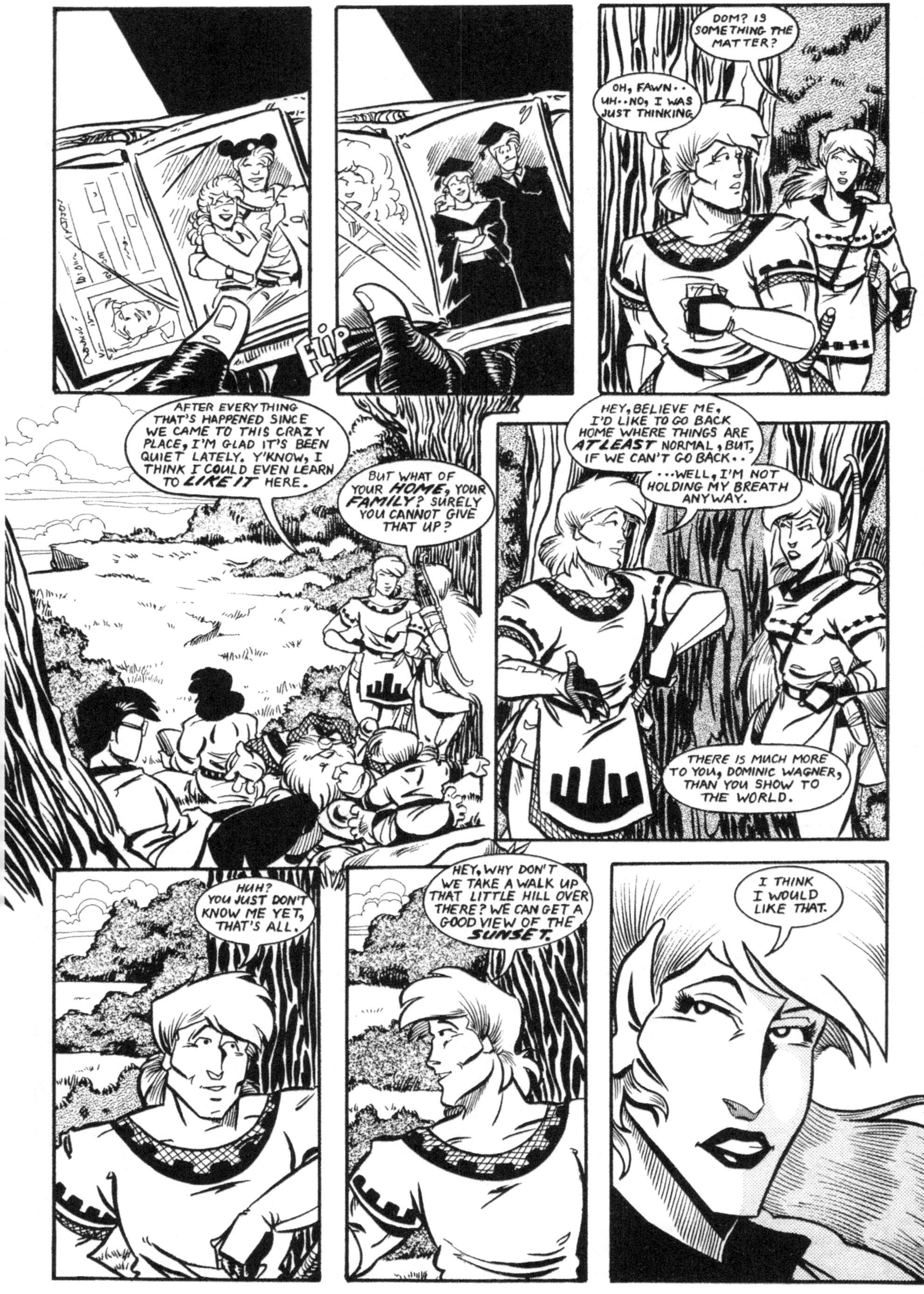

FLIP
DOM? IS SOMETHING THE MATTER?
OH, FAWN.. UH..NO, I WAS JUST THINKING.
AFTER EVERYTHING THAT'S HAPPENED SINCE WE CAME TO THIS CRAZY PLACE, I'M GLAD IT'S BEEN QUIET LATELY. Y'KNOW, I THINK I COULD EVEN LEARN TO LIKE IT HERE.
BUT WHAT OF YOUR HOME, YOUR FAMILY? SURELY YOU CANNOT GIVE THAT UP?
HEY, BELIEVE ME, I'D LIKE TO GO BACK HOME WHERE THINGS ARE ATLEAST NORMAL, BUT, IF WE CAN'T GO BACK..
...WELL, I'M NOT HOLDING MY BREATH ANYWAY.
THERE IS MUCH MORE TO YOU, DOMINIC WAGNER, THAN YOU SHOW TO THE WORLD.
HUH? YOU JUST DON'T KNOW ME YET, THAT'S ALL.
HEY, WHY DON'T WE TAKE A WALK UP THAT LITTLE HILL OVER THERE? WE CAN GET A GOOD VIEW OF THE SUNSET.
I THINK I WOULD LIKE THAT.

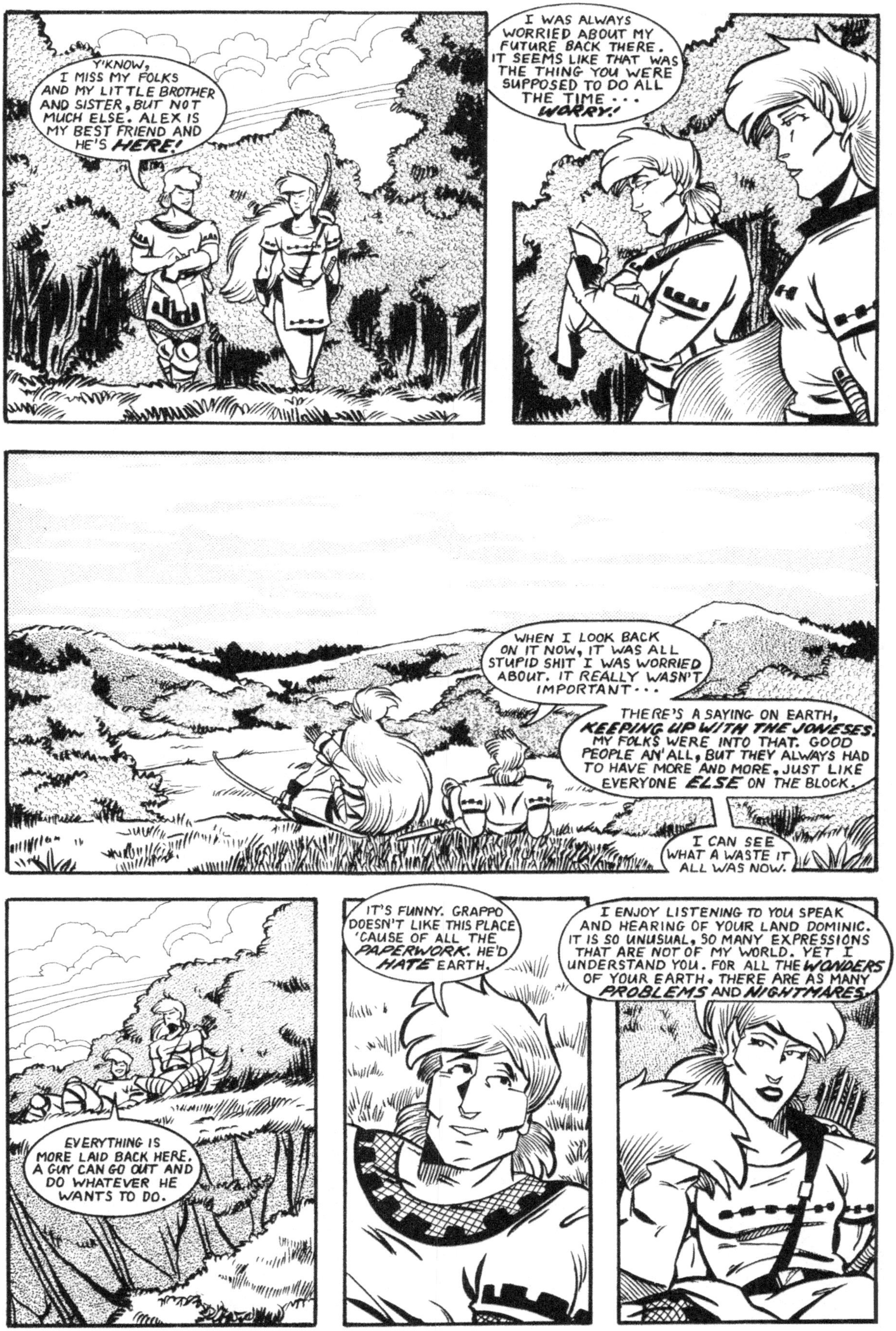
Y'KNOW, I MISS MY FOLKS AND MY LITTLE BROTHER AND SISTER, BUT NOT MUCH ELSE. ALEX IS MY BEST FRIEND AND HE'S HERE!
I WAS ALWAYS WORRIED ABOUT MY FUTURE BACK THERE. IT SEEMS LIKE THAT WAS THE THING YOU WERE SUPPOSED TO DO ALL THE TIME... WORRY!
WHEN I LOOK BACK ON IT NOW, IT WAS ALL STUPID SHIT I WAS WORRIED ABOUT. IT REALLY WASN'T IMPORTANT...
THERE'S A SAYING ON EARTH, KEEPING UP WITH THE JONESES. MY FOLKS WERE INTO THAT. GOOD PEOPLE AN' ALL, BUT THEY ALWAYS HAD TO HAVE MORE AND MORE, JUST LIKE EVERYONE ELSE ON THE BLOCK.
I CAN SEE WHAT A WASTE IT ALL WAS NOW.
EVERYTHING IS MORE LAID BACK HERE. A GUY CAN GO OUT AND DO WHATEVER HE WANTS TO DO.
IT'S FUNNY. GRAPPO DOESN'T LIKE THIS PLACE 'CAUSE OF ALL THE PAPERWORK. HE'D HATE EARTH.
I ENJOY LISTENING TO YOU SPEAK AND HEARING OF YOUR LAND DOMINIC. IT IS SO UNUSUAL, SO MANY EXPRESSIONS THAT ARE NOT OF MY WORLD. YET I UNDERSTAND YOU. FOR ALL THE WONDERS OF YOUR EARTH, THERE ARE AS MANY PROBLEMS AND NIGHTMARES.

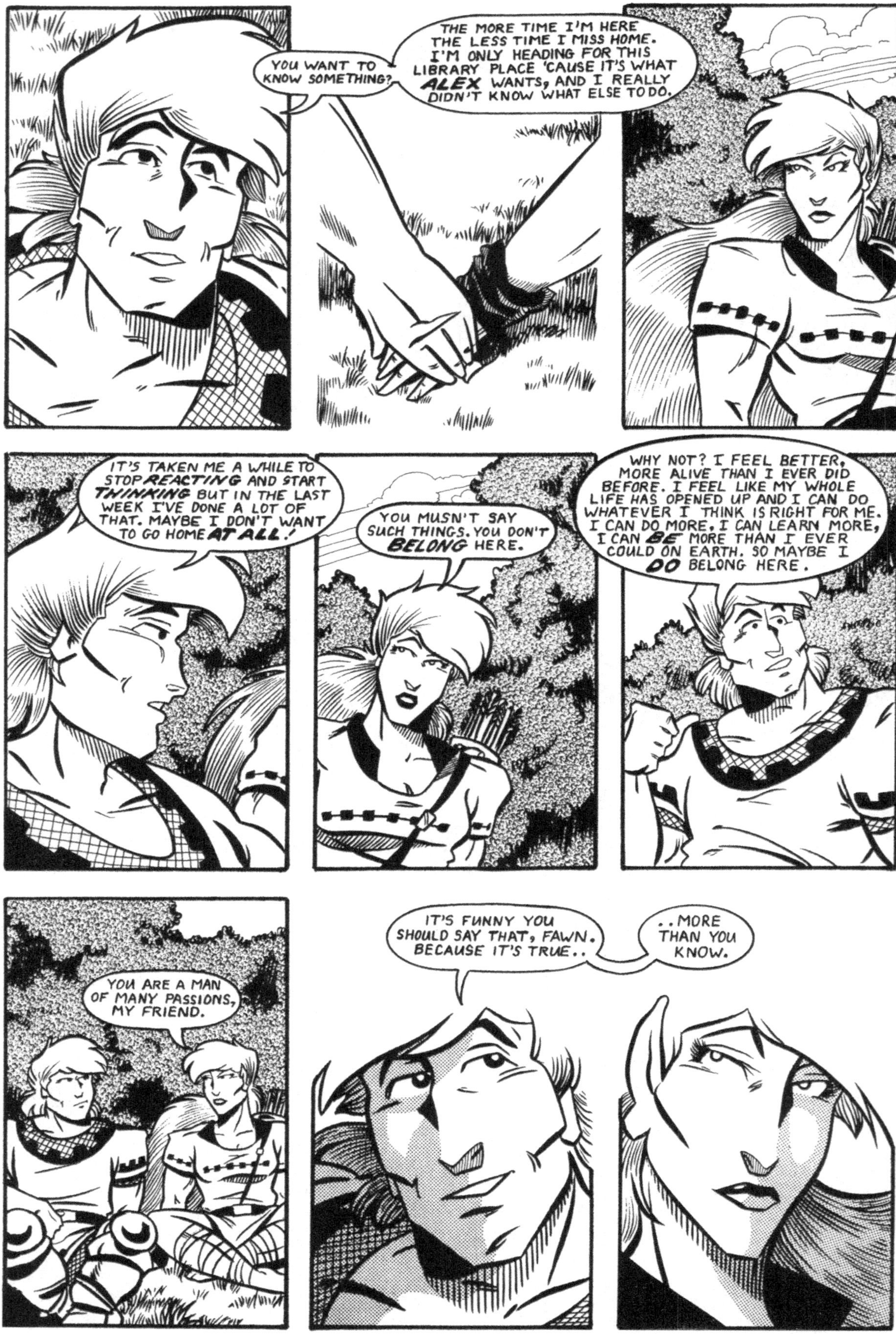

YOU WANT TO KNOW SOMETHING?
THE MORE TIME I'M HERE THE LESS TIME I MISS HOME. I'M ONLY HEADING FOR THIS LIBRARY PLACE 'CAUSE IT'S WHAT ALEX WANTS, AND I REALLY DIDN'T KNOW WHAT ELSE TO DO.
IT'S TAKEN ME A WHILE TO STOP REACTING AND START THINKING BUT IN THE LAST WEEK I'VE DONE A LOT OF THAT. MAYBE I DON'T WANT TO GO HOME AT ALL!
YOU MUSN'T SAY SUCH THINGS. YOU DON'T BELONG HERE.
WHY NOT? I FEEL BETTER, MORE ALIVE THAN I EVER DID BEFORE. I FEEL LIKE MY WHOLE LIFE HAS OPENED UP AND I CAN DO WHATEVER I THINK IS RIGHT FOR ME. I CAN DO MORE, I CAN LEARN MORE, I CAN BE MORE THAN I EVER COULD ON EARTH. SO MAYBE I DO BELONG HERE.
YOU ARE A MAN OF MANY PASSIONS, MY FRIEND.
IT'S FUNNY YOU SHOULD SAY THAT, FAWN. BECAUSE IT'S TRUE..
..MORE THAN YOU KNOW.

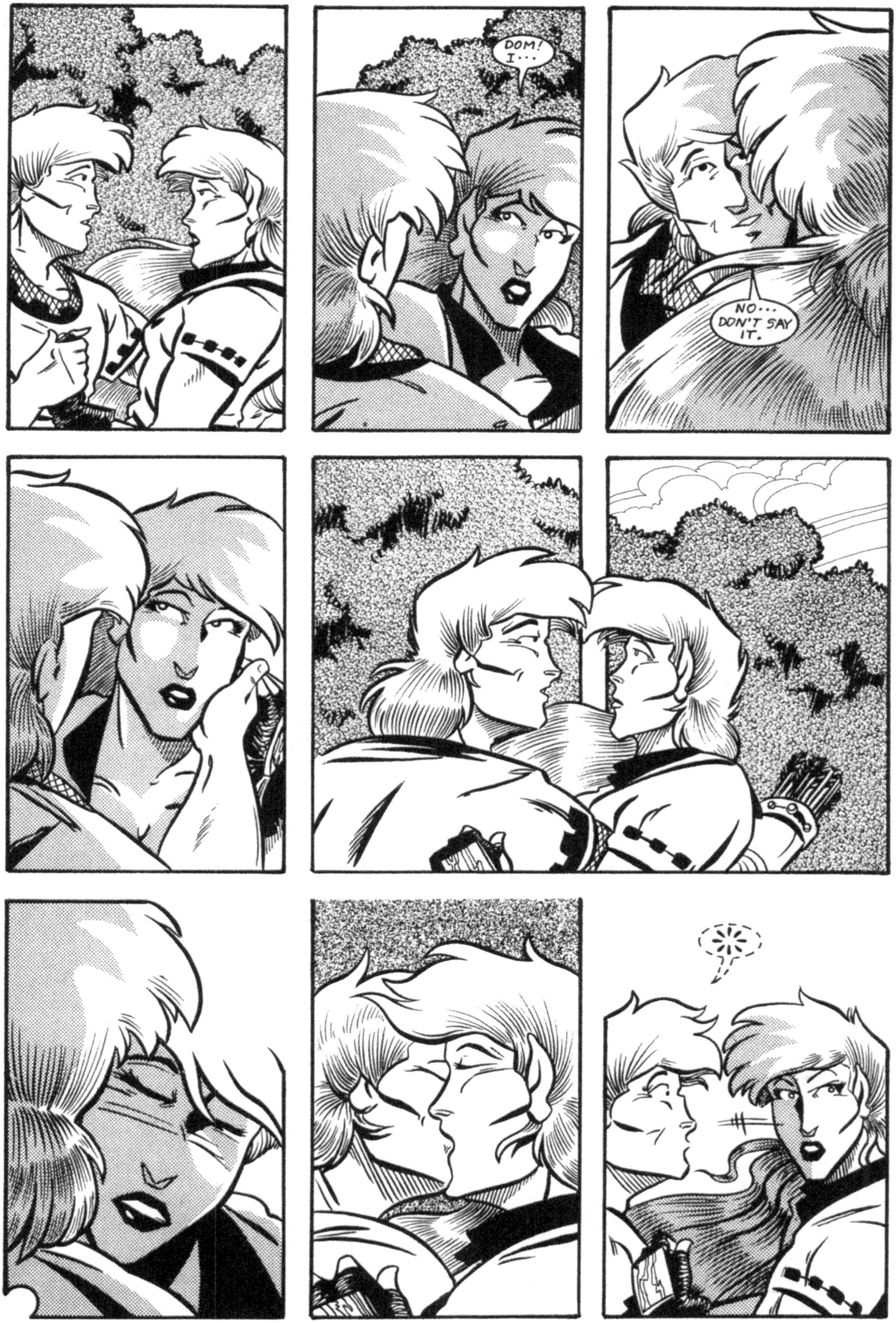
DOM! I...
NO... DON'T SAY IT.

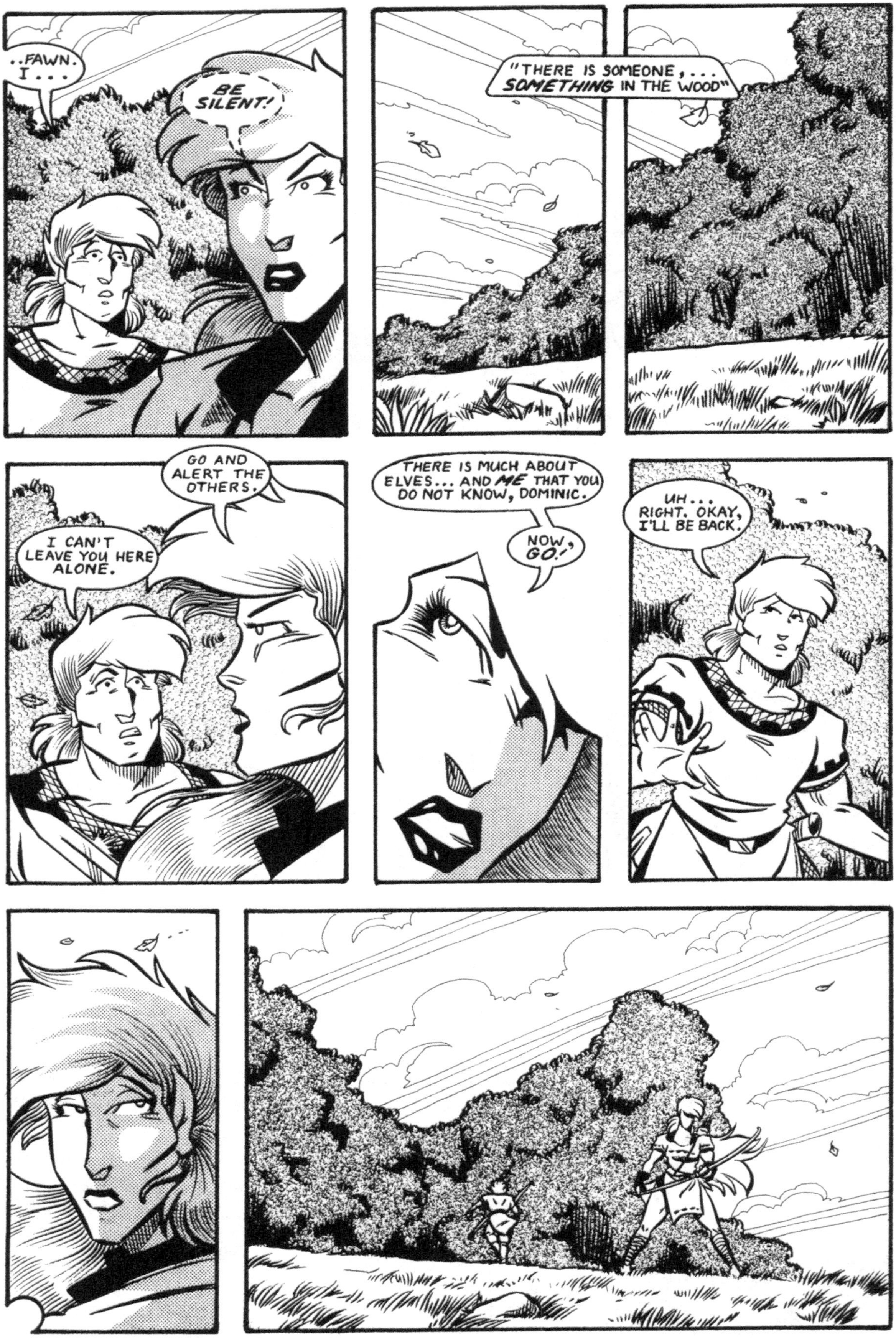

..FAWN. I . . .
BE SILENT!
"THERE IS SOMEONE, . . . SOMETHING IN THE WOOD"
GO AND ALERT THE OTHERS.
I CAN'T LEAVE YOU HERE ALONE.
THERE IS MUCH ABOUT ELVES . . . AND ME THAT YOU DO NOT KNOW, DOMINIC.
NOW, GO!
UH . . . RIGHT. OKAY, I'LL BE BACK.

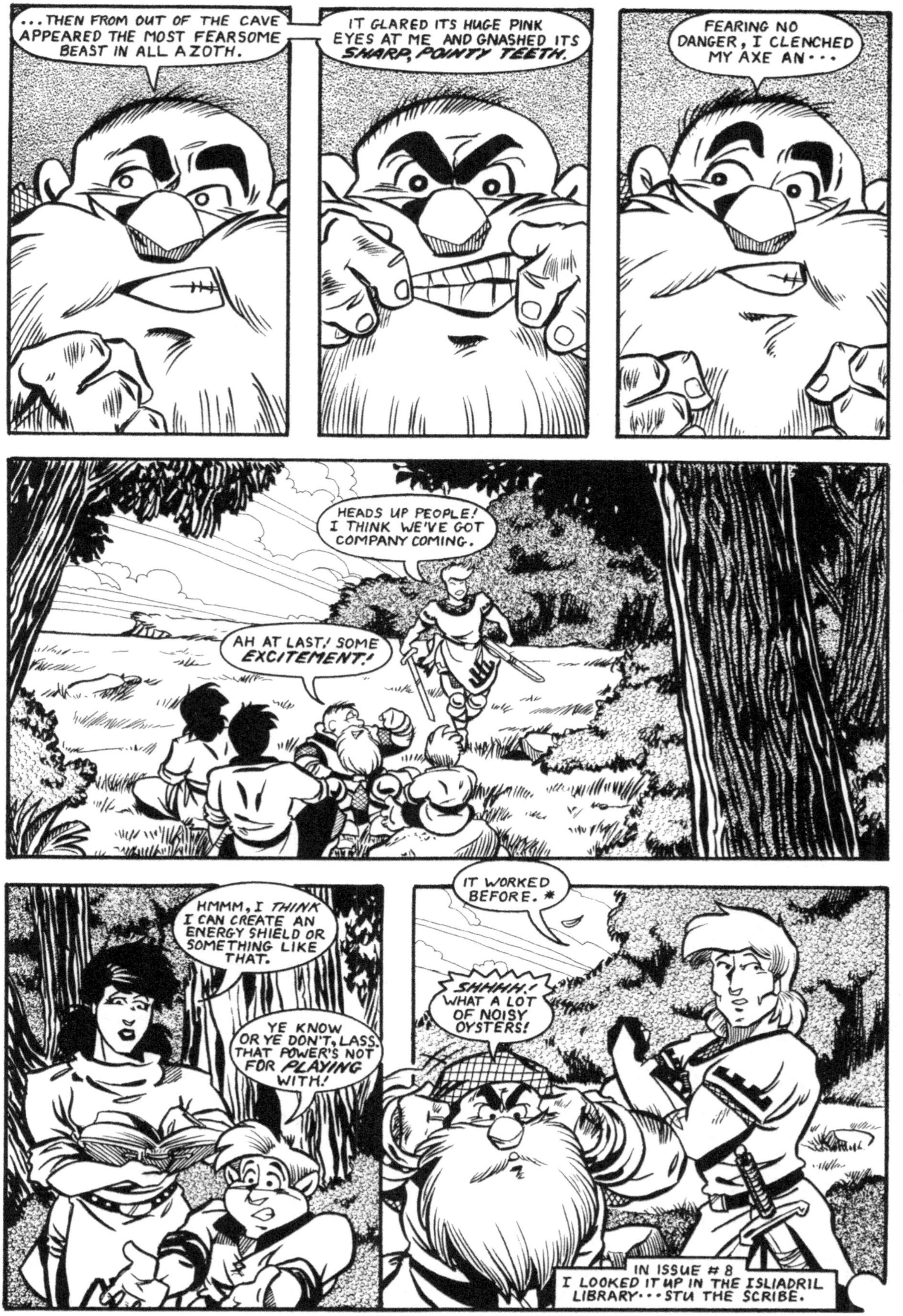
...THEN FROM OUT OF THE CAVE APPEARED THE MOST FEARSOME BEAST IN ALL AZOTH.
IT GLARED ITS HUGE PINK EYES AT ME AND GNASHED ITS *SHARP, POINTY TEETH.*
FEARING NO DANGER, I CLENCHED MY AXE AN...
HEADS UP PEOPLE! I THINK WE'VE GOT COMPANY COMING.
AH AT LAST! SOME *EXCITEMENT!*
HMMM, I *THINK* I CAN CREATE AN ENERGY SHIELD OR SOMETHING LIKE THAT.
YE KNOW OR YE DON'T, LASS. THAT POWER'S NOT FOR *PLAYING* WITH!
IT WORKED BEFORE.*
SHHHH! WHAT A LOT OF NOISY OYSTERS!
* IN ISSUE # 8 I LOOKED IT UP IN THE ISLIADRIL LIBRARY...STU THE SCRIBE.

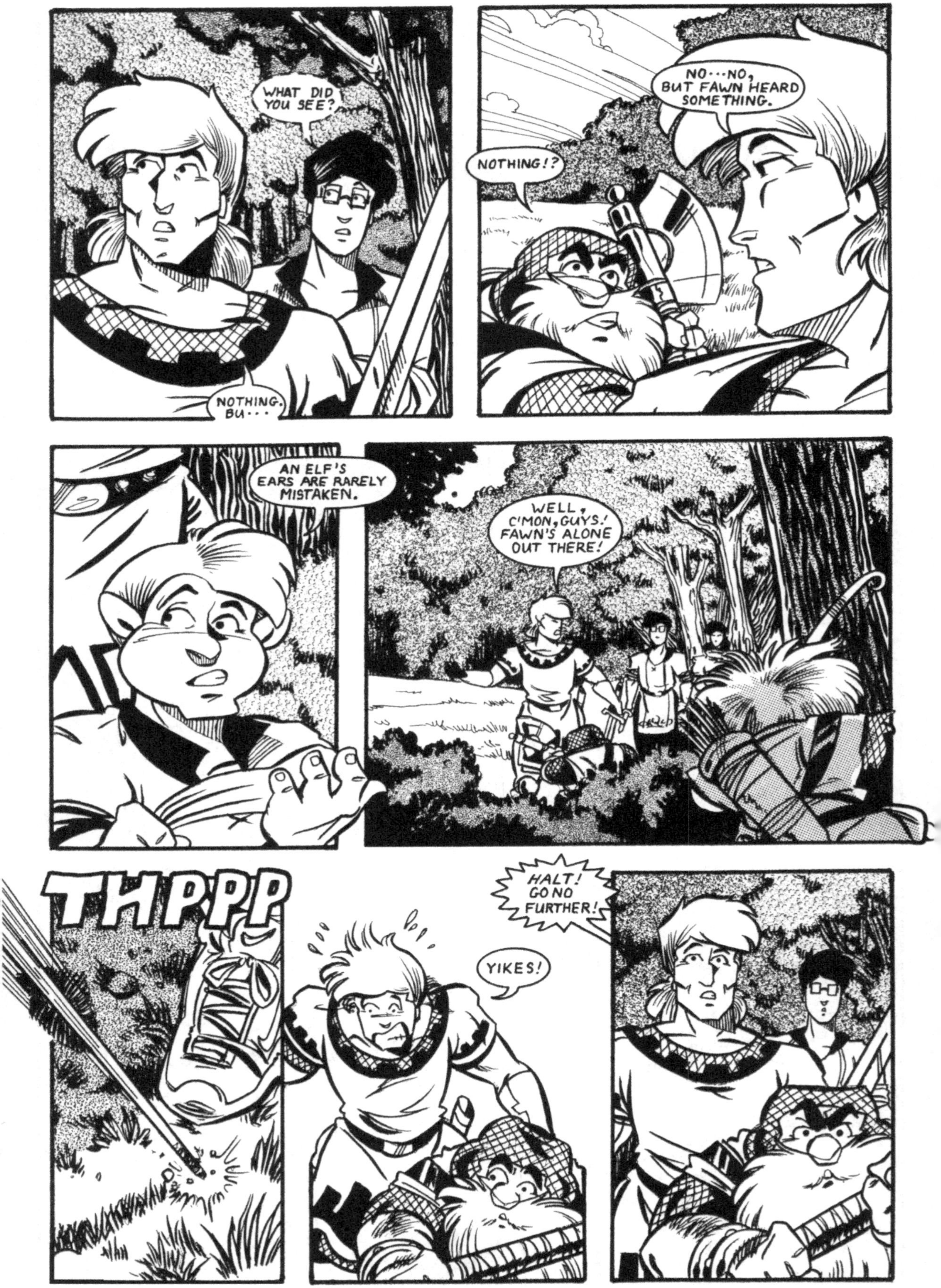

WHAT DID YOU SEE?
NOTHING. BU···
NOTHING!?
NO···NO, BUT FAWN HEARD SOMETHING.
AN ELF'S EARS ARE RARELY MISTAKEN.
WELL, C'MON, GUYS! FAWN'S ALONE OUT THERE!
THPPP
YIKES!
HALT! GO NO FURTHER!

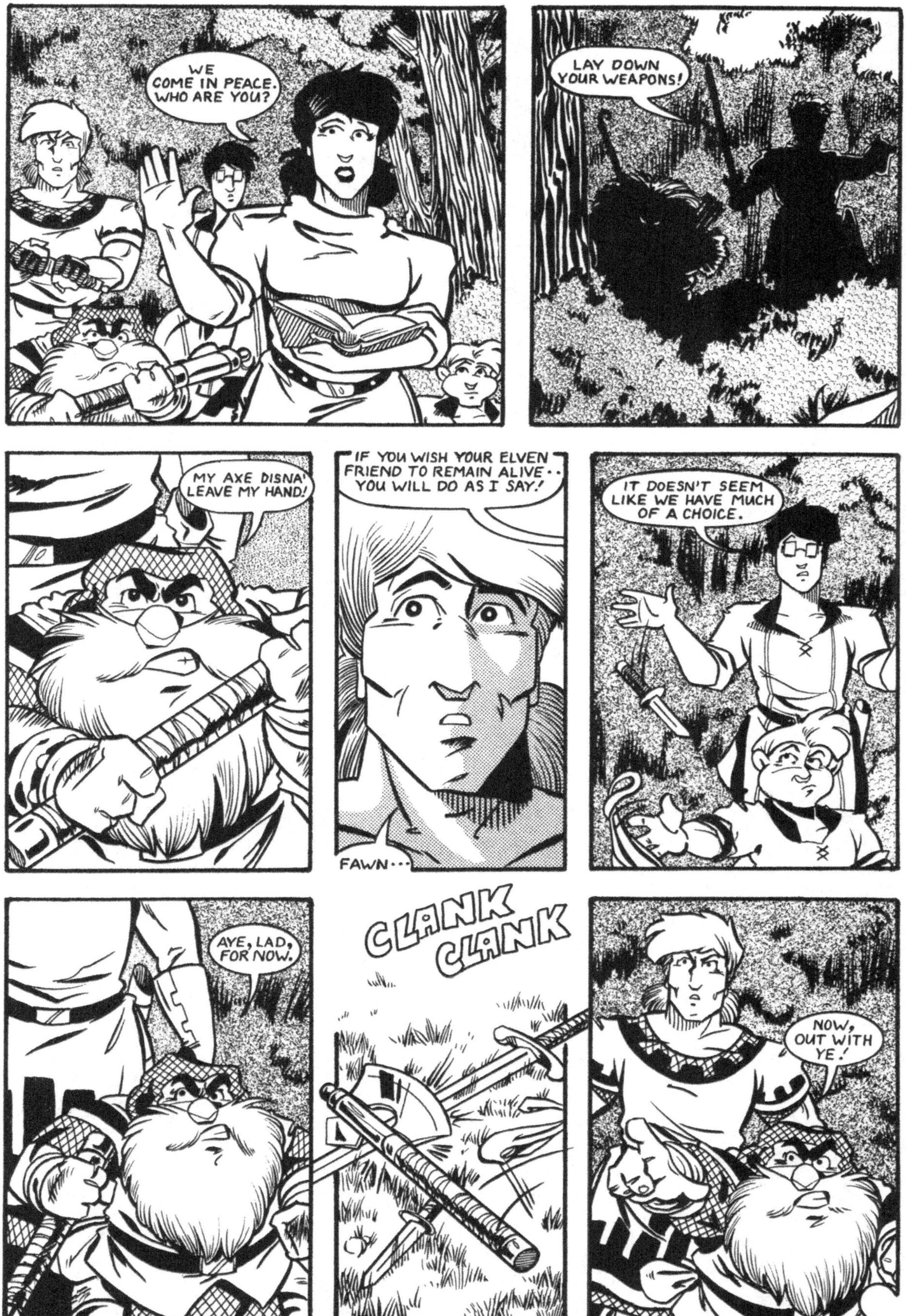
WE COME IN PEACE. WHO ARE YOU?
LAY DOWN YOUR WEAPONS!
MY AXE DISNA' LEAVE MY HAND!
IF YOU WISH YOUR ELVEN FRIEND TO REMAIN ALIVE.. YOU WILL DO AS I SAY!
FAWN...
IT DOESN'T SEEM LIKE WE HAVE MUCH OF A CHOICE.
AYE, LAD, FOR NOW.
CLANK CLANK
NOW, OUT WITH YE!

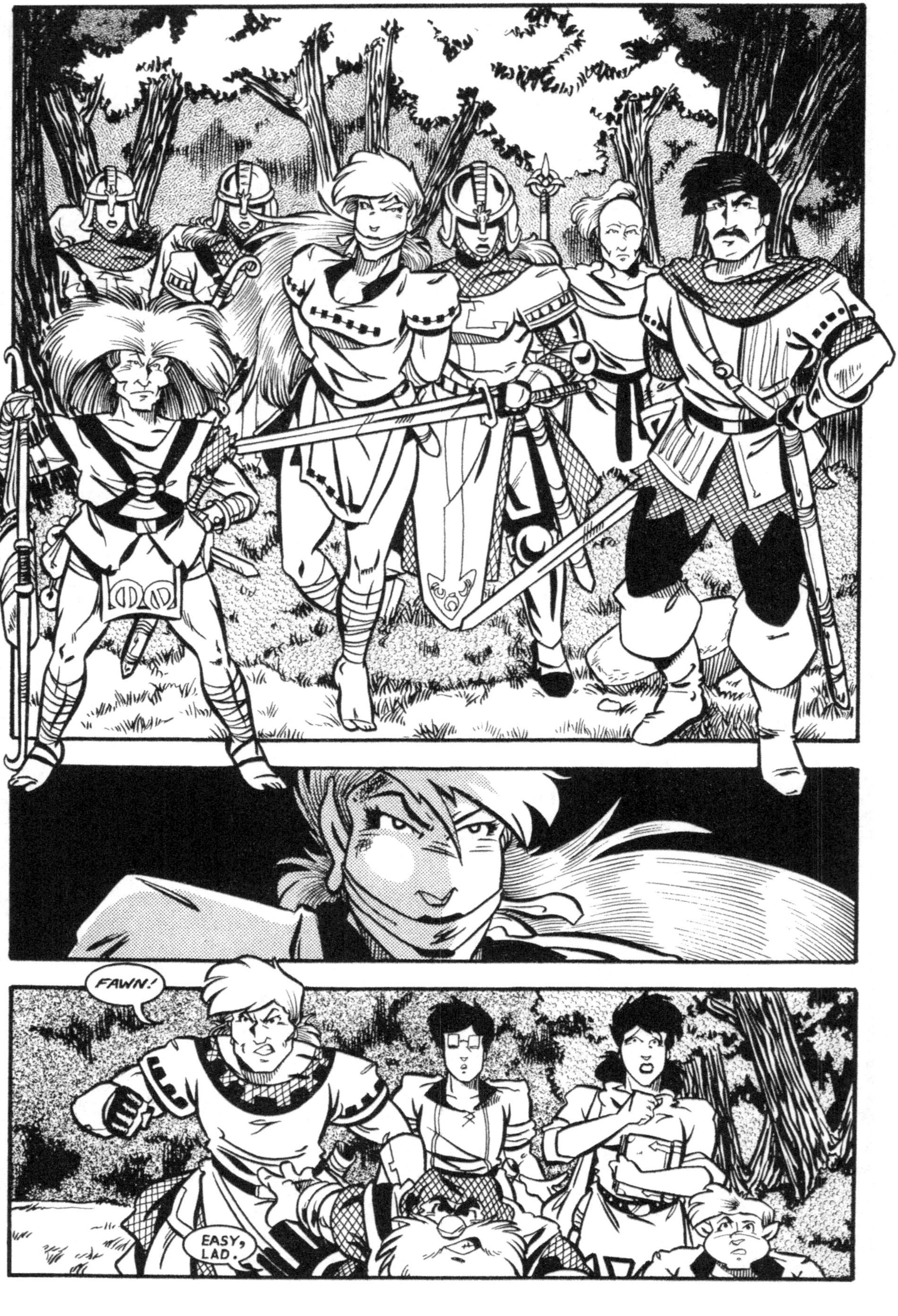
FAWN!
EASY, LAD.

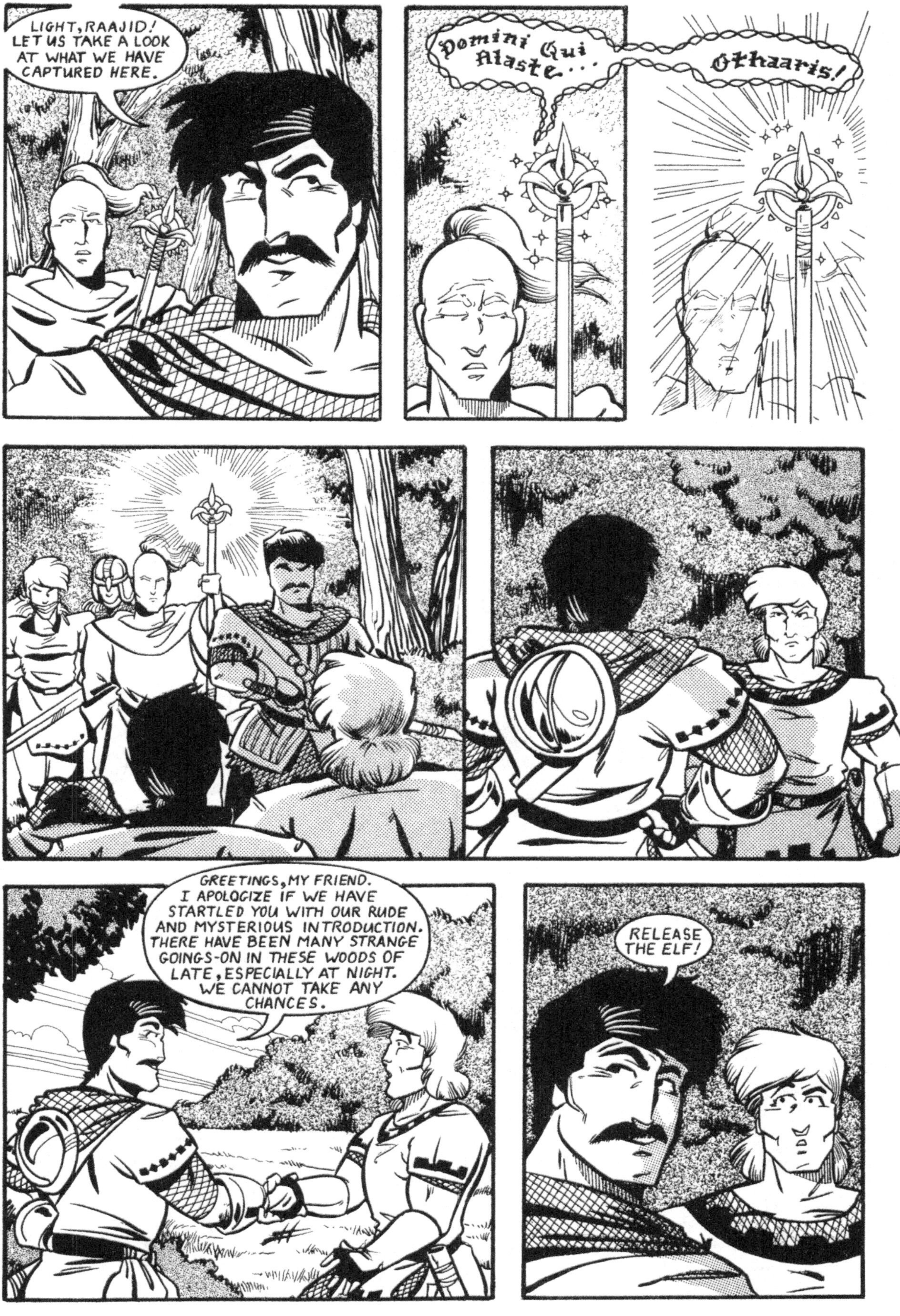

LIGHT, RAAJID! LET US TAKE A LOOK AT WHAT WE HAVE CAPTURED HERE.
Domini Qui Alaste....
Othaaris!
GREETINGS, MY FRIEND. I APOLOGIZE IF WE HAVE STARTLED YOU WITH OUR RUDE AND MYSTERIOUS INTRODUCTION. THERE HAVE BEEN MANY STRANGE GOINGS-ON IN THESE WOODS OF LATE, ESPECIALLY AT NIGHT. WE CANNOT TAKE ANY CHANCES.
RELEASE THE ELF!

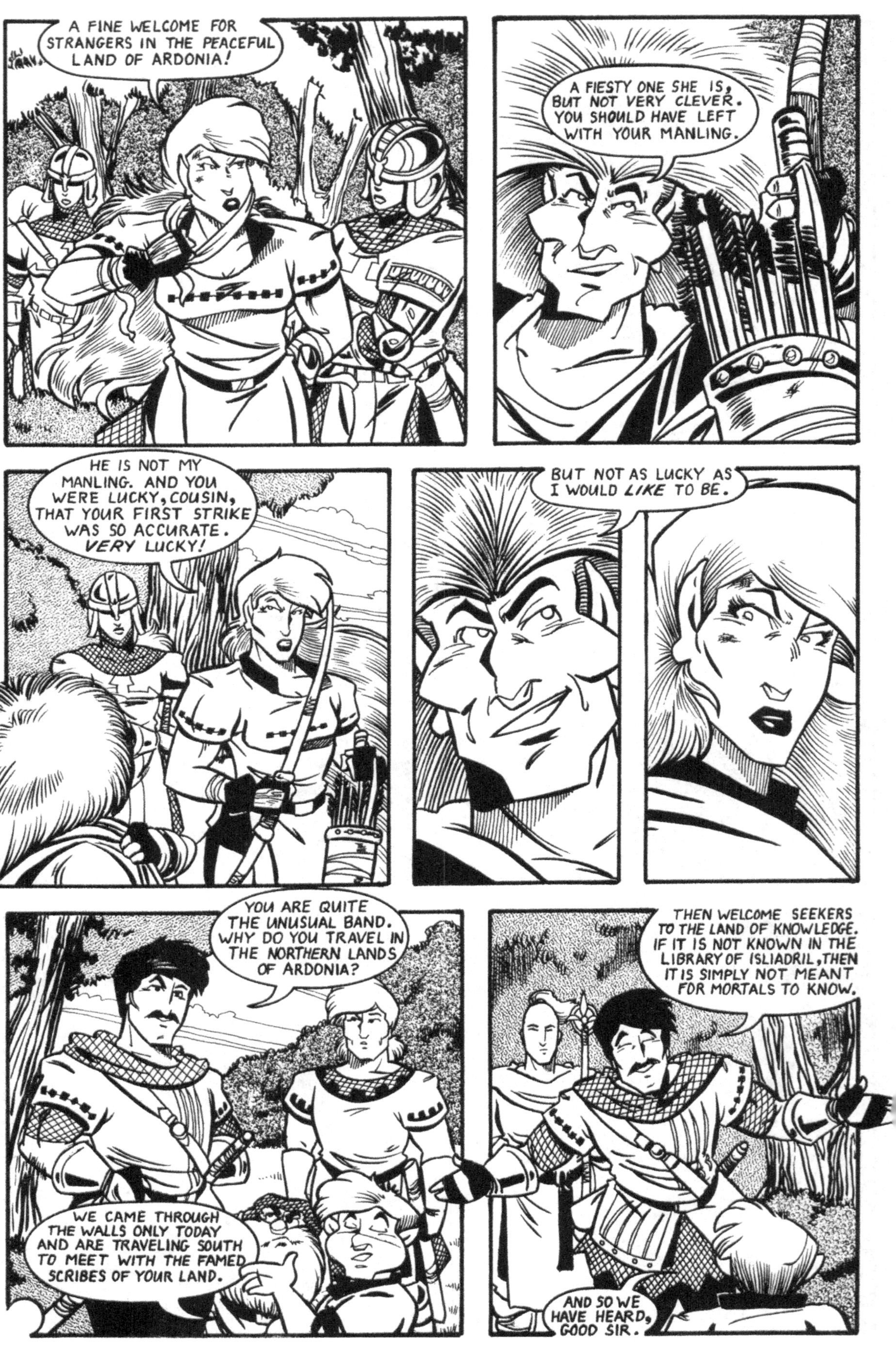
A FINE WELCOME FOR STRANGERS IN THE PEACEFUL LAND OF ARDONIA!
A FIESTY ONE SHE IS, BUT NOT VERY CLEVER. YOU SHOULD HAVE LEFT WITH YOUR MANLING.
HE IS NOT MY MANLING. AND YOU WERE LUCKY, COUSIN, THAT YOUR FIRST STRIKE WAS SO ACCURATE. VERY LUCKY!
BUT NOT AS LUCKY AS I WOULD LIKE TO BE.
YOU ARE QUITE THE UNUSUAL BAND. WHY DO YOU TRAVEL IN THE NORTHERN LANDS OF ARDONIA?
WE CAME THROUGH THE WALLS ONLY TODAY AND ARE TRAVELING SOUTH TO MEET WITH THE FAMED SCRIBES OF YOUR LAND.
THEN WELCOME SEEKERS TO THE LAND OF KNOWLEDGE. IF IT IS NOT KNOWN IN THE LIBRARY OF ISLIADRIL, THEN IT IS SIMPLY NOT MEANT FOR MORTALS TO KNOW.
AND SO WE HAVE HEARD, GOOD SIR.

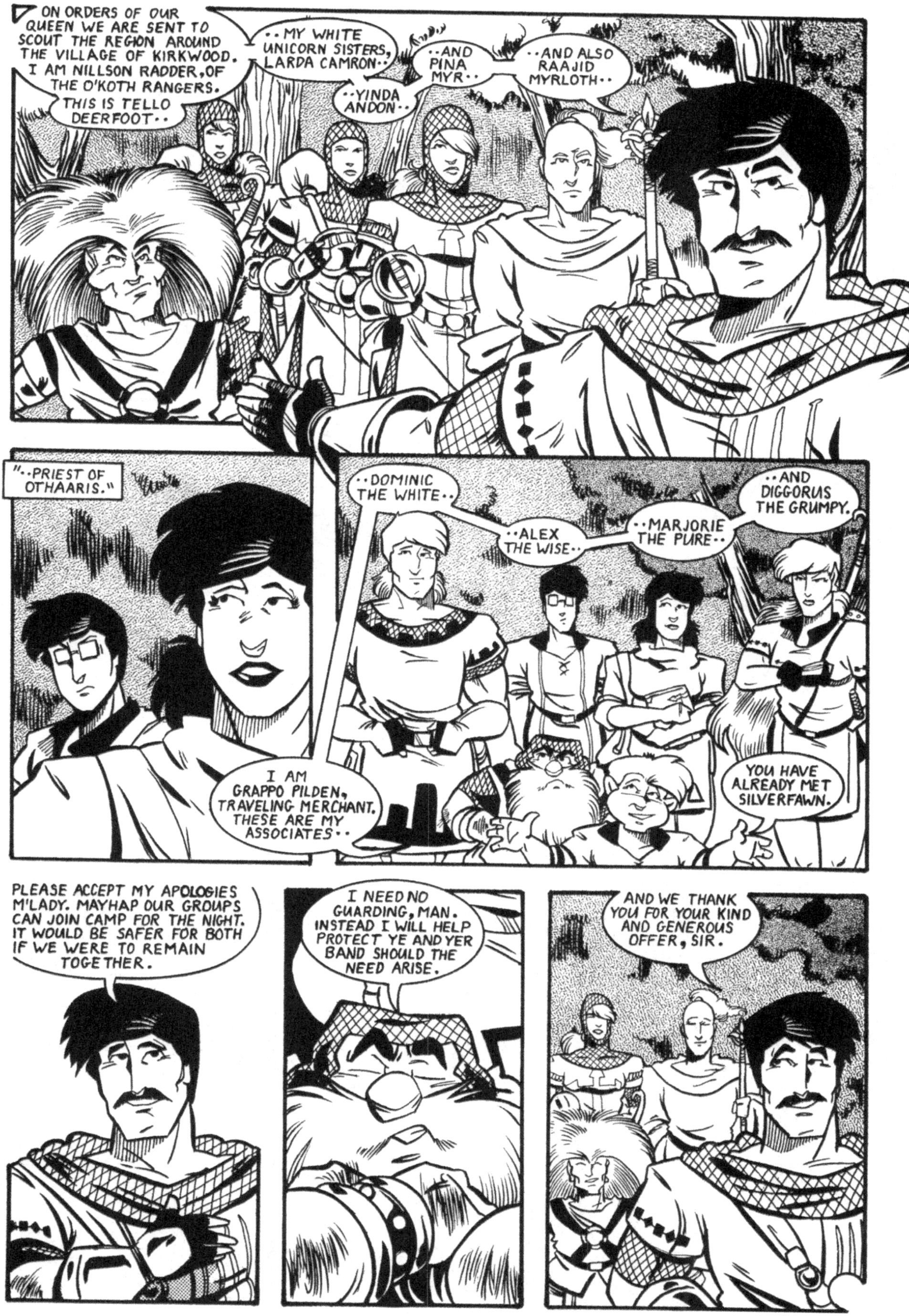
ON ORDERS OF OUR QUEEN WE ARE SENT TO SCOUT THE REGION AROUND THE VILLAGE OF KIRKWOOD. I AM NILLSON RADDER, OF THE O'KOTH RANGERS.
THIS IS TELLO DEERFOOT··
··MY WHITE UNICORN SISTERS, LARDA CAMRON··
··YINDA ANDON··
··AND PINA MYR··
··AND ALSO RAAJID MYRLOTH··
"··PRIEST OF OTHAARIS."
I AM GRAPPO PILDEN, TRAVELING MERCHANT. THESE ARE MY ASSOCIATES··
··DOMINIC THE WHITE··
··ALEX THE WISE··
··MARJORIE THE PURE··
··AND DIGGORUS THE GRUMPY.
YOU HAVE ALREADY MET SILVERFAWN.
PLEASE ACCEPT MY APOLOGIES M'LADY. MAYHAP OUR GROUPS CAN JOIN CAMP FOR THE NIGHT. IT WOULD BE SAFER FOR BOTH IF WE WERE TO REMAIN TOGETHER.
I NEED NO GUARDING, MAN. INSTEAD I WILL HELP PROTECT YE AND YER BAND SHOULD THE NEED ARISE.
AND WE THANK YOU FOR YOUR KIND AND GENEROUS OFFER, SIR.

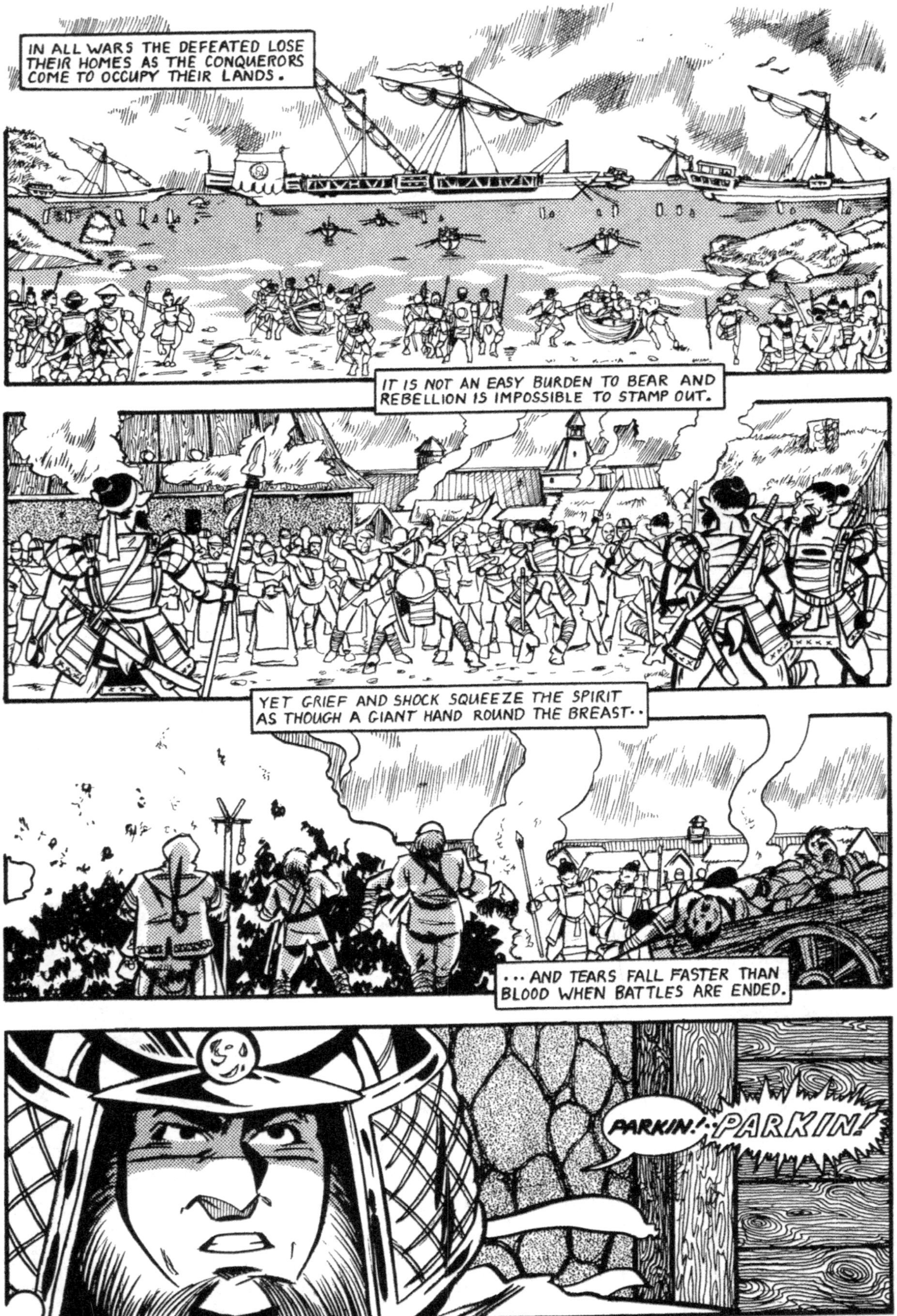
IN ALL WARS THE DEFEATED LOSE THEIR HOMES AS THE CONQUERORS COME TO OCCUPY THEIR LANDS.
IT IS NOT AN EASY BURDEN TO BEAR AND REBELLION IS IMPOSSIBLE TO STAMP OUT.
YET GRIEF AND SHOCK SQUEEZE THE SPIRIT AS THOUGH A GIANT HAND ROUND THE BREAST..
...AND TEARS FALL FASTER THAN BLOOD WHEN BATTLES ARE ENDED.
PARKIN!
PARKIN!

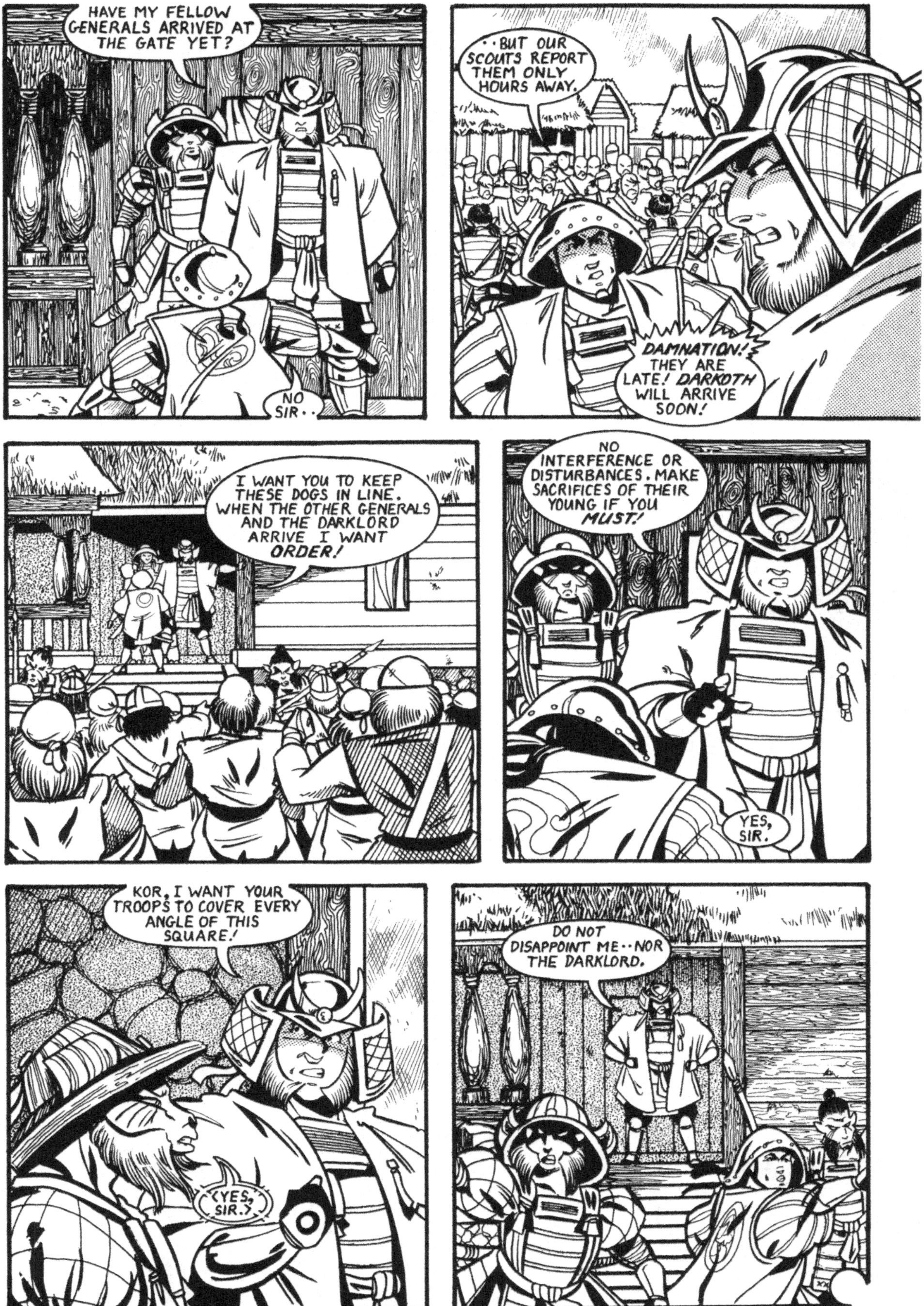
HAVE MY FELLOW GENERALS ARRIVED AT THE GATE YET?
NO SIR··
··BUT OUR SCOUTS REPORT THEM ONLY HOURS AWAY.
DAMNATION!
THEY ARE LATE! DARKOTH WILL ARRIVE SOON!
I WANT YOU TO KEEP THESE DOGS IN LINE. WHEN THE OTHER GENERALS AND THE DARKLORD ARRIVE I WANT ORDER!
NO INTERFERENCE OR DISTURBANCES. MAKE SACRIFICES OF THEIR YOUNG IF YOU MUST!
YES, SIR.
KOR, I WANT YOUR TROOPS TO COVER EVERY ANGLE OF THIS SQUARE!
<YES, SIR.>
DO NOT DISAPPOINT ME··NOR THE DARKLORD.

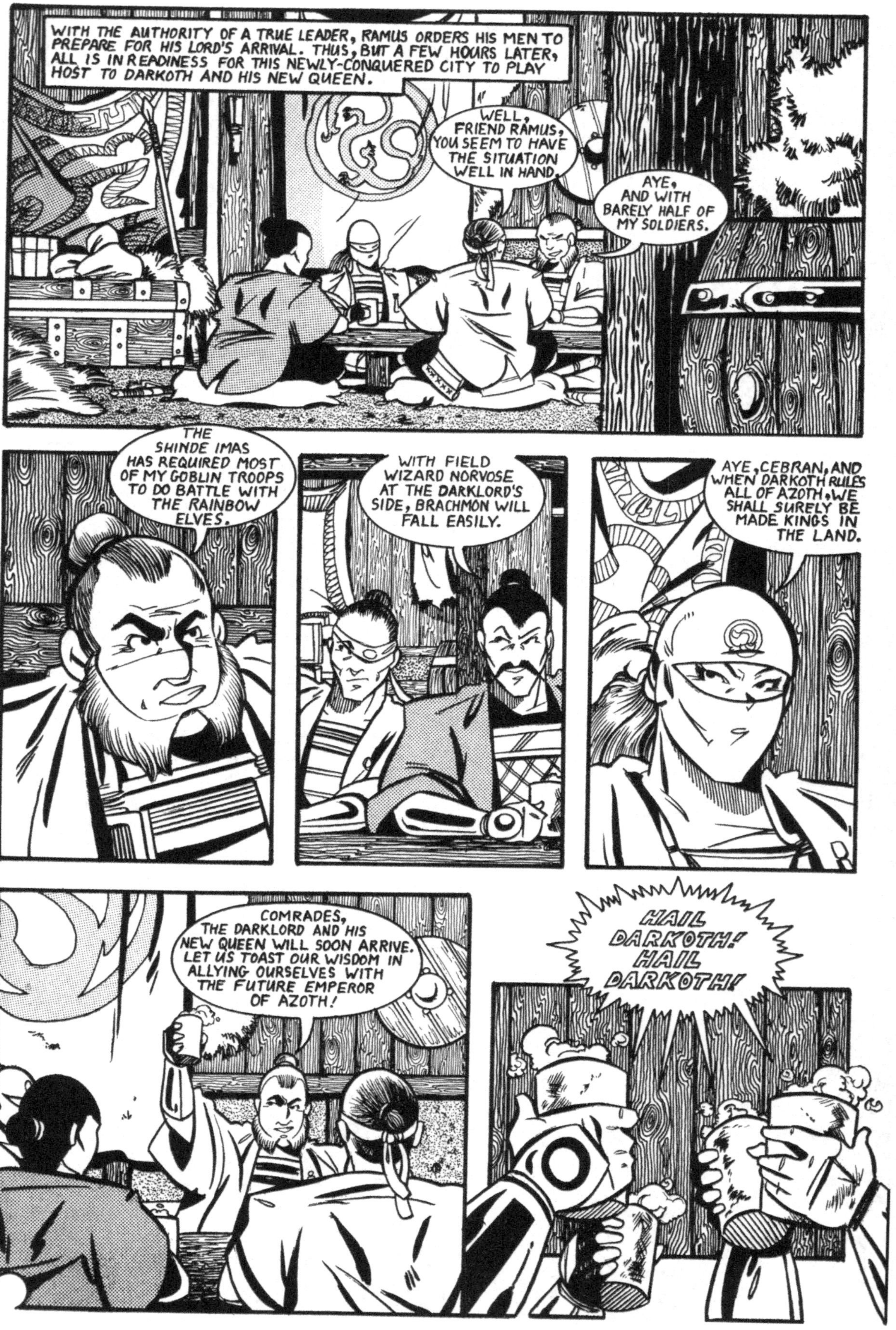
WITH THE AUTHORITY OF A TRUE LEADER, RAMUS ORDERS HIS MEN TO PREPARE FOR HIS LORD'S ARRIVAL. THUS, BUT A FEW HOURS LATER, ALL IS IN READINESS FOR THIS NEWLY-CONQUERED CITY TO PLAY HOST TO DARKOTH AND HIS NEW QUEEN.
WELL, FRIEND RAMUS, YOU SEEM TO HAVE THE SITUATION WELL IN HAND.
AYE, AND WITH BARELY HALF OF MY SOLDIERS.
THE SHINDE IMAS HAS REQUIRED MOST OF MY GOBLIN TROOPS TO DO BATTLE WITH THE RAINBOW ELVES.
WITH FIELD WIZARD NORVOSE AT THE DARKLORD'S SIDE, BRACHMON WILL FALL EASILY.
AYE, CEBRAN, AND WHEN DARKOTH RULES ALL OF AZOTH, WE SHALL SURELY BE MADE KINGS IN THE LAND.
COMRADES, THE DARKLORD AND HIS NEW QUEEN WILL SOON ARRIVE. LET US TOAST OUR WISDOM IN ALLYING OURSELVES WITH THE FUTURE EMPEROR OF AZOTH!
HAIL DARKOTH! HAIL DARKOTH!

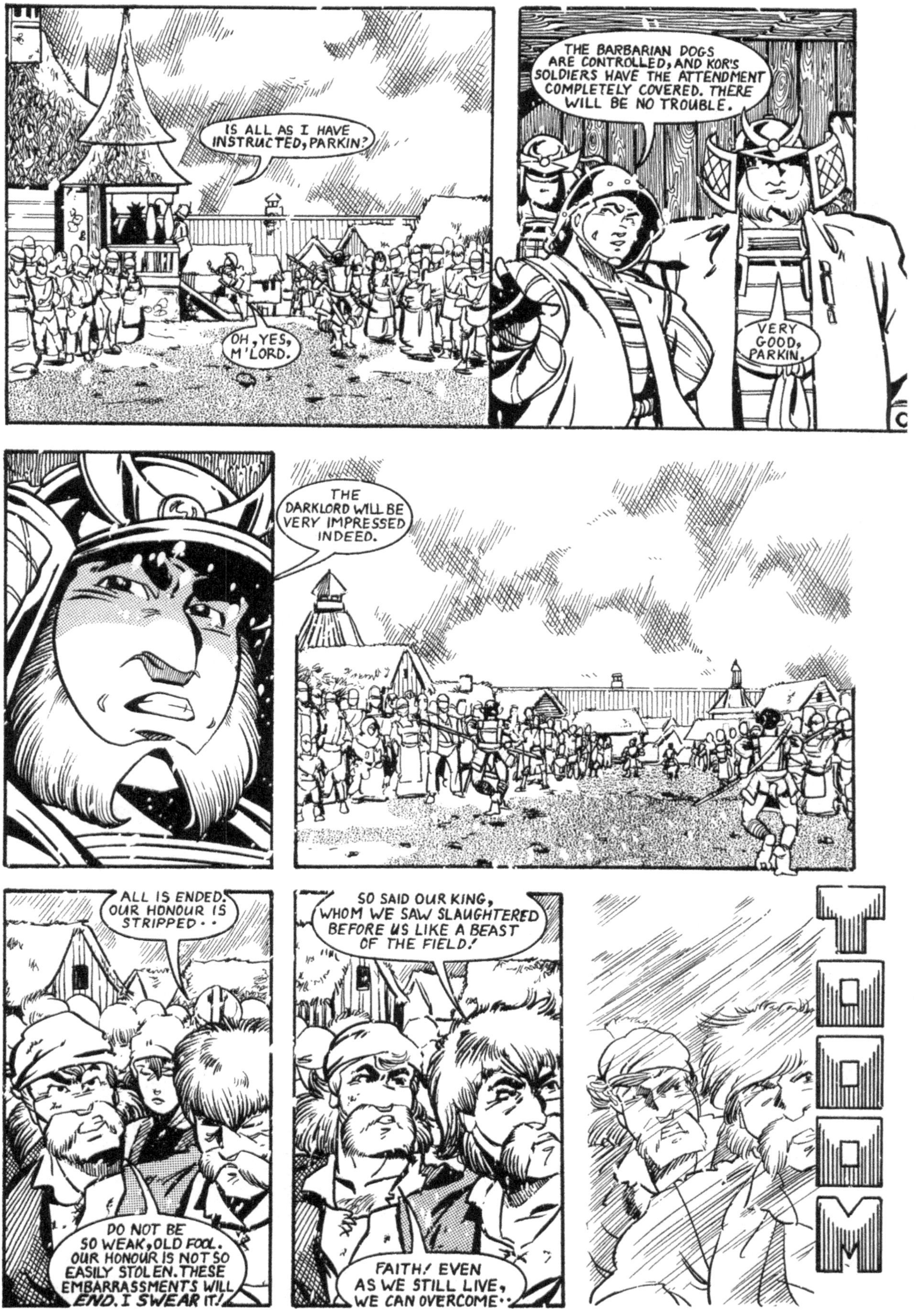
IS ALL AS I HAVE INSTRUCTED, PARKIN?
OH, YES, M'LORD.
THE BARBARIAN DOGS ARE CONTROLLED, AND KOR'S SOLDIERS HAVE THE ATTENDMENT COMPLETELY COVERED. THERE WILL BE NO TROUBLE.
VERY GOOD, PARKIN.
THE DARKLORD WILL BE VERY IMPRESSED INDEED.
ALL IS ENDED. OUR HONOUR IS STRIPPED . .
DO NOT BE SO WEAK, OLD FOOL. OUR HONOUR IS NOT SO EASILY STOLEN. THESE EMBARRASSMENTS WILL *END*. I *SWEAR* IT!
SO SAID OUR KING, WHOM WE SAW SLAUGHTERED BEFORE US LIKE A BEAST OF THE FIELD!
FAITH! EVEN AS WE STILL LIVE, WE CAN OVERCOME . .
TOOOM

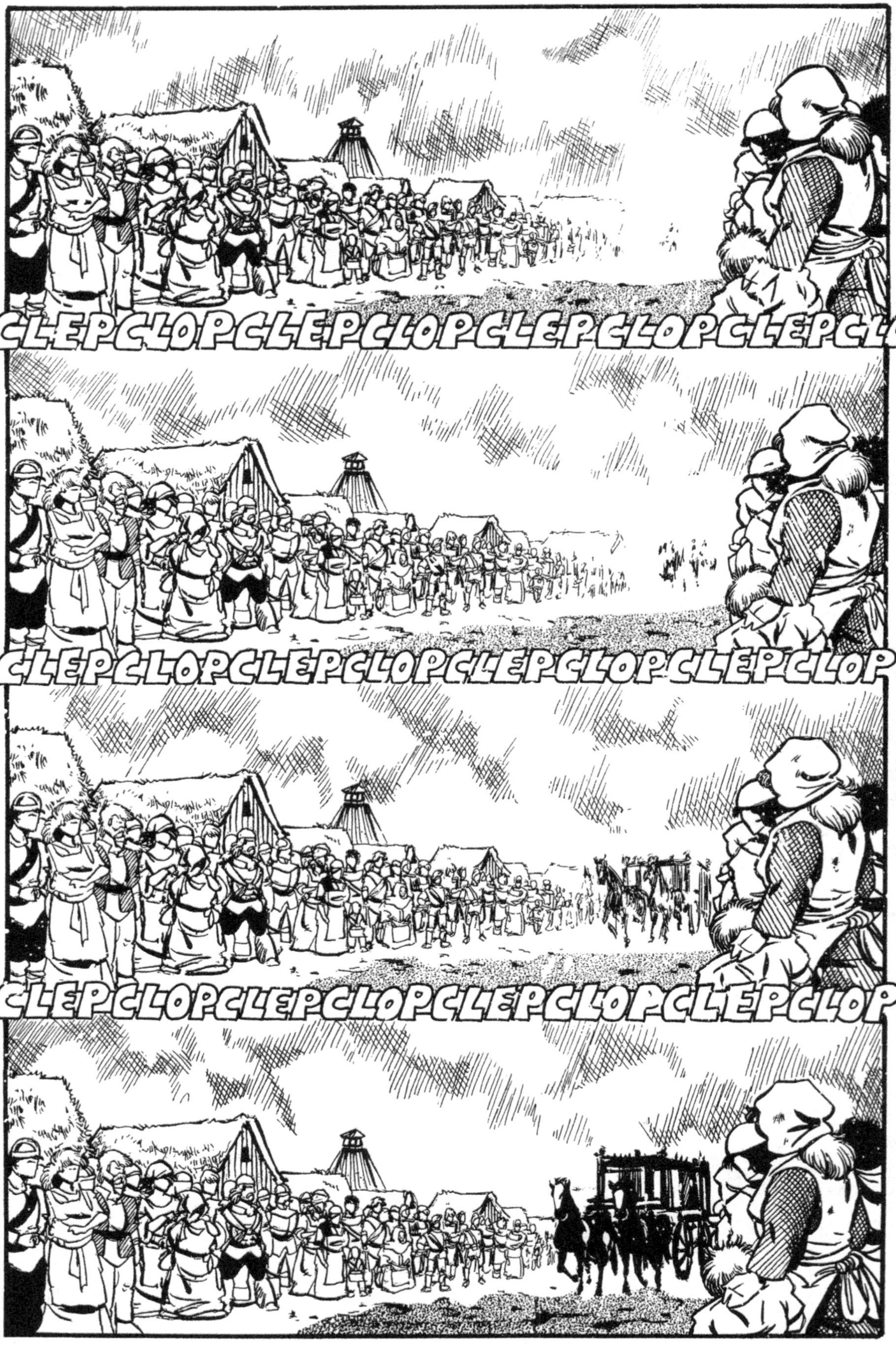
CLEPCLOPCLEPCLOPCLEPCLOPCLEPCLOP
CLEPCLOPCLEPCLOPCLEPCLOPCLEPCLOP
CLEPCLOPCLEPCLOPCLEPCLOPCLEPCLOP

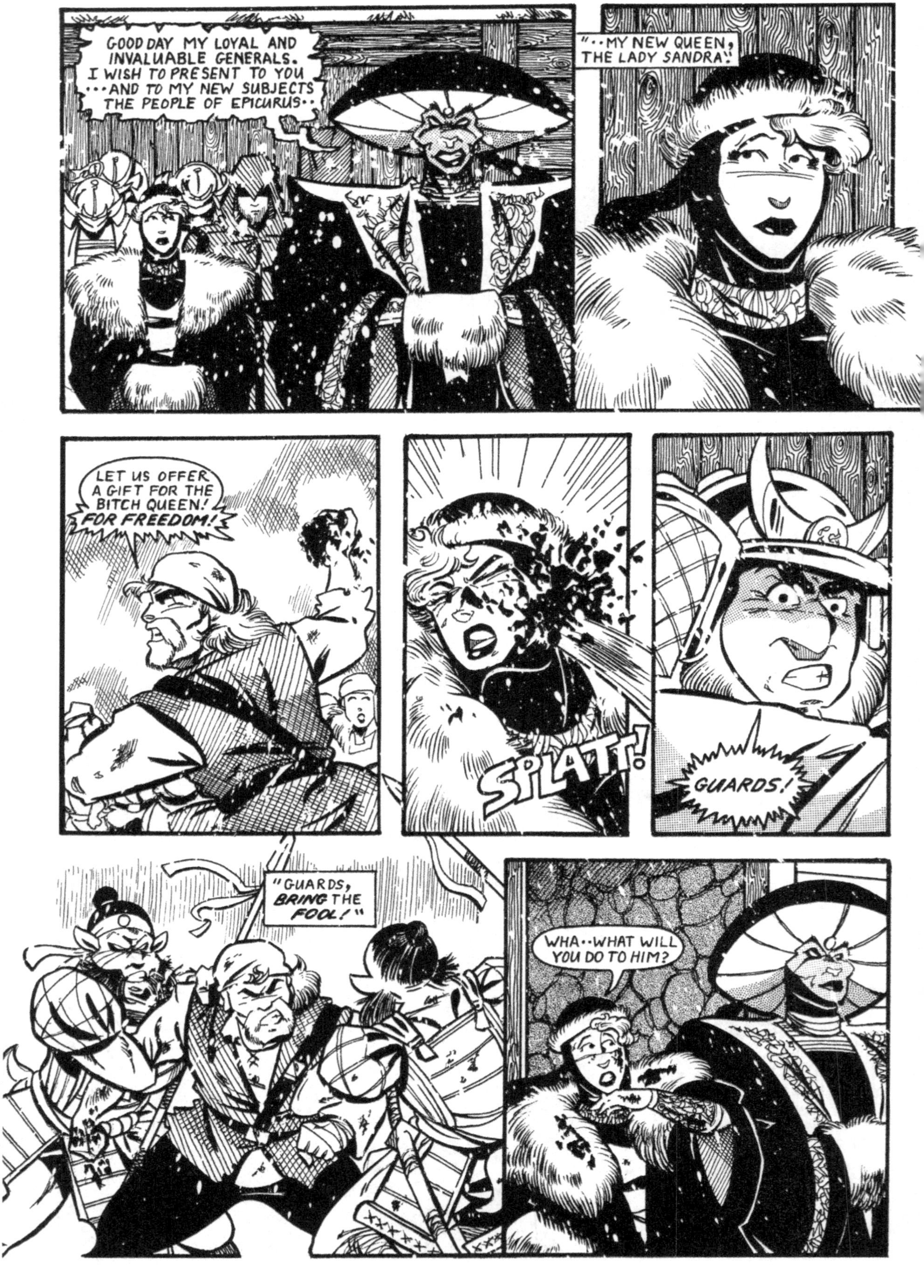
GOOD DAY MY LOYAL AND INVALUABLE GENERALS. I WISH TO PRESENT TO YOU ...AND TO MY NEW SUBJECTS THE PEOPLE OF EPICURUS..
"..MY NEW QUEEN, THE LADY SANDRA!"
LET US OFFER A GIFT FOR THE BITCH QUEEN! FOR FREEDOM!
SPLATT!
GUARDS!
"GUARDS, BRING THE FOOL!"
WHA..WHAT WILL YOU DO TO HIM?

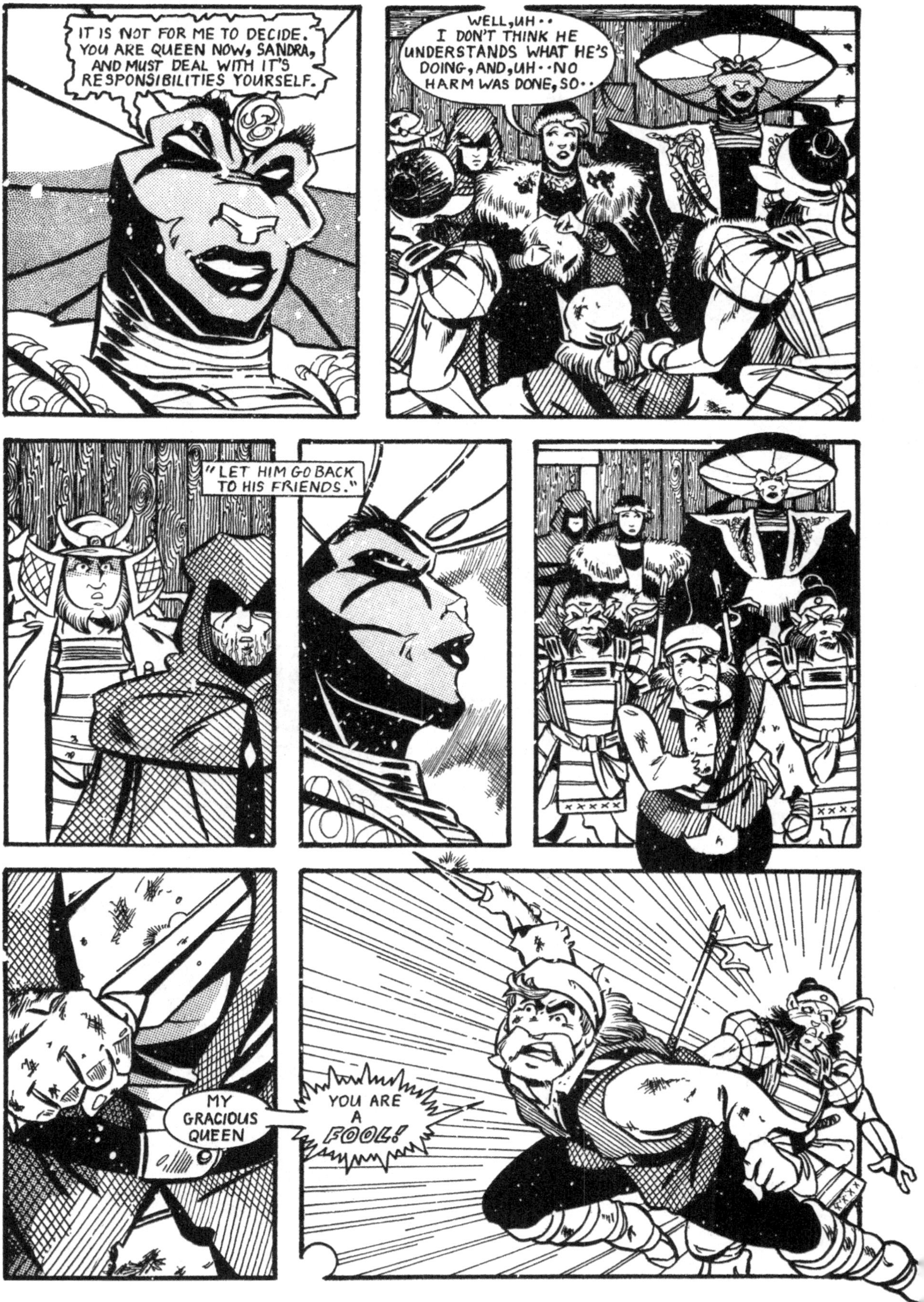
IT IS NOT FOR ME TO DECIDE. YOU ARE QUEEN NOW, SANDRA, AND MUST DEAL WITH IT'S RESPONSIBILITIES YOURSELF.
WELL, UH.. I DON'T THINK HE UNDERSTANDS WHAT HE'S DOING, AND, UH.. NO HARM WAS DONE, SO..
"LET HIM GO BACK TO HIS FRIENDS."
MY GRACIOUS QUEEN
YOU ARE A FOOL!

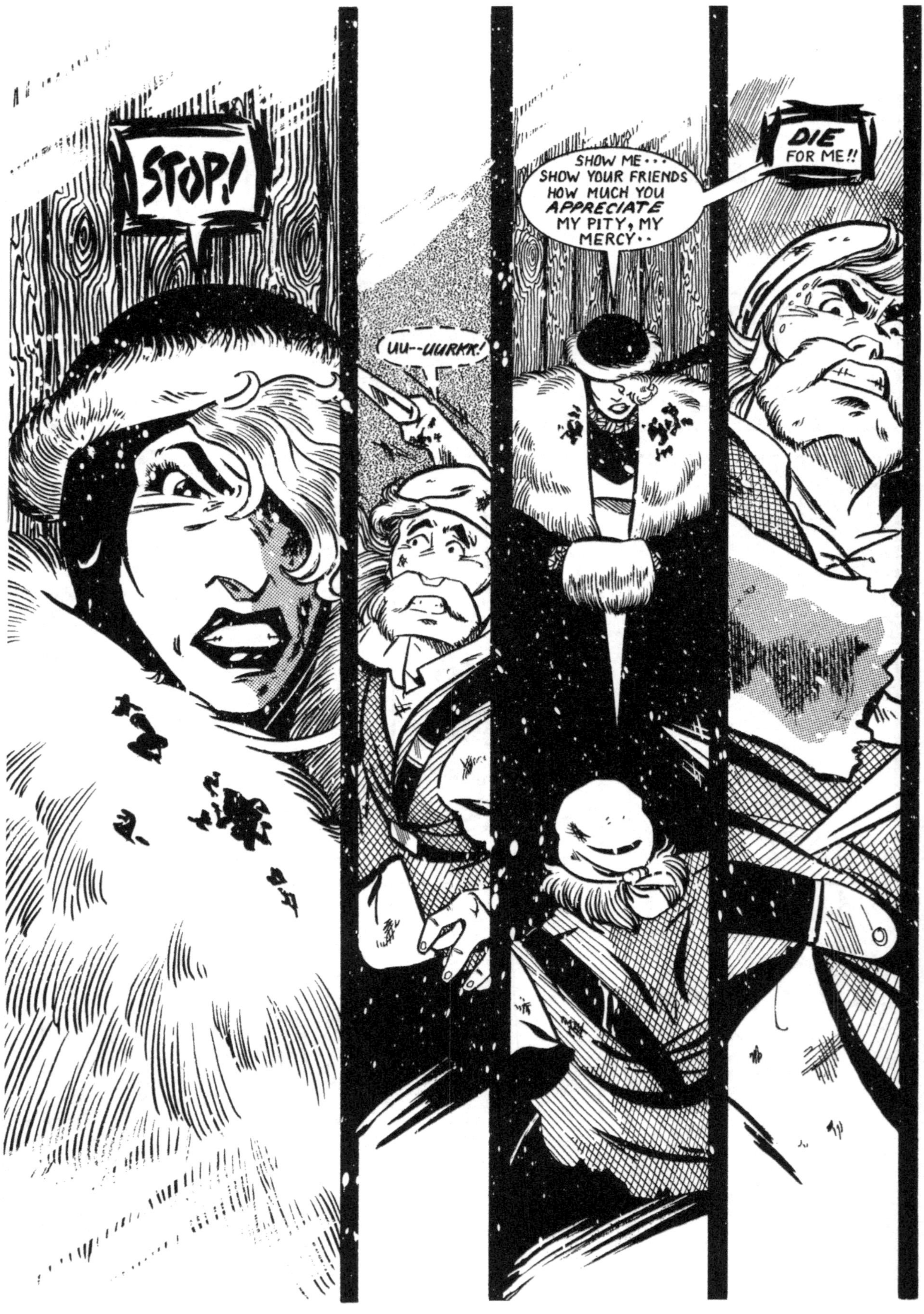
STOP!
UU--UURKK!
SHOW ME... SHOW YOUR FRIENDS HOW MUCH YOU APPRECIATE MY PITY, MY MERCY..
DIE FOR ME!!

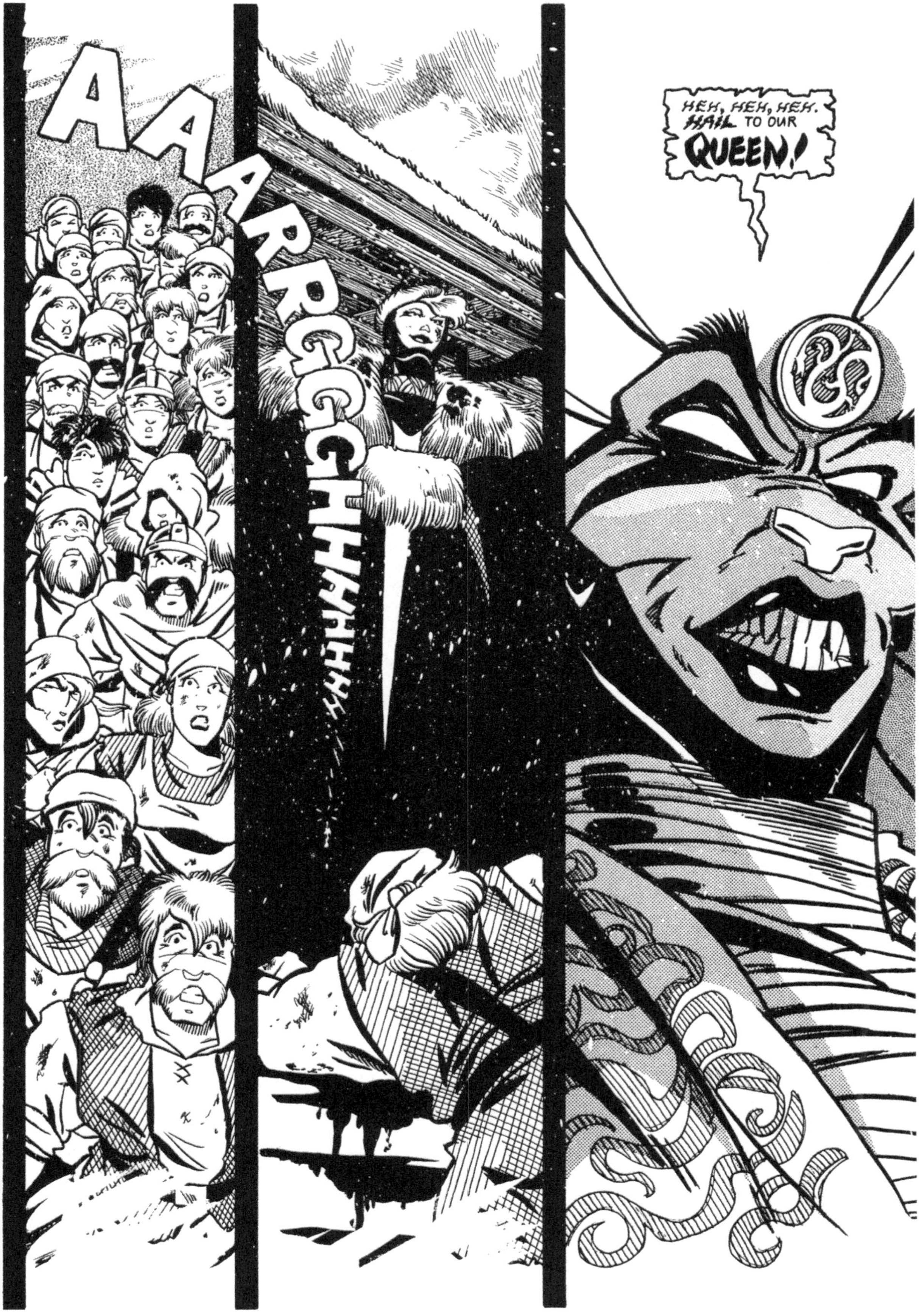

AAAARRGGGHHHHHHH
HEH, HEH, HEH. HAIL TO OUR QUEEN!

LEGENDLORE

THE REALM - VOLUME ONE

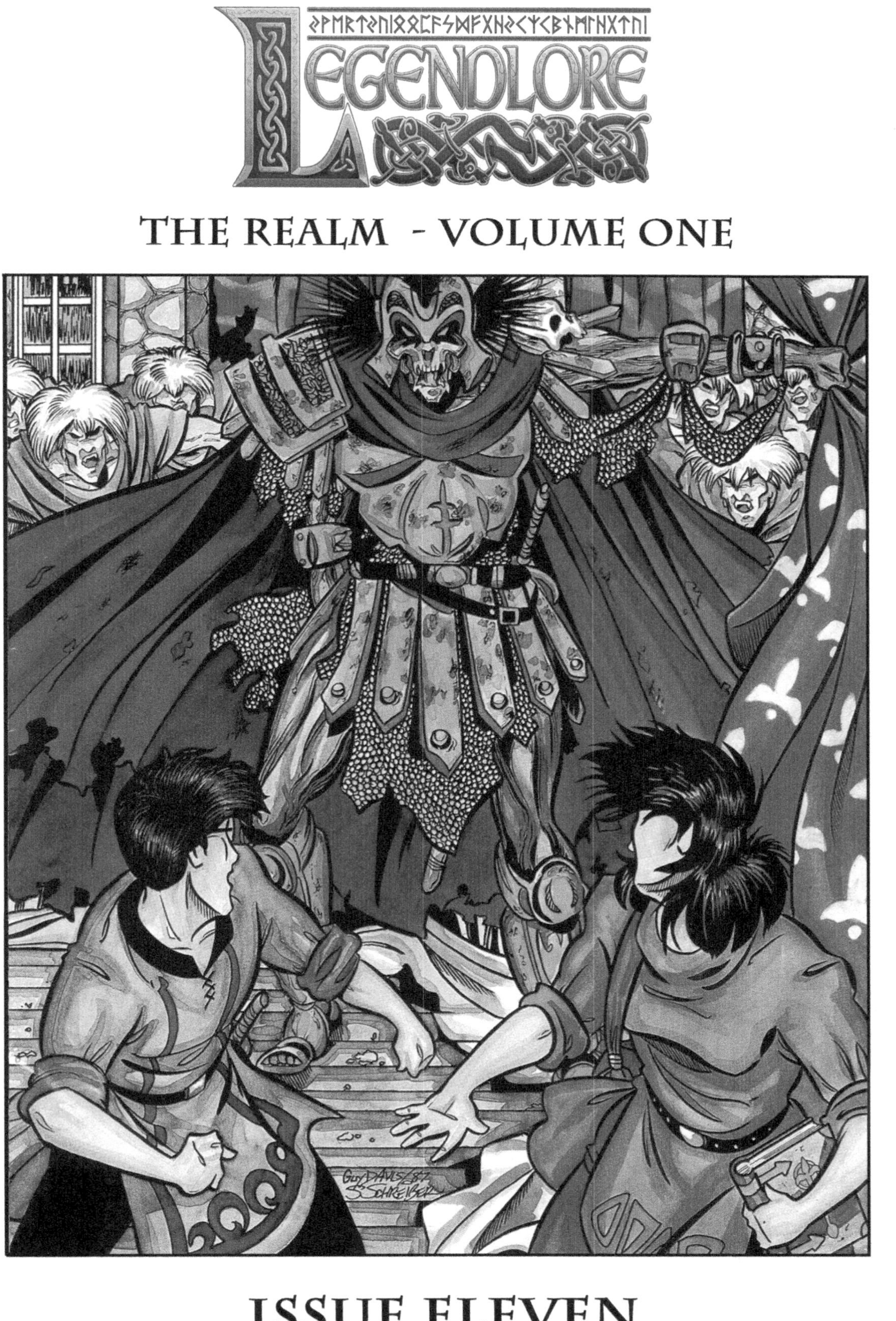

ISSUE ELEVEN

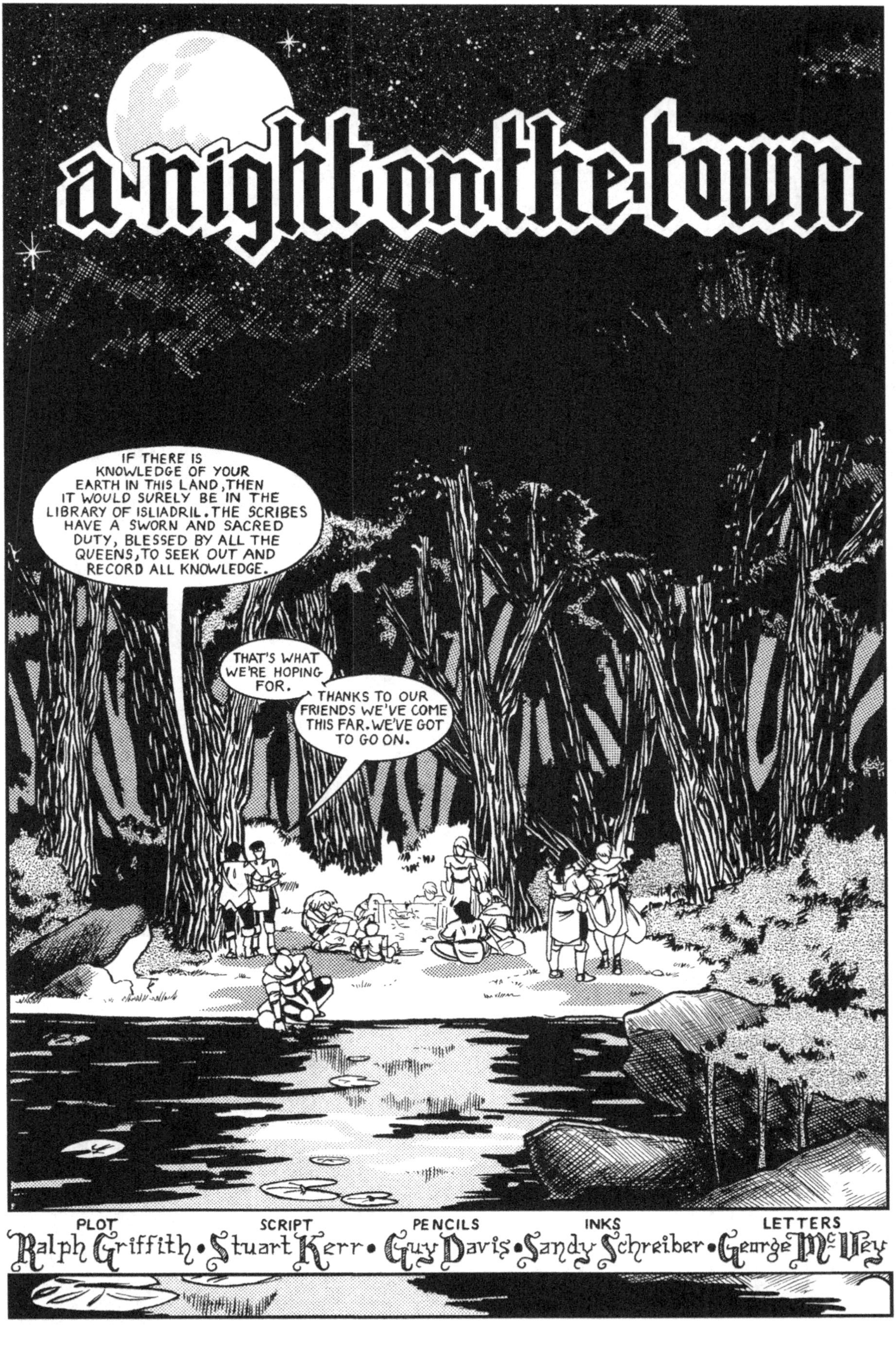
a night on the town
IF THERE IS KNOWLEDGE OF YOUR EARTH IN THIS LAND, THEN IT WOULD SURELY BE IN THE LIBRARY OF ISLIADRIL. THE SCRIBES HAVE A SWORN AND SACRED DUTY, BLESSED BY ALL THE QUEENS, TO SEEK OUT AND RECORD ALL KNOWLEDGE.
THAT'S WHAT WE'RE HOPING FOR.
THANKS TO OUR FRIENDS WE'VE COME THIS FAR. WE'VE GOT TO GO ON.
PLOT Ralph Griffith • SCRIPT Stuart Kerr • PENCILS Guy Davis • INKS Sandy Schreiber • LETTERS George McVey

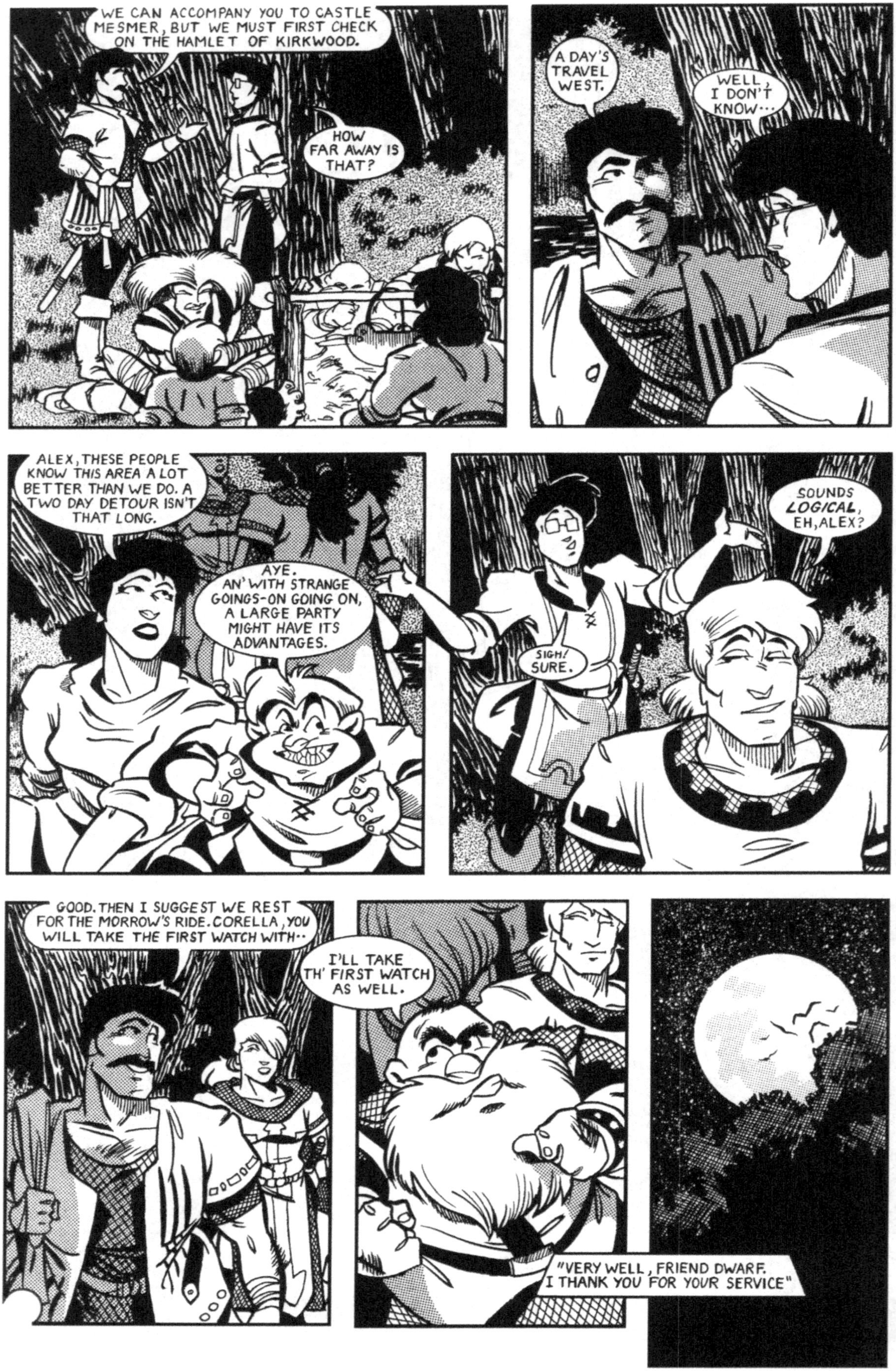
WE CAN ACCOMPANY YOU TO CASTLE MESMER, BUT WE MUST FIRST CHECK ON THE HAMLET OF KIRKWOOD.
HOW FAR AWAY IS THAT?
A DAY'S TRAVEL WEST.
WELL, I DON'T KNOW...
ALEX, THESE PEOPLE KNOW THIS AREA A LOT BETTER THAN WE DO. A TWO DAY DETOUR ISN'T THAT LONG.
AYE. AN' WITH STRANGE GOINGS-ON GOING ON, A LARGE PARTY MIGHT HAVE ITS ADVANTAGES.
SOUNDS LOGICAL, EH, ALEX?
SIGH! SURE.
GOOD. THEN I SUGGEST WE REST FOR THE MORROW'S RIDE. CORELLA, YOU WILL TAKE THE FIRST WATCH WITH..
I'LL TAKE TH' FIRST WATCH AS WELL.
"VERY WELL, FRIEND DWARF. I THANK YOU FOR YOUR SERVICE"

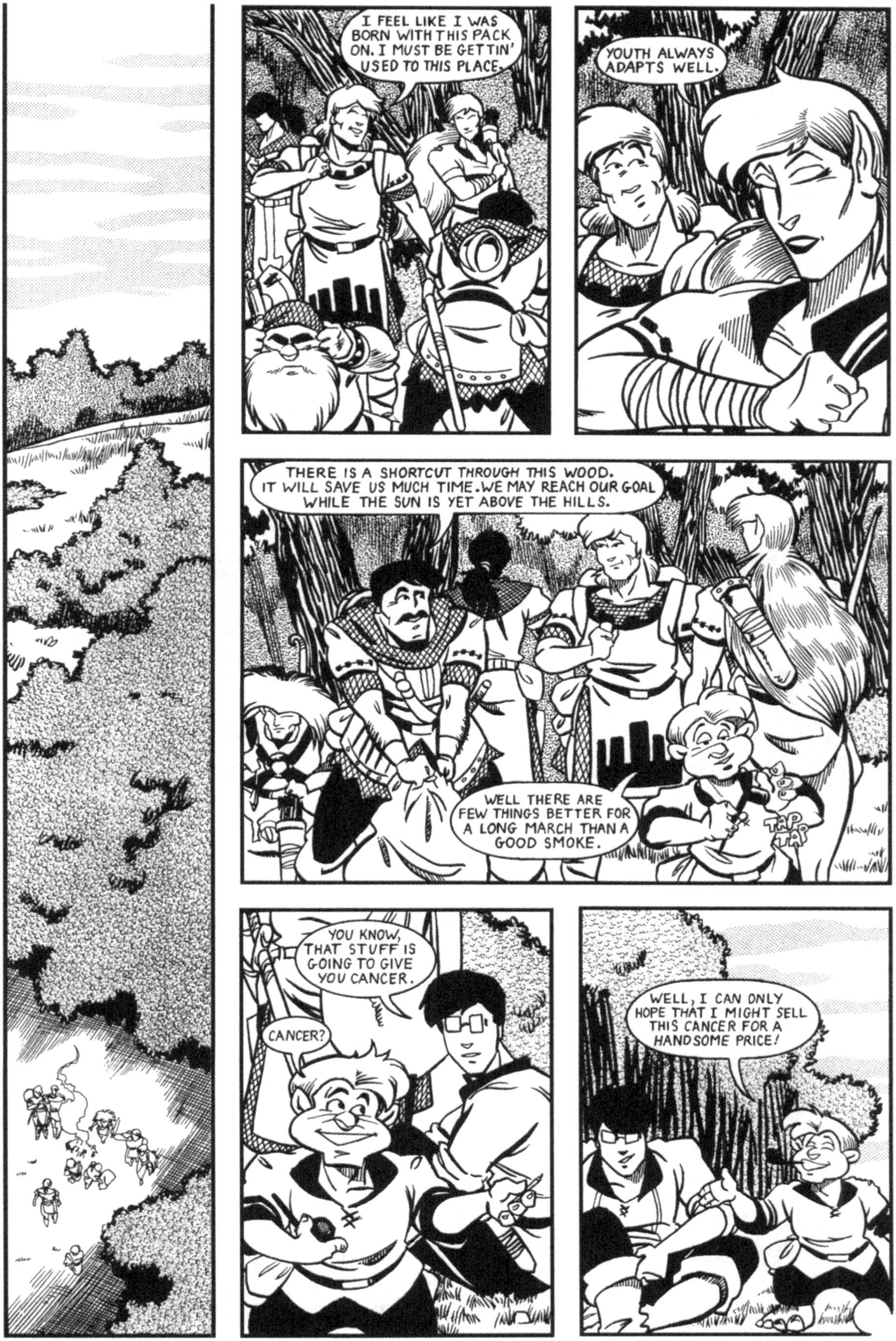
I FEEL LIKE I WAS BORN WITH THIS PACK ON. I MUST BE GETTIN' USED TO THIS PLACE.
YOUTH ALWAYS ADAPTS WELL.
THERE IS A SHORTCUT THROUGH THIS WOOD. IT WILL SAVE US MUCH TIME. WE MAY REACH OUR GOAL WHILE THE SUN IS YET ABOVE THE HILLS.
WELL THERE ARE FEW THINGS BETTER FOR A LONG MARCH THAN A GOOD SMOKE.
TAP TAP
YOU KNOW, THAT STUFF IS GOING TO GIVE YOU CANCER.
CANCER?
WELL, I CAN ONLY HOPE THAT I MIGHT SELL THIS CANCER FOR A HANDSOME PRICE!

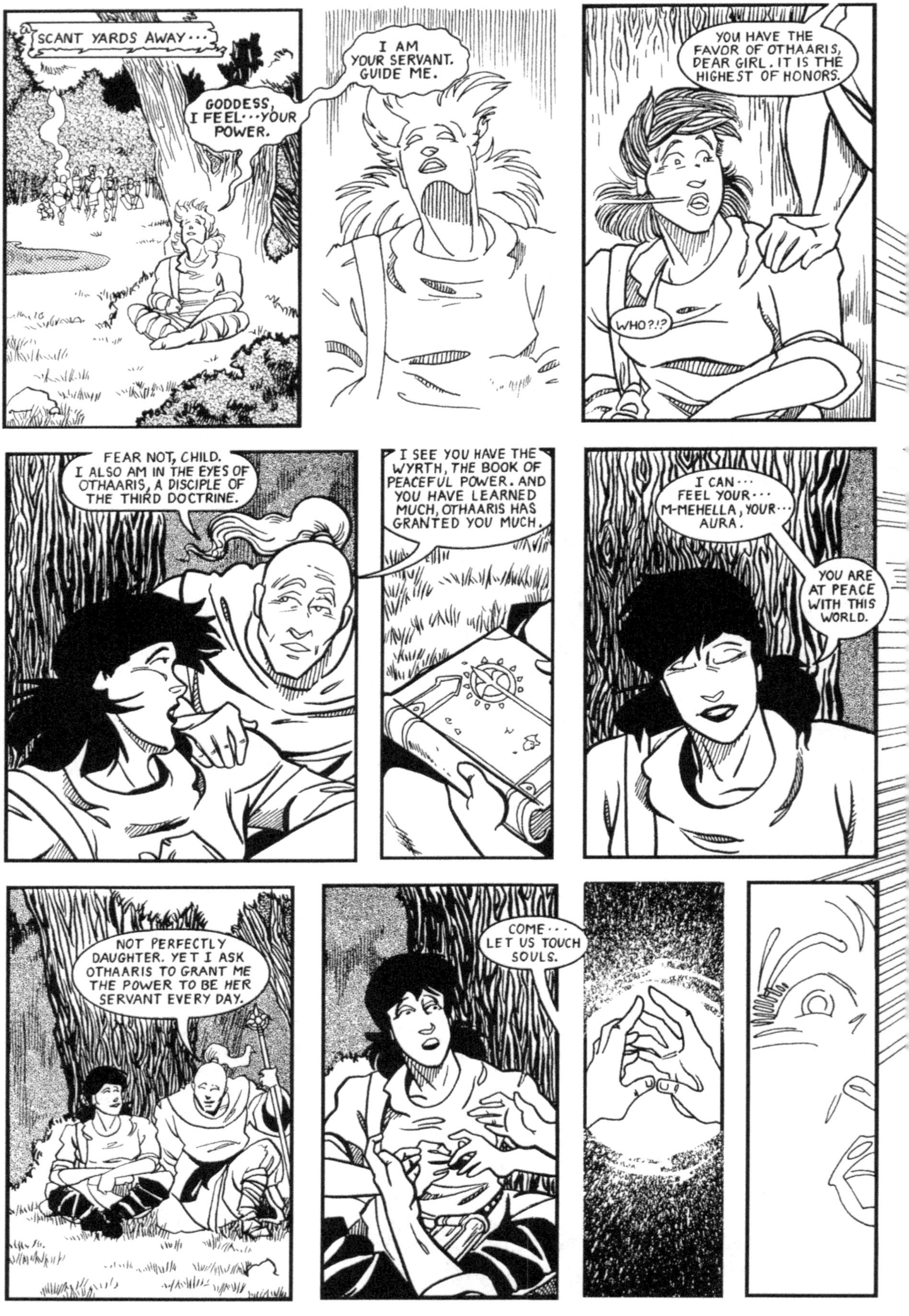
SCANT YARDS AWAY...
GODDESS, I FEEL...YOUR POWER.
I AM YOUR SERVANT. GUIDE ME.
YOU HAVE THE FAVOR OF OTHAARIS, DEAR GIRL. IT IS THE HIGHEST OF HONORS.
WHO?!?
FEAR NOT, CHILD. I ALSO AM IN THE EYES OF OTHAARIS, A DISCIPLE OF THE THIRD DOCTRINE.
I SEE YOU HAVE THE WYRTH, THE BOOK OF PEACEFUL POWER. AND YOU HAVE LEARNED MUCH, OTHAARIS HAS GRANTED YOU MUCH.
I CAN... FEEL YOUR... M-MEHELLA, YOUR... AURA.
YOU ARE AT PEACE WITH THIS WORLD.
NOT PERFECTLY DAUGHTER. YET I ASK OTHAARIS TO GRANT ME THE POWER TO BE HER SERVANT EVERY DAY.
COME... LET US TOUCH SOULS.

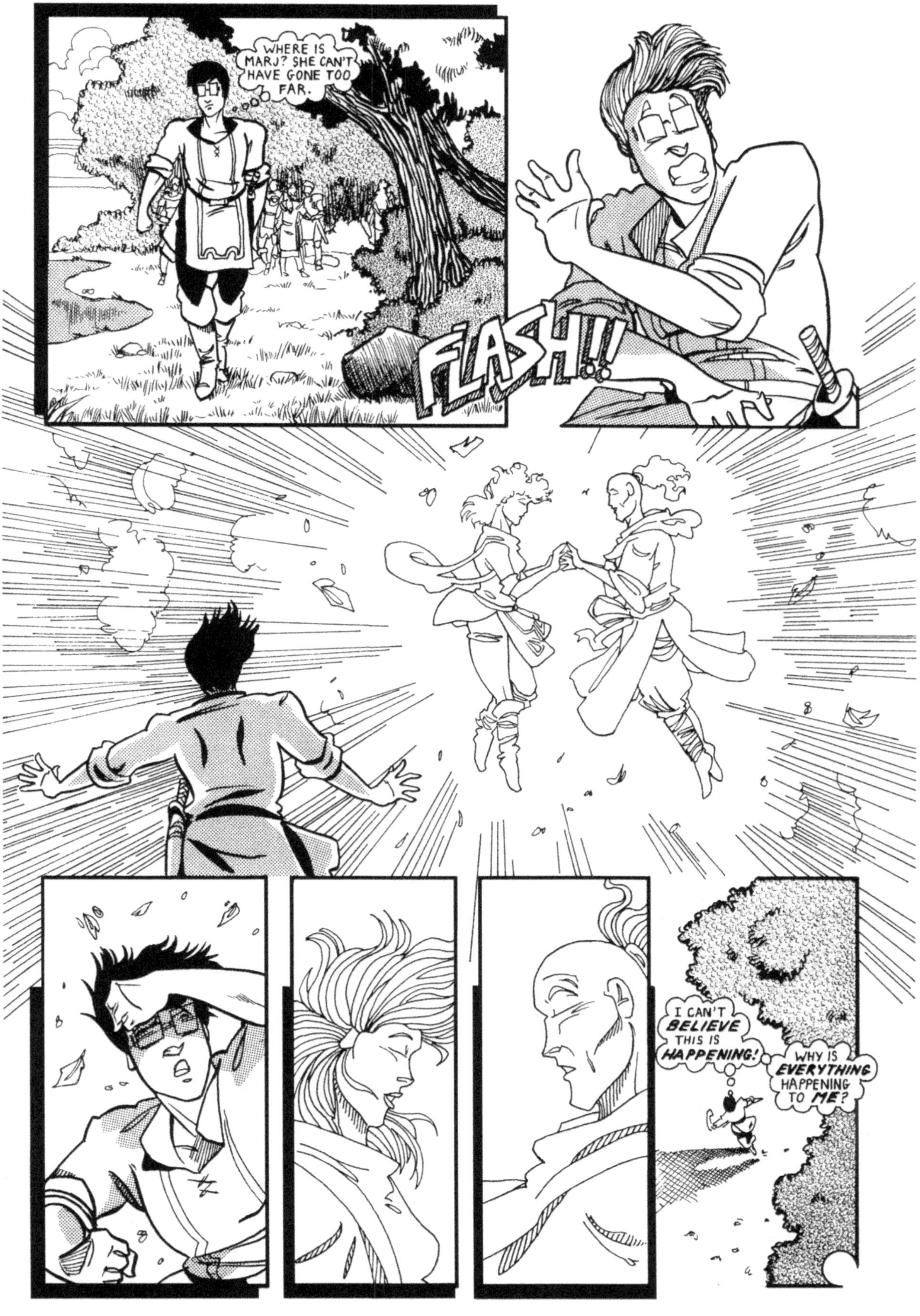
WHERE IS MARJ? SHE CAN'T HAVE GONE TOO FAR.
FLASH!!
I CAN'T BELIEVE THIS IS HAPPENING!
WHY IS EVERYTHING HAPPENING TO ME?

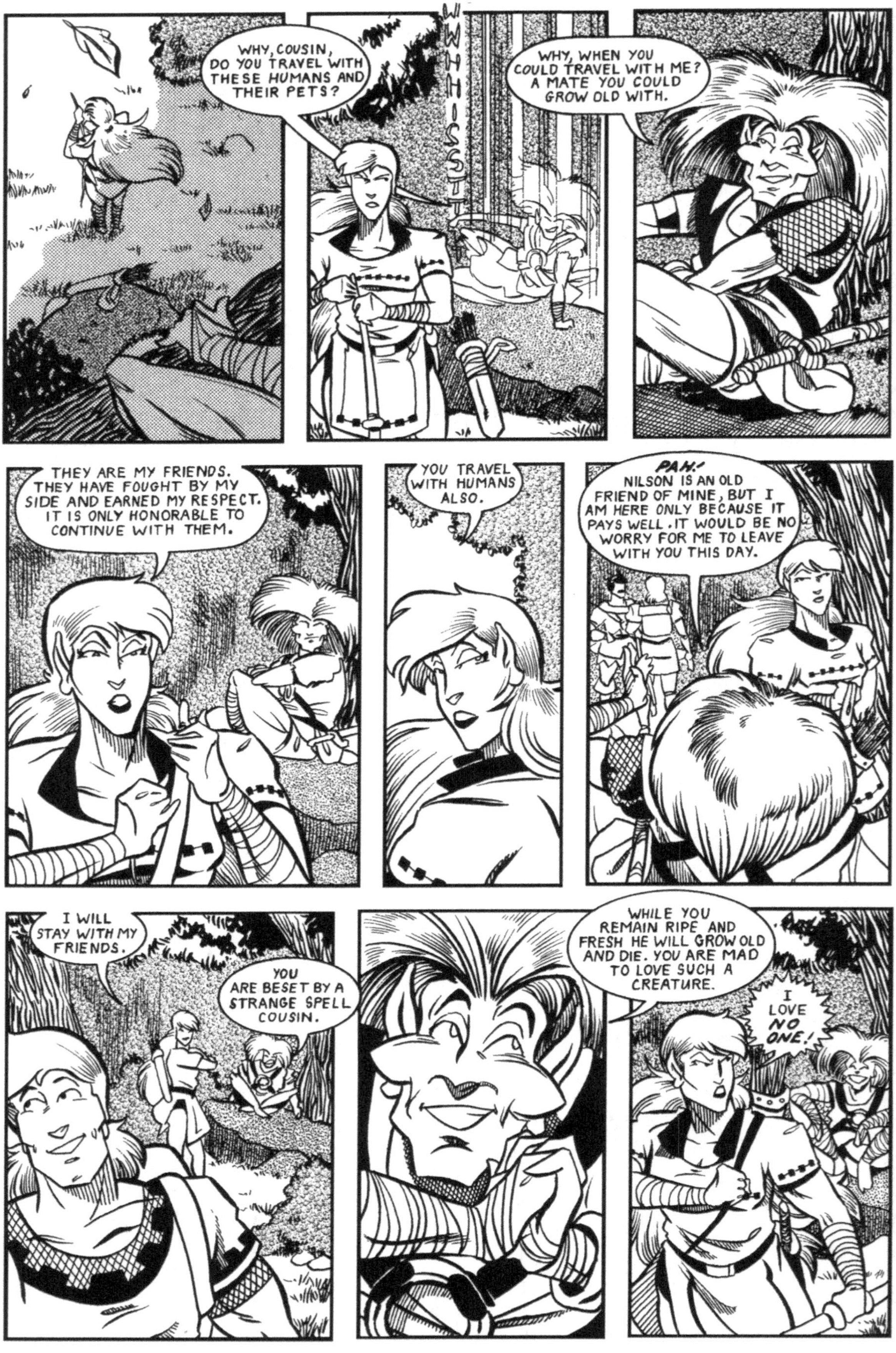
WHY, COUSIN, DO YOU TRAVEL WITH THESE HUMANS AND THEIR PETS?
WHISST
WHY, WHEN YOU COULD TRAVEL WITH ME? A MATE YOU COULD GROW OLD WITH.
THEY ARE MY FRIENDS. THEY HAVE FOUGHT BY MY SIDE AND EARNED MY RESPECT. IT IS ONLY HONORABLE TO CONTINUE WITH THEM.
YOU TRAVEL WITH HUMANS ALSO.
PAH!
NILSON IS AN OLD FRIEND OF MINE, BUT I AM HERE ONLY BECAUSE IT PAYS WELL. IT WOULD BE NO WORRY FOR ME TO LEAVE WITH YOU THIS DAY.
I WILL STAY WITH MY FRIENDS.
YOU ARE BESET BY A STRANGE SPELL COUSIN.
WHILE YOU REMAIN RIPE AND FRESH HE WILL GROW OLD AND DIE. YOU ARE MAD TO LOVE SUCH A CREATURE.
I LOVE NO ONE!

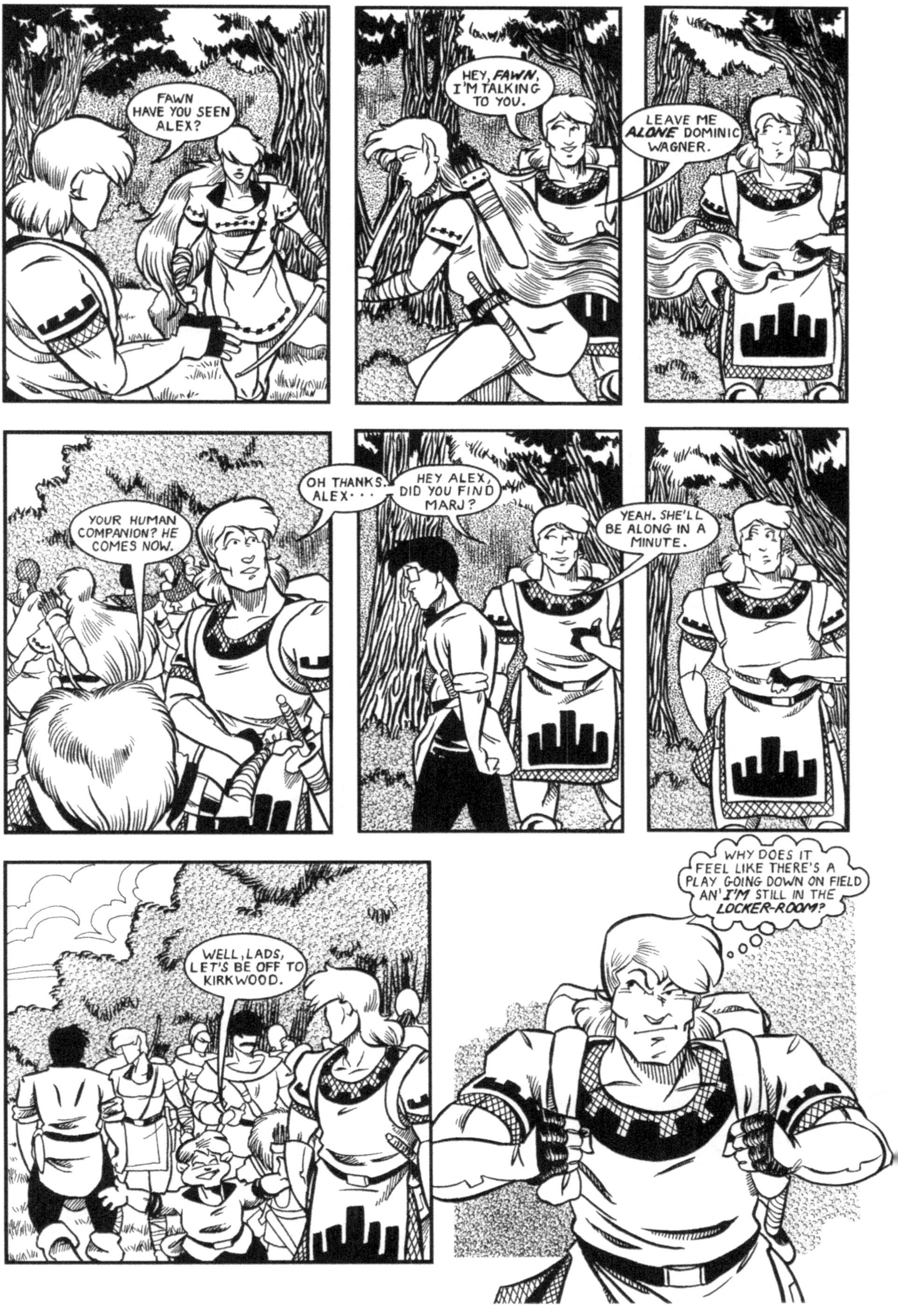
FAWN HAVE YOU SEEN ALEX?
HEY, FAWN, I'M TALKING TO YOU.
LEAVE ME ALONE DOMINIC WAGNER.
YOUR HUMAN COMPANION? HE COMES NOW.
OH THANKS. ALEX...
HEY ALEX, DID YOU FIND MARJ?
YEAH. SHE'LL BE ALONG IN A MINUTE.
WELL, LADS, LET'S BE OFF TO KIRKWOOD.
WHY DOES IT FEEL LIKE THERE'S A PLAY GOING DOWN ON FIELD AN' I'M STILL IN THE LOCKER-ROOM?

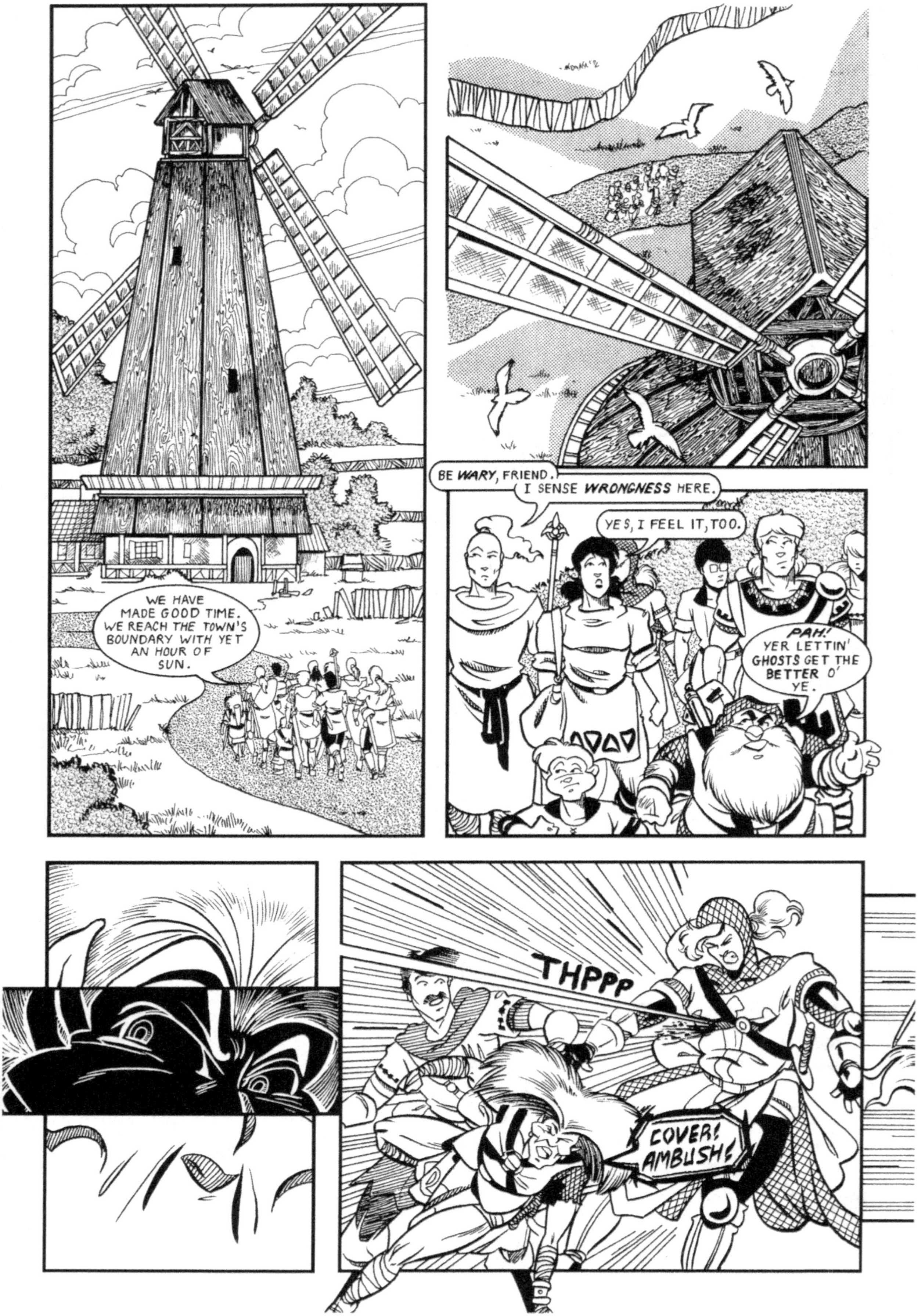

WE HAVE MADE GOOD TIME. WE REACH THE TOWN'S BOUNDARY WITH YET AN HOUR OF SUN.
BE WARY, FRIEND.
I SENSE WRONGNESS HERE.
YES, I FEEL IT, TOO.
PAH! YER LETTIN' GHOSTS GET THE BETTER O' YE.
THPPP
COVER! AMBUSH!

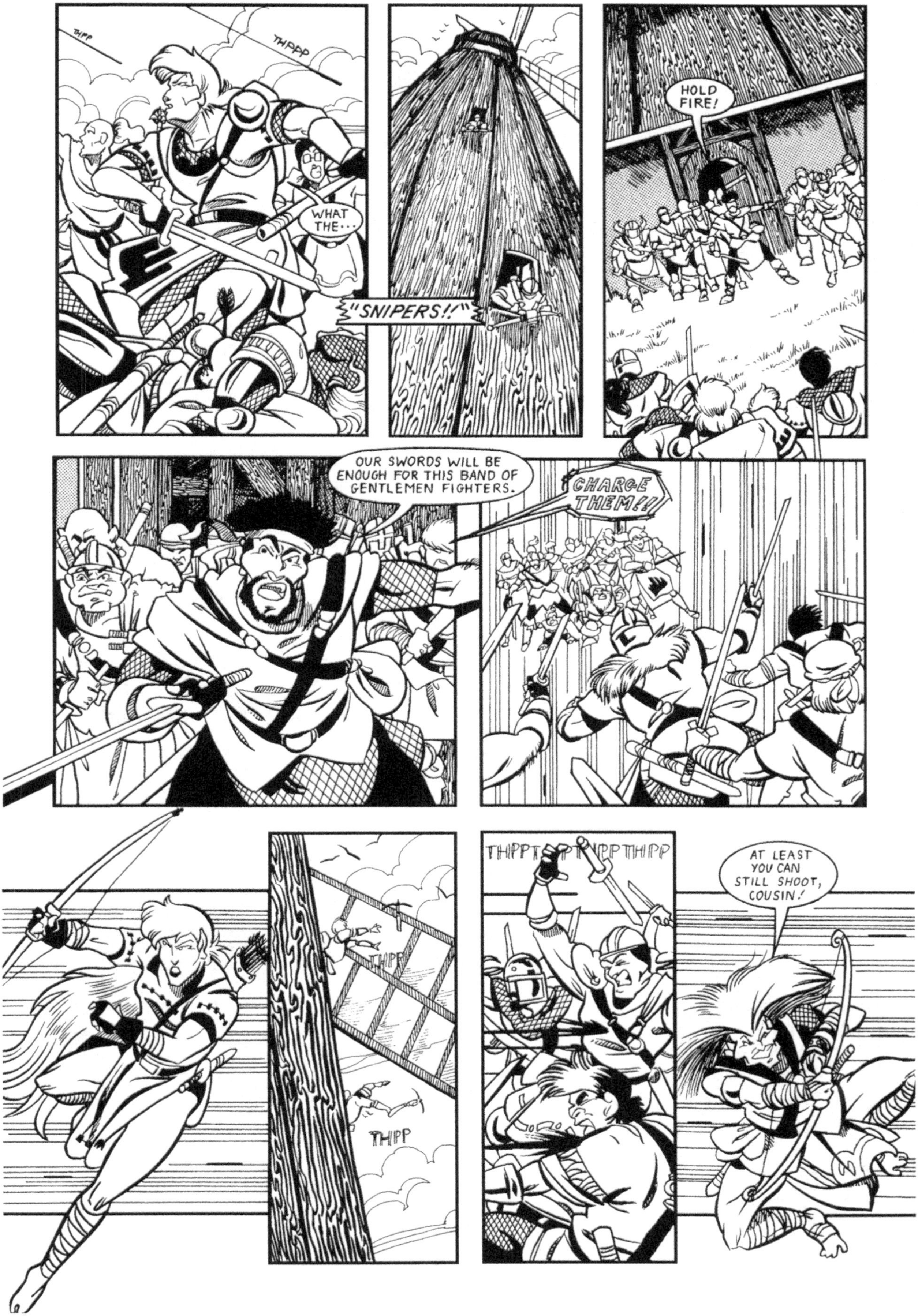

THPP
THPPP
WHAT THE...
"SNIPERS!!"
HOLD FIRE!
OUR SWORDS WILL BE ENOUGH FOR THIS BAND OF GENTLEMEN FIGHTERS.
CHARGE THEM!!
THPP
THPP
THPPTHPPTHPPTHPP
AT LEAST YOU CAN STILL SHOOT, COUSIN!

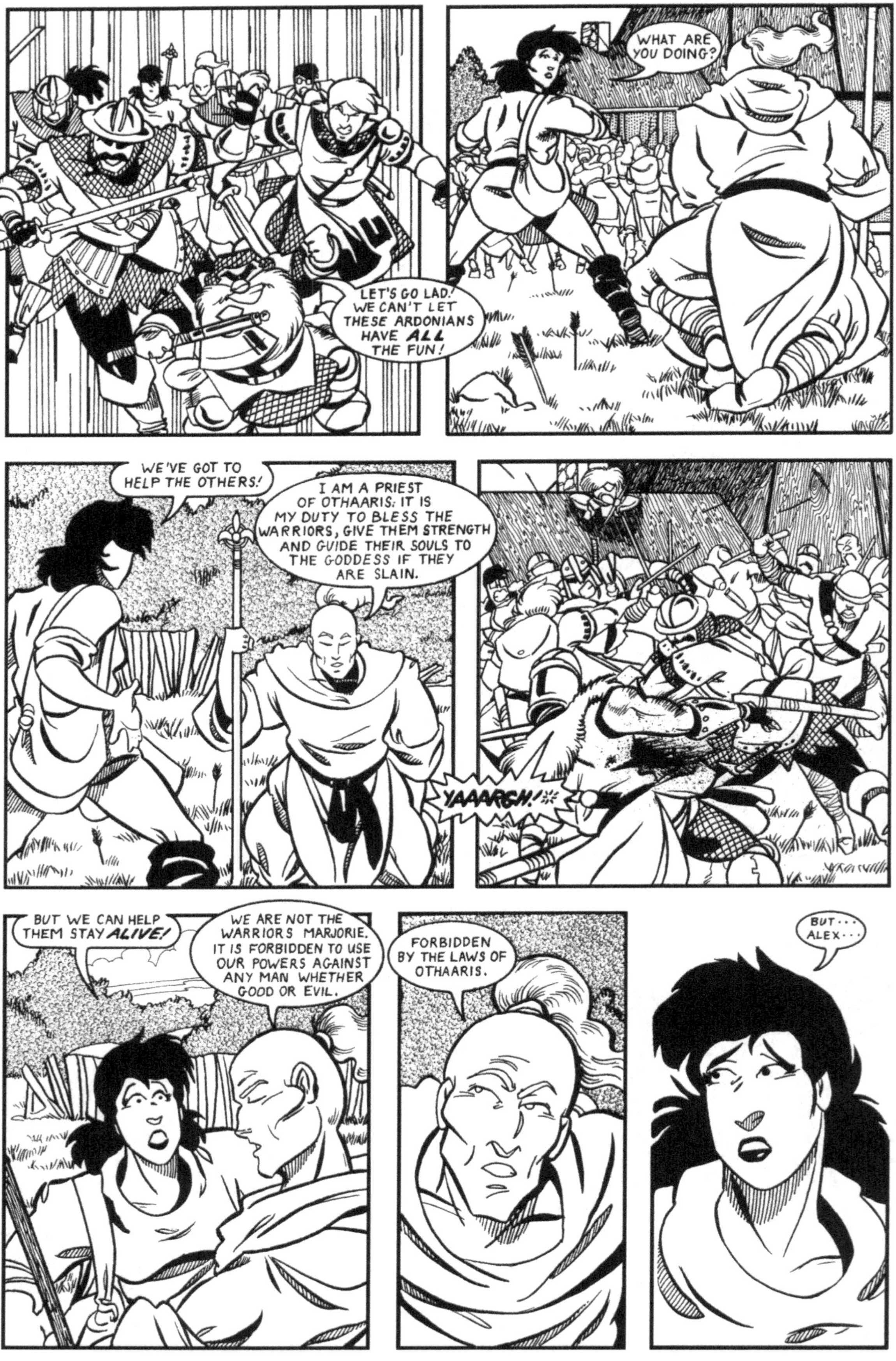
LET'S GO LAD! WE CAN'T LET THESE ARDONIANS HAVE ALL THE FUN!
WHAT ARE YOU DOING?
WE'VE GOT TO HELP THE OTHERS!
I AM A PRIEST OF OTHAARIS: IT IS MY DUTY TO BLESS THE WARRIORS, GIVE THEM STRENGTH AND GUIDE THEIR SOULS TO THE GODDESS IF THEY ARE SLAIN.
YAAARGH!
BUT WE CAN HELP THEM STAY ALIVE!
WE ARE NOT THE WARRIORS MARJORIE. IT IS FORBIDDEN TO USE OUR POWERS AGAINST ANY MAN WHETHER GOOD OR EVIL.
FORBIDDEN BY THE LAWS OF OTHAARIS.
BUT... ALEX...

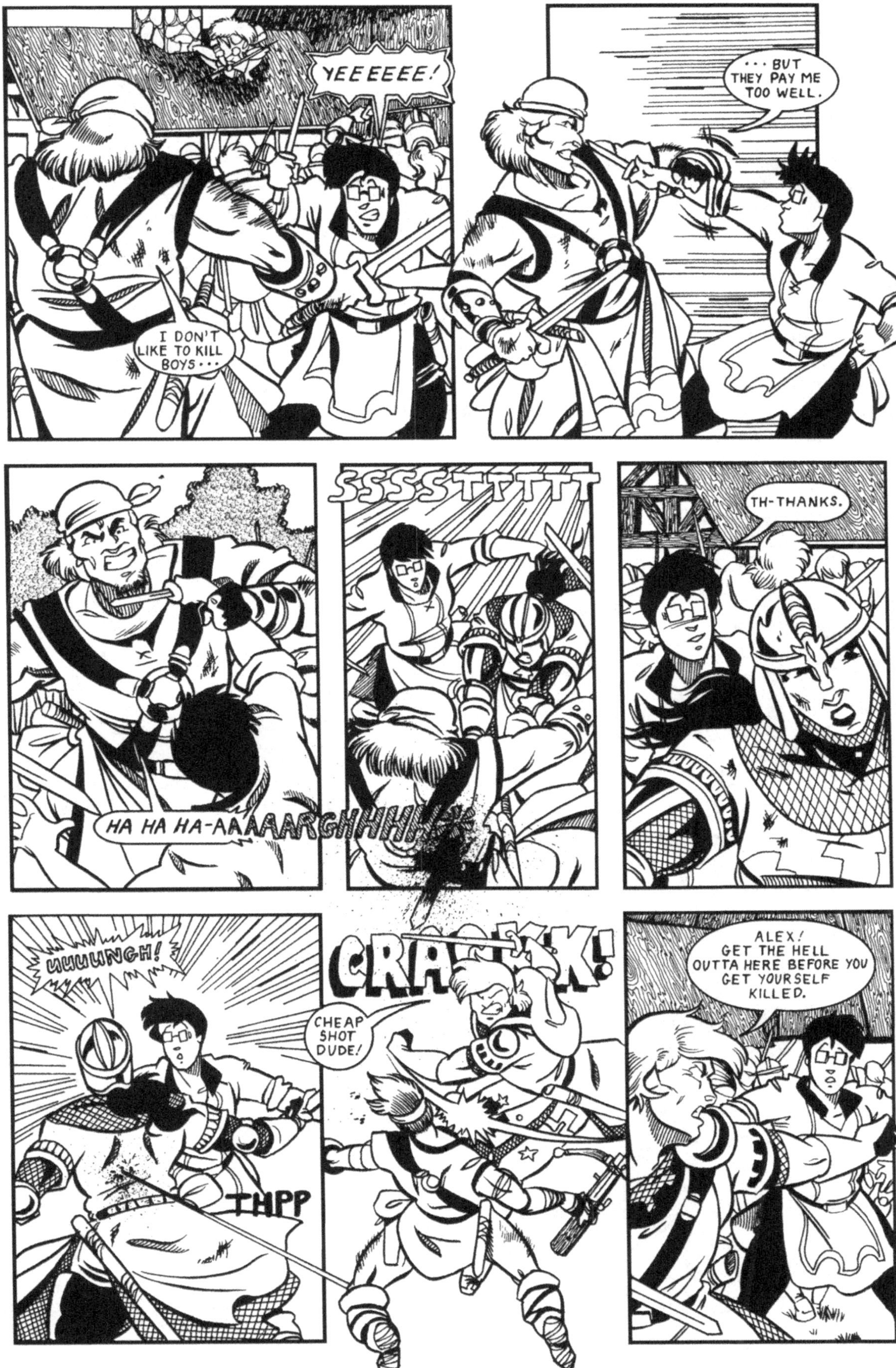
YEEEEEE!
I DON'T LIKE TO KILL BOYS...
...BUT THEY PAY ME TOO WELL.
HA HA HA-AAAAARGHHHH!
SSSSTTTTT
TH-THANKS.
UUUUNGH!
THPP
CRACKK!
CHEAP SHOT DUDE!
ALEX! GET THE HELL OUTTA HERE BEFORE YOU GET YOURSELF KILLED.

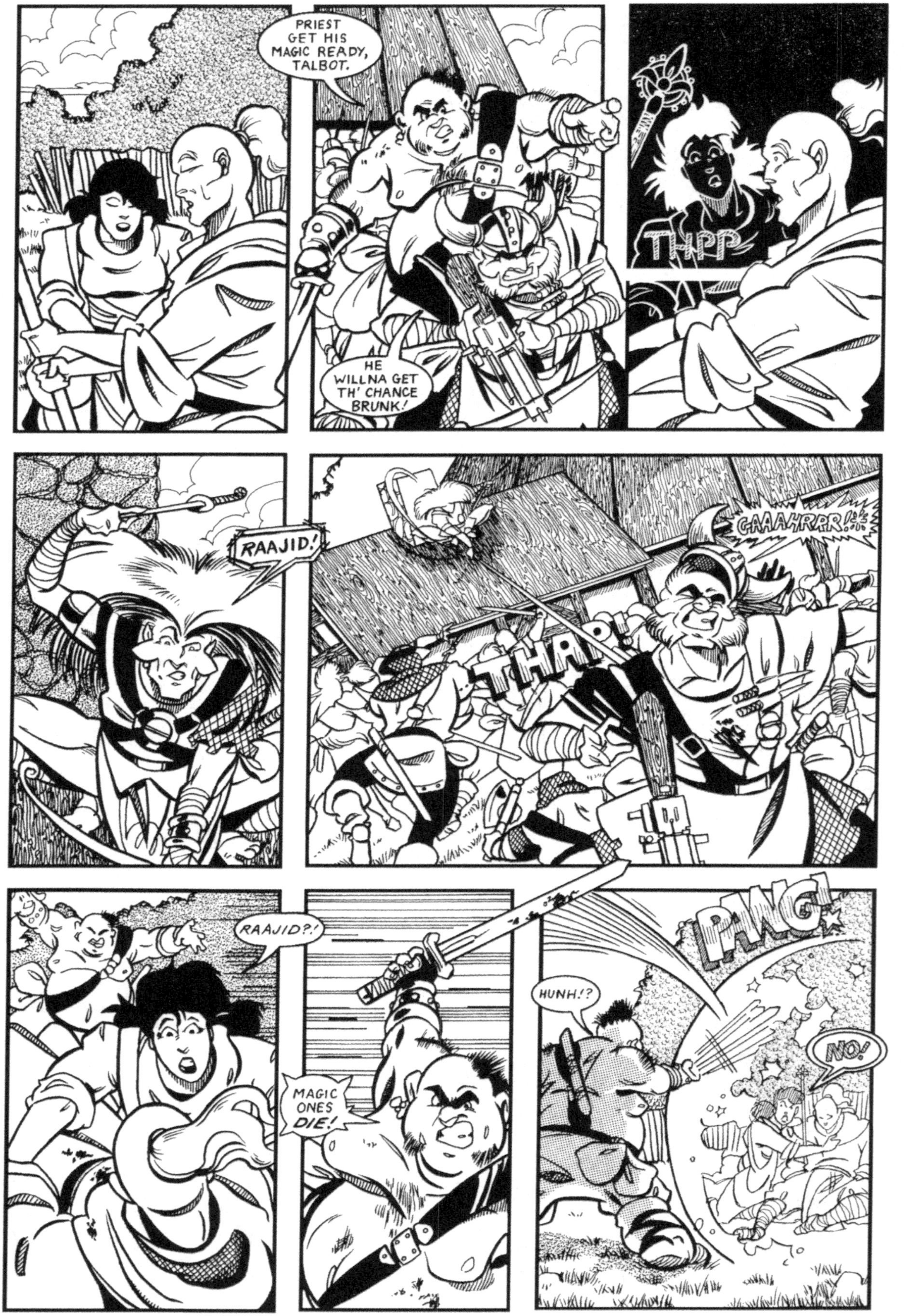
PRIEST GET HIS MAGIC READY, TALBOT.
HE WILLNA GET TH' CHANCE BRUNK!
THPP
RAAJID!
GAAAHRRR!!
THAP!
RAAJID?!
MAGIC ONES DIE!
PANG!
HUNH!?
NO!

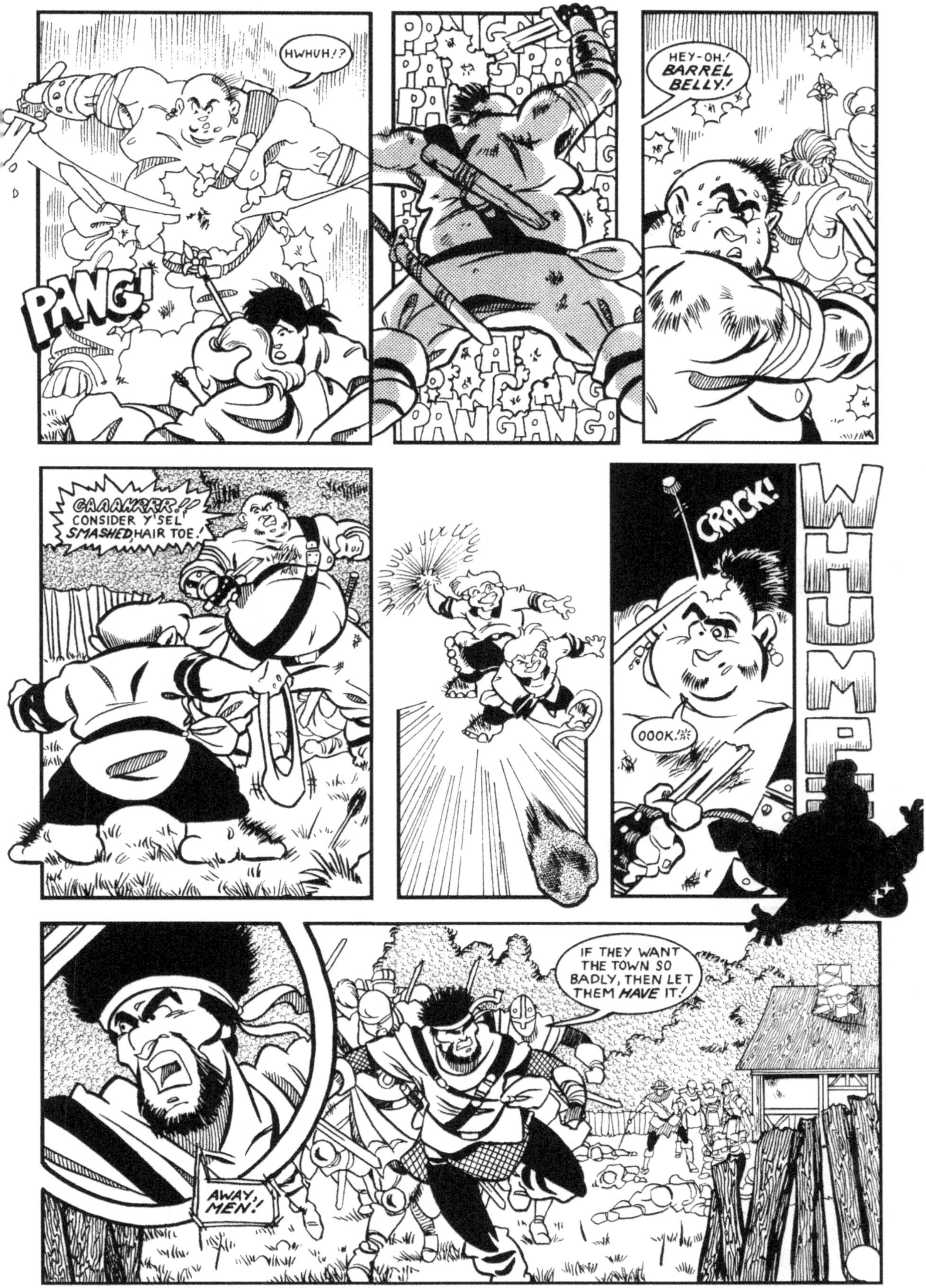

HWHUH!?
PANG!
PANG PANG PANG
HEY-OH! BARREL BELLY!
GAAAHRRR!! CONSIDER Y'SEL' SMASHED, HAIR TOE!
CRACK!
WHUMP!
OOOK.
IF THEY WANT THE TOWN SO BADLY, THEN LET THEM HAVE IT!
AWAY, MEN!

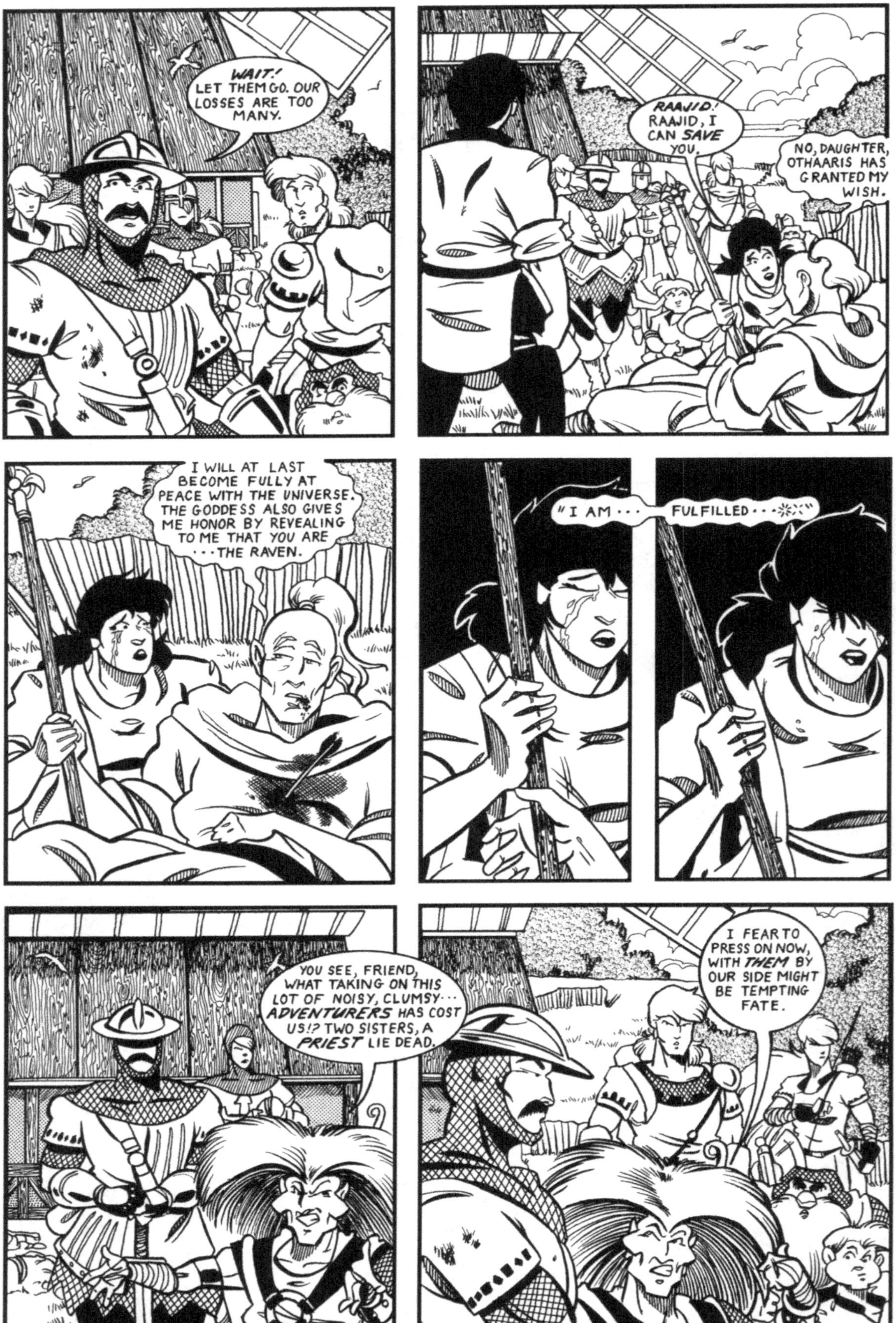
WAIT! LET THEM GO. OUR LOSSES ARE TOO MANY.
RAAJID! RAAJID, I CAN SAVE YOU.
NO, DAUGHTER, OTHAARIS HAS GRANTED MY WISH.
I WILL AT LAST BECOME FULLY AT PEACE WITH THE UNIVERSE. THE GODDESS ALSO GIVES ME HONOR BY REVEALING TO ME THAT YOU ARE ...THE RAVEN.
"I AM ...
FULFILLED ...
YOU SEE, FRIEND, WHAT TAKING ON THIS LOT OF NOISY, CLUMSY... ADVENTURERS HAS COST US!? TWO SISTERS, A PRIEST LIE DEAD.
I FEAR TO PRESS ON NOW, WITH THEM BY OUR SIDE MIGHT BE TEMPTING FATE.

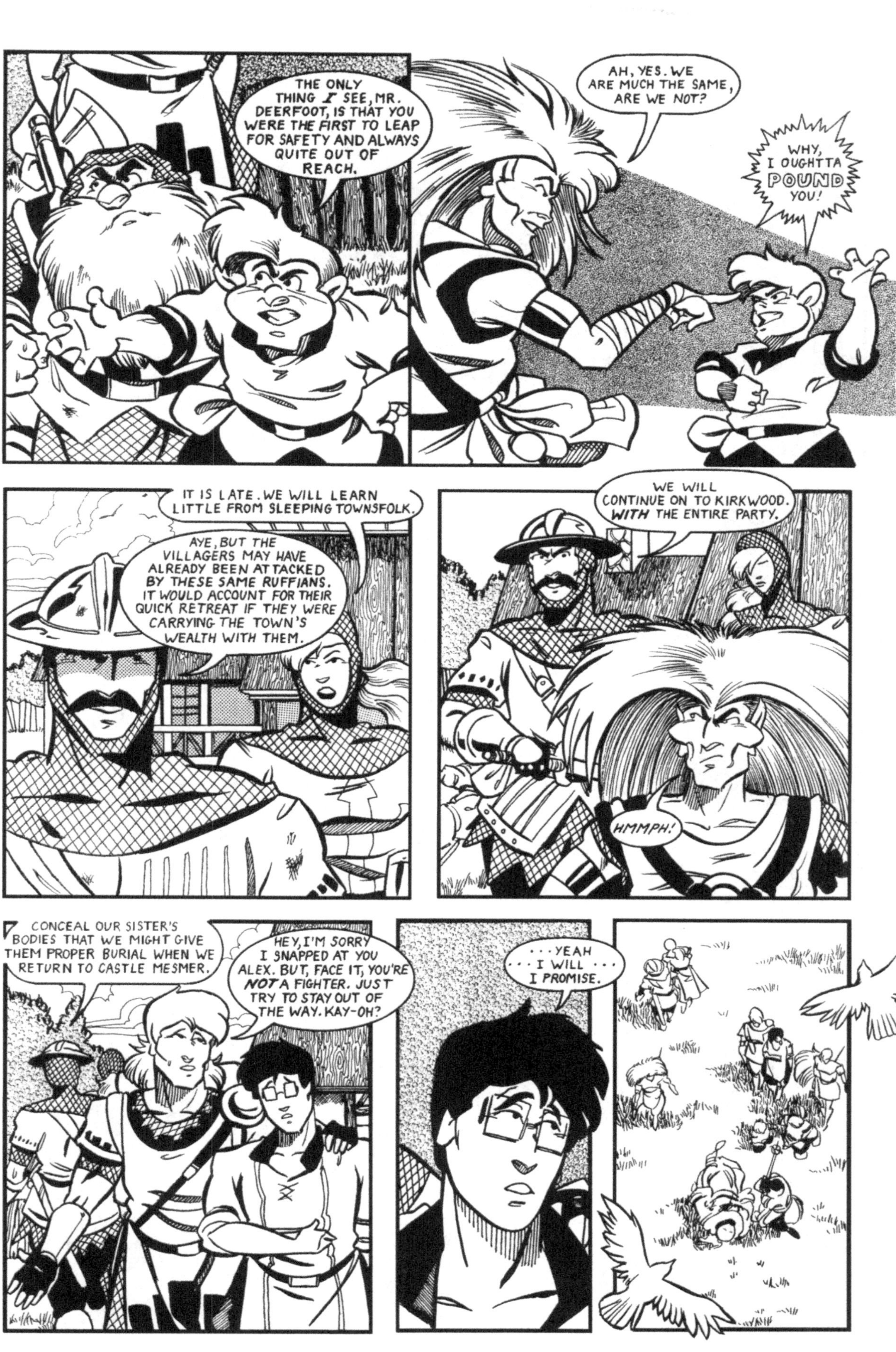
THE ONLY THING I SEE, MR. DEERFOOT, IS THAT YOU WERE THE FIRST TO LEAP FOR SAFETY AND ALWAYS QUITE OUT OF REACH.
AH, YES. WE ARE MUCH THE SAME, ARE WE NOT?
WHY, I OUGHTTA POUND YOU!
IT IS LATE. WE WILL LEARN LITTLE FROM SLEEPING TOWNSFOLK.
AYE, BUT THE VILLAGERS MAY HAVE ALREADY BEEN ATTACKED BY THESE SAME RUFFIANS. IT WOULD ACCOUNT FOR THEIR QUICK RETREAT IF THEY WERE CARRYING THE TOWN'S WEALTH WITH THEM.
WE WILL CONTINUE ON TO KIRKWOOD. WITH THE ENTIRE PARTY.
HMMPH!
CONCEAL OUR SISTER'S BODIES THAT WE MIGHT GIVE THEM PROPER BURIAL WHEN WE RETURN TO CASTLE MESMER.
HEY, I'M SORRY I SNAPPED AT YOU ALEX. BUT, FACE IT, YOU'RE NOT A FIGHTER. JUST TRY TO STAY OUT OF THE WAY. KAY-OH?
...YEAH ...I WILL... I PROMISE.

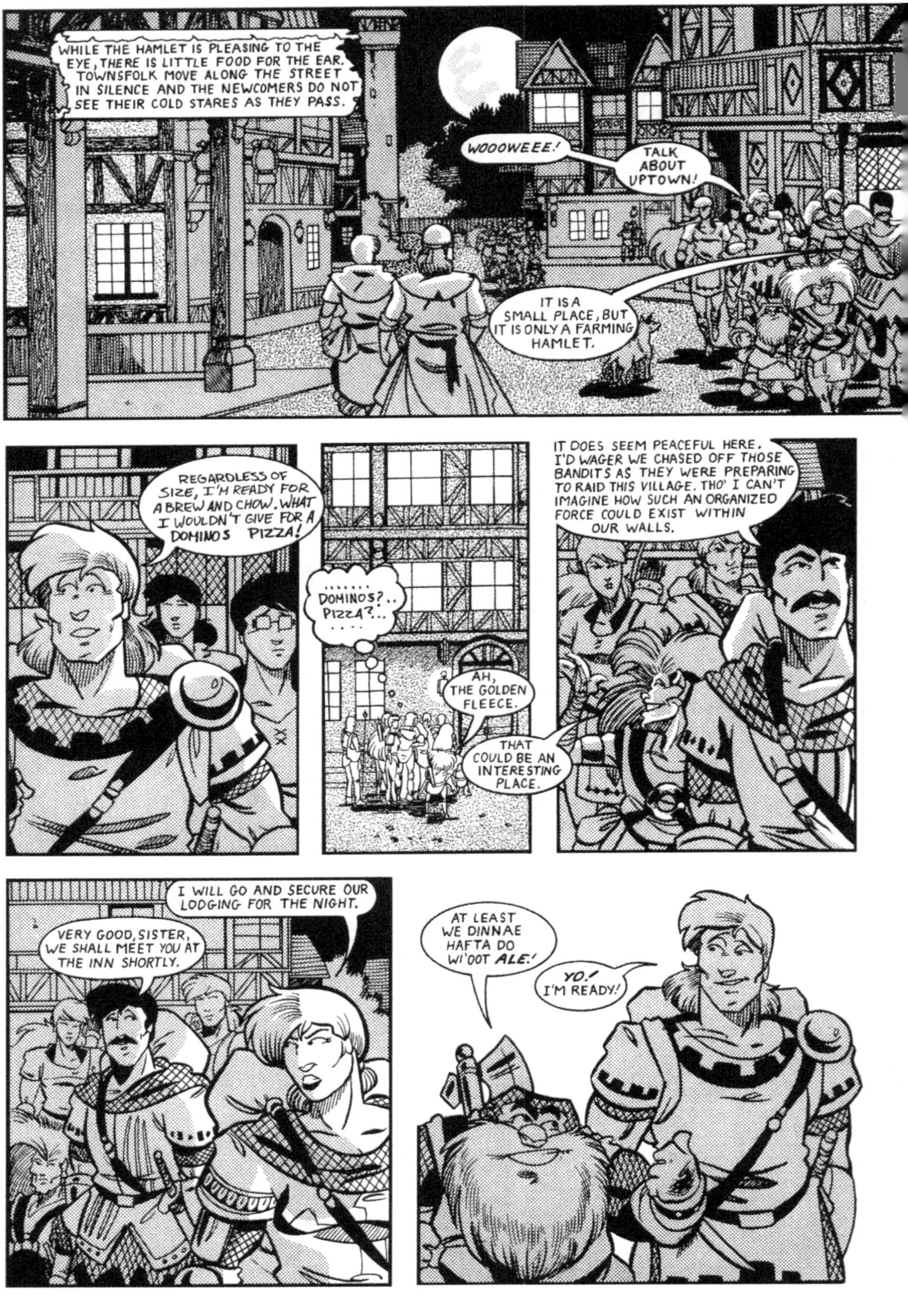
WHILE THE HAMLET IS PLEASING TO THE EYE, THERE IS LITTLE FOOD FOR THE EAR. TOWNSFOLK MOVE ALONG THE STREET IN SILENCE AND THE NEWCOMERS DO NOT SEE THEIR COLD STARES AS THEY PASS.
WOOOWEEE!
TALK ABOUT UPTOWN!
IT IS A SMALL PLACE, BUT IT IS ONLY A FARMING HAMLET.
REGARDLESS OF SIZE, I'M READY FOR A BREW AND CHOW. WHAT I WOULDN'T GIVE FOR A DOMINOS PIZZA!
.... DOMINOS?.. PIZZA?... ....
AH, THE GOLDEN FLEECE.
THAT COULD BE AN INTERESTING PLACE.
IT DOES SEEM PEACEFUL HERE. I'D WAGER WE CHASED OFF THOSE BANDITS AS THEY WERE PREPARING TO RAID THIS VILLAGE. THO' I CAN'T IMAGINE HOW SUCH AN ORGANIZED FORCE COULD EXIST WITHIN OUR WALLS.
I WILL GO AND SECURE OUR LODGING FOR THE NIGHT.
VERY GOOD, SISTER, WE SHALL MEET YOU AT THE INN SHORTLY.
AT LEAST WE DINNAE HAFTA DO WI'OOT ALE!
YO! I'M READY!

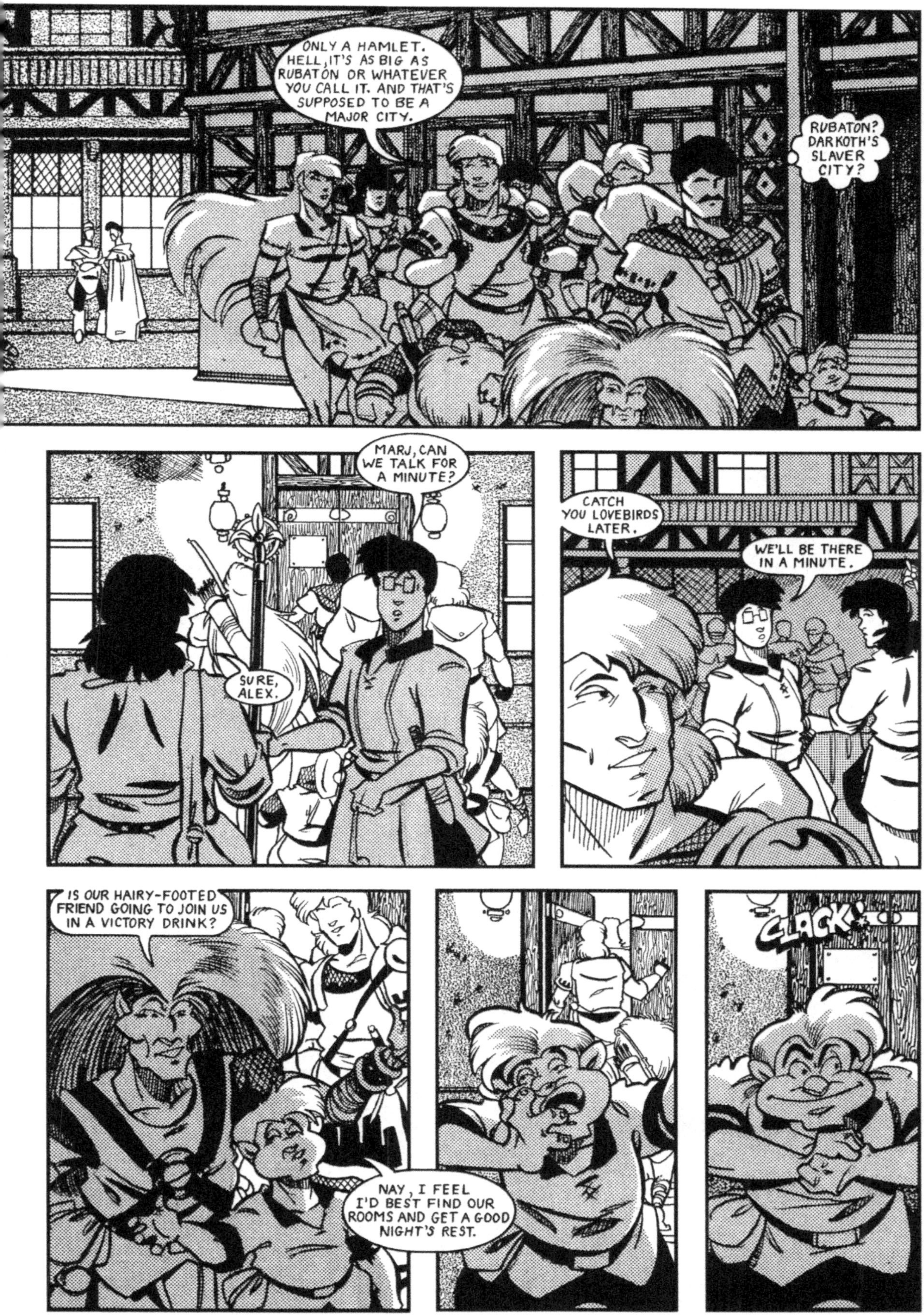
ONLY A HAMLET. HELL, IT'S AS BIG AS RUBATON OR WHATEVER YOU CALL IT. AND THAT'S SUPPOSED TO BE A MAJOR CITY.
RUBATON? DARKOTH'S SLAVER CITY?
MARJ, CAN WE TALK FOR A MINUTE?
SURE, ALEX.
CATCH YOU LOVEBIRDS LATER.
WE'LL BE THERE IN A MINUTE.
IS OUR HAIRY-FOOTED FRIEND GOING TO JOIN US IN A VICTORY DRINK?
NAY, I FEEL I'D BEST FIND OUR ROOMS AND GET A GOOD NIGHT'S REST.
CLACK!

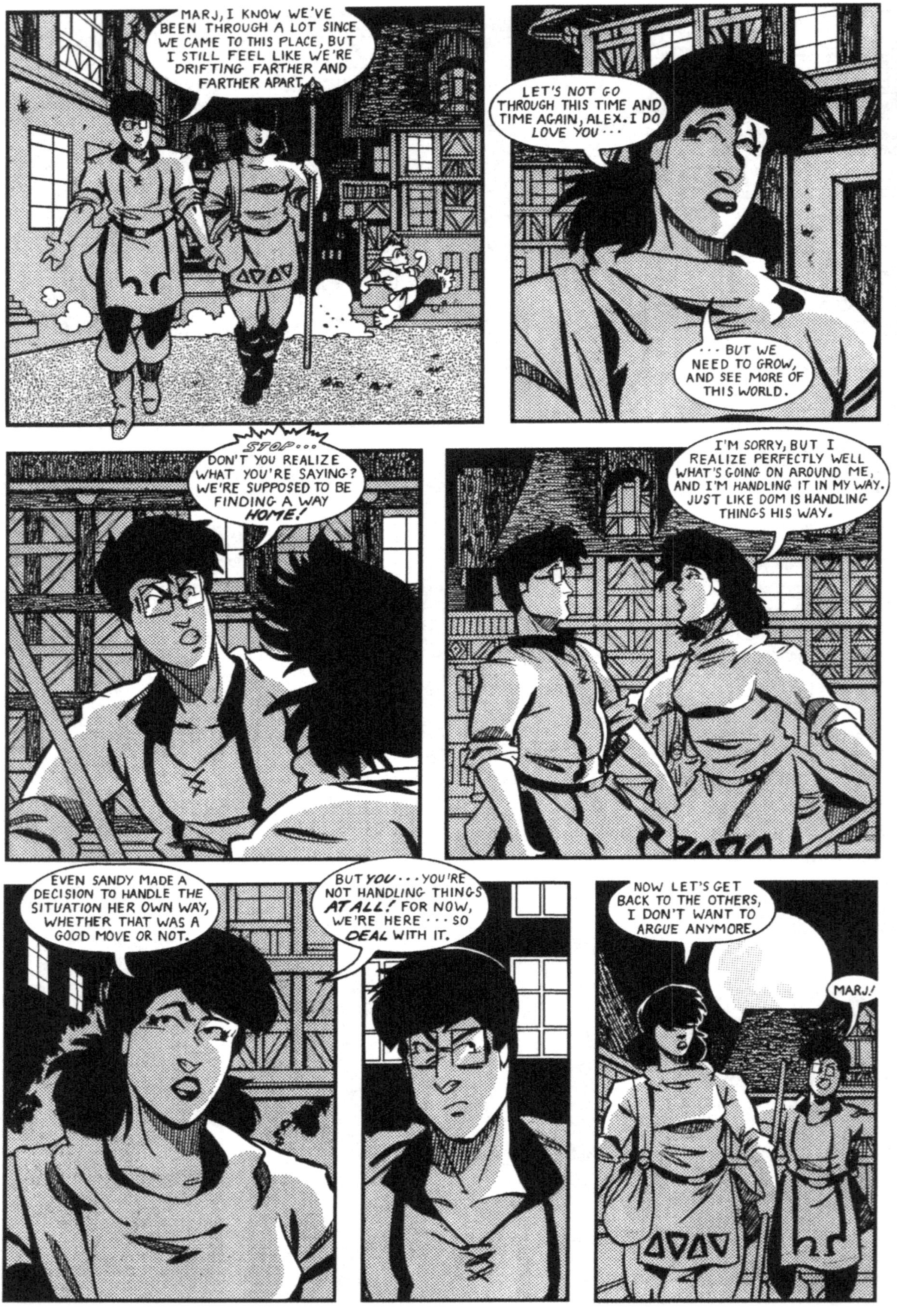
MARJ, I KNOW WE'VE BEEN THROUGH A LOT SINCE WE CAME TO THIS PLACE, BUT I STILL FEEL LIKE WE'RE DRIFTING FARTHER AND FARTHER APART.
LET'S NOT GO THROUGH THIS TIME AND TIME AGAIN, ALEX. I DO LOVE YOU...
...BUT WE NEED TO GROW, AND SEE MORE OF THIS WORLD.
STOP... DON'T YOU REALIZE WHAT YOU'RE SAYING? WE'RE SUPPOSED TO BE FINDING A WAY HOME!
I'M SORRY, BUT I REALIZE PERFECTLY WELL WHAT'S GOING ON AROUND ME, AND I'M HANDLING IT IN MY WAY. JUST LIKE DOM IS HANDLING THINGS HIS WAY.
EVEN SANDY MADE A DECISION TO HANDLE THE SITUATION HER OWN WAY, WHETHER THAT WAS A GOOD MOVE OR NOT.
BUT YOU... YOU'RE NOT HANDLING THINGS AT ALL! FOR NOW, WE'RE HERE... SO DEAL WITH IT.
NOW LET'S GET BACK TO THE OTHERS, I DON'T WANT TO ARGUE ANYMORE.
MARJ!

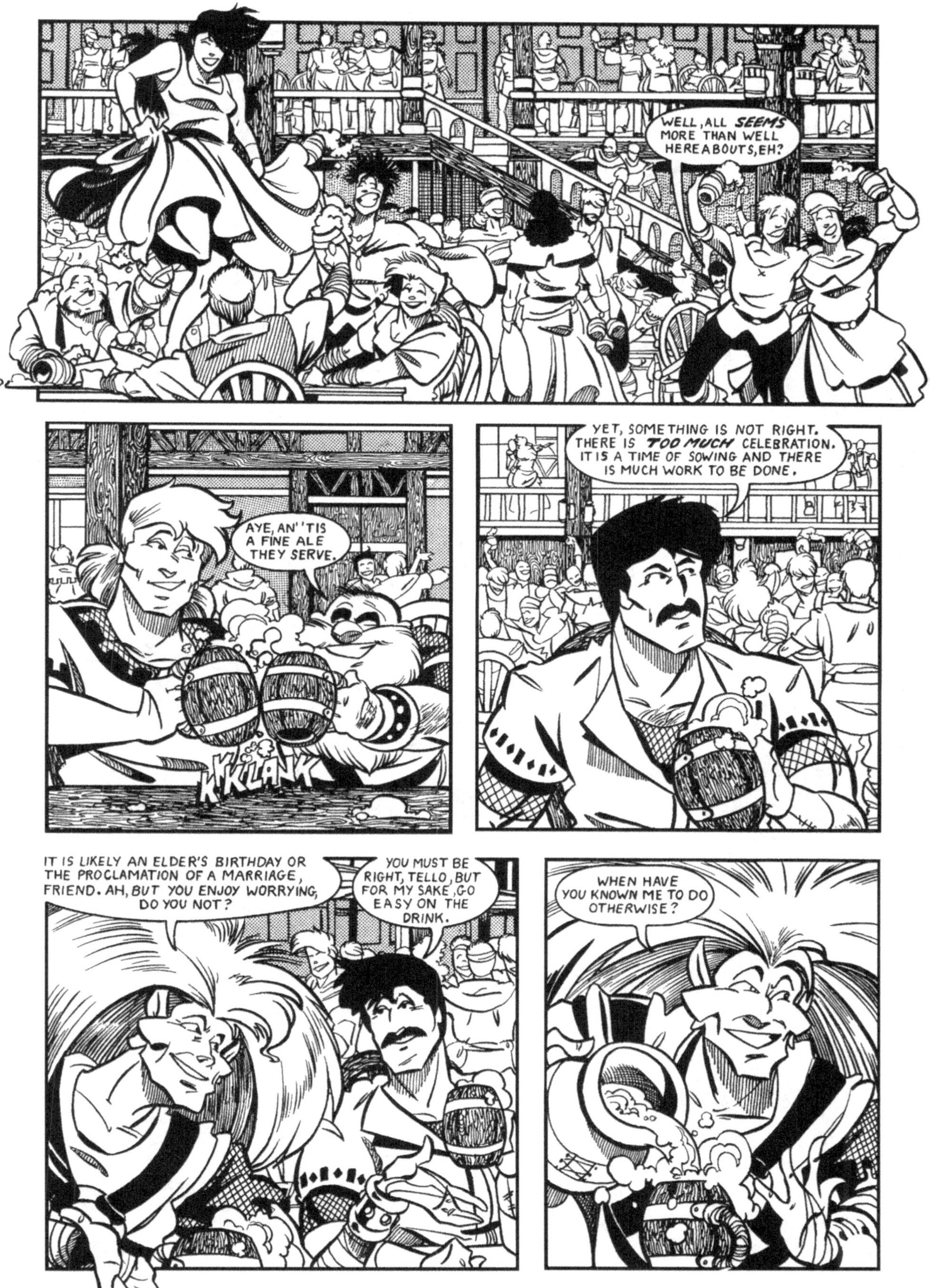
WELL, ALL SEEMS MORE THAN WELL HEREABOUTS, EH?
AYE, AN' 'TIS A FINE ALE THEY SERVE.
KKLANK
YET, SOMETHING IS NOT RIGHT. THERE IS TOO MUCH CELEBRATION. IT IS A TIME OF SOWING AND THERE IS MUCH WORK TO BE DONE.
IT IS LIKELY AN ELDER'S BIRTHDAY OR THE PROCLAMATION OF A MARRIAGE, FRIEND. AH, BUT YOU ENJOY WORRYING, DO YOU NOT?
YOU MUST BE RIGHT, TELLO, BUT FOR MY SAKE, GO EASY ON THE DRINK.
WHEN HAVE YOU KNOWN ME TO DO OTHERWISE?

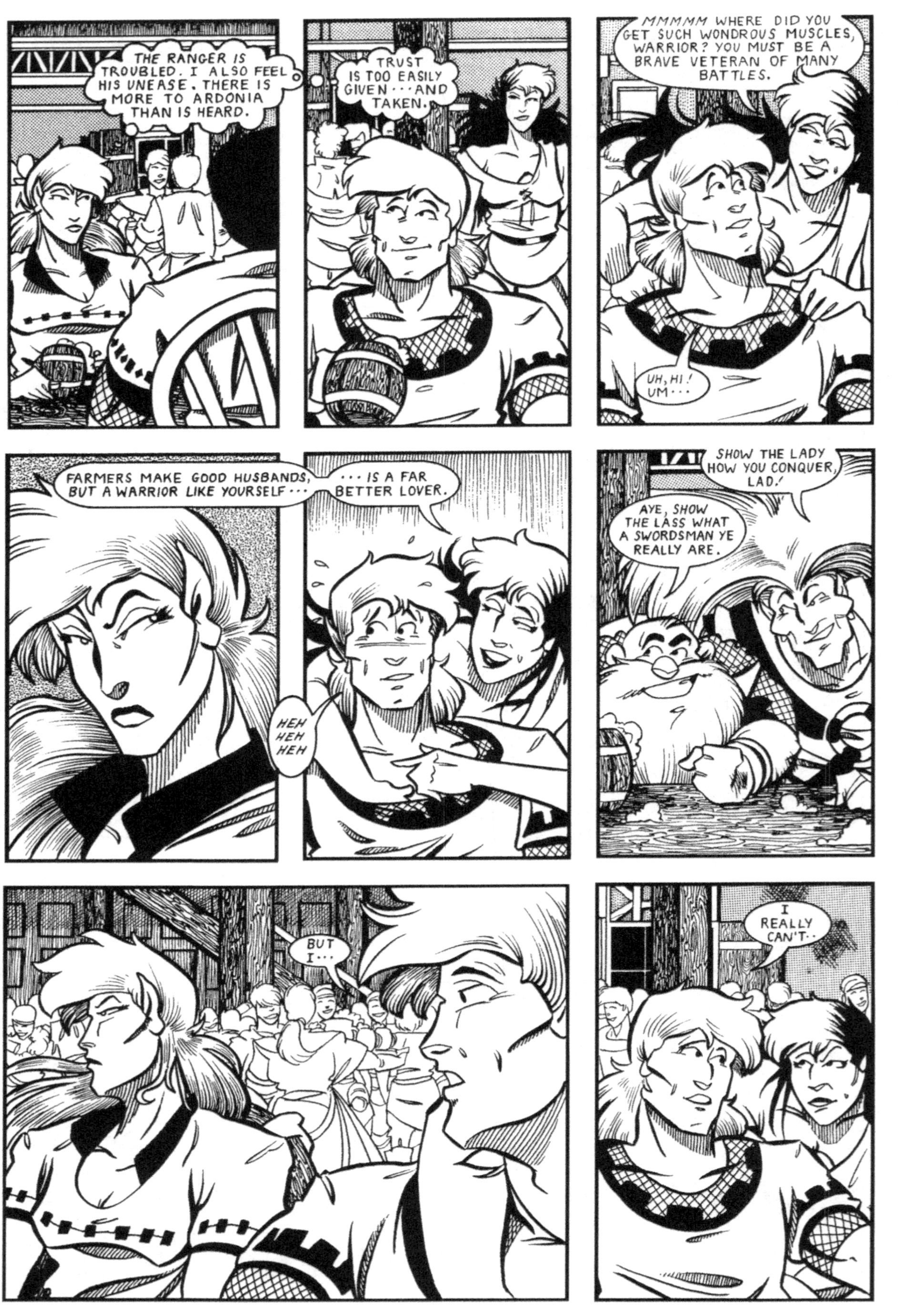
THE RANGER IS TROUBLED. I ALSO FEEL HIS UNEASE. THERE IS MORE TO ARDONIA THAN IS HEARD.
TRUST IS TOO EASILY GIVEN ··· AND TAKEN.
MMMMM WHERE DID YOU GET SUCH WONDROUS MUSCLES, WARRIOR? YOU MUST BE A BRAVE VETERAN OF MANY BATTLES.
UH, HI! UM···
FARMERS MAKE GOOD HUSBANDS, BUT A WARRIOR LIKE YOURSELF···
··· IS A FAR BETTER LOVER.
HEH HEH HEH
SHOW THE LADY HOW YOU CONQUER, LAD!
AYE, SHOW THE LASS WHAT A SWORDSMAN YE REALLY ARE.
BUT I···
I REALLY CAN'T··

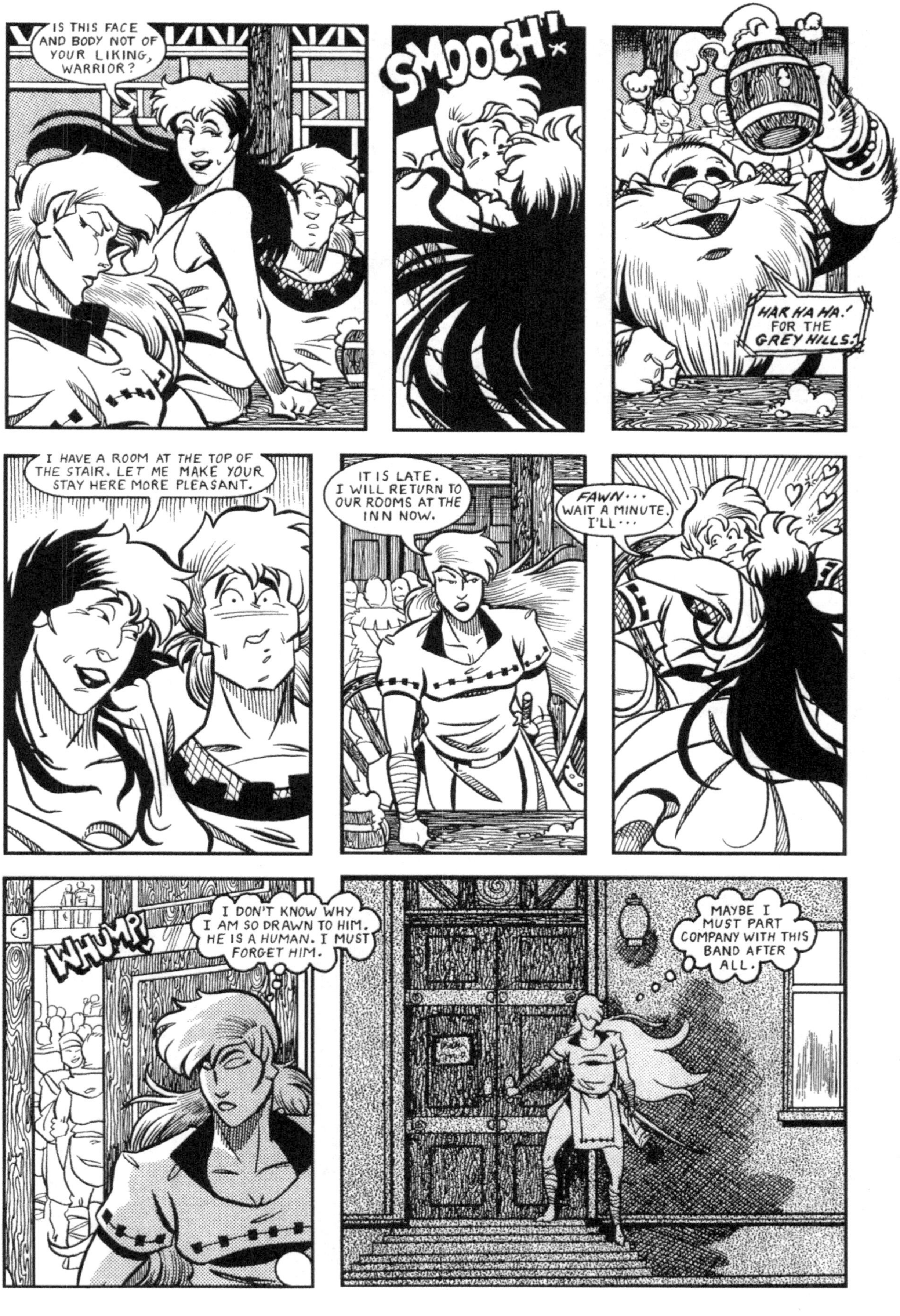
IS THIS FACE AND BODY NOT OF YOUR LIKING, WARRIOR?
SMOOCH!
HAR HA HA! FOR THE GREY HILLS!
I HAVE A ROOM AT THE TOP OF THE STAIR. LET ME MAKE YOUR STAY HERE MORE PLEASANT.
IT IS LATE. I WILL RETURN TO OUR ROOMS AT THE INN NOW.
FAWN... WAIT A MINUTE. I'LL...
WHUMP!
I DON'T KNOW WHY I AM SO DRAWN TO HIM. HE IS A HUMAN. I MUST FORGET HIM.
MAYBE I MUST PART COMPANY WITH THIS BAND AFTER ALL.

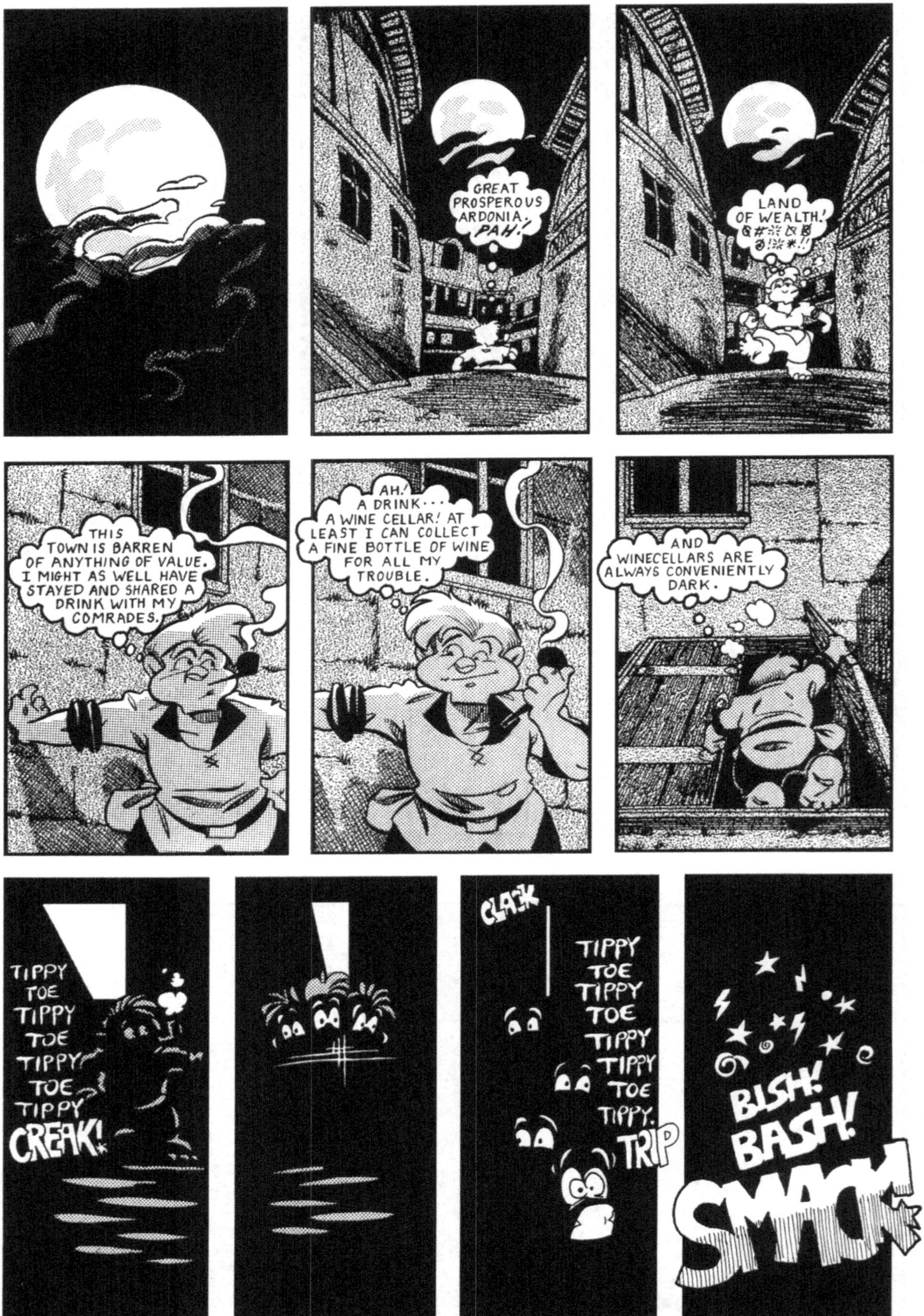
GREAT PROSPEROUS ARDONIA. PAH!
LAND OF WEALTH!
THIS TOWN IS BARREN OF ANYTHING OF VALUE. I MIGHT AS WELL HAVE STAYED AND SHARED A DRINK WITH MY COMRADES.
AH! A DRINK... A WINE CELLAR! AT LEAST I CAN COLLECT A FINE BOTTLE OF WINE FOR ALL MY TROUBLE.
AND WINECELLARS ARE ALWAYS CONVENIENTLY DARK.
TIPPY TOE TIPPY TOE TIPPY TOE TIPPY
CREAK!
CLACK
TIPPY TOE TIPPY TOE TIPPY TIPPY TOE TIPPY.
TRIP
BISH! BASH!
SMACK

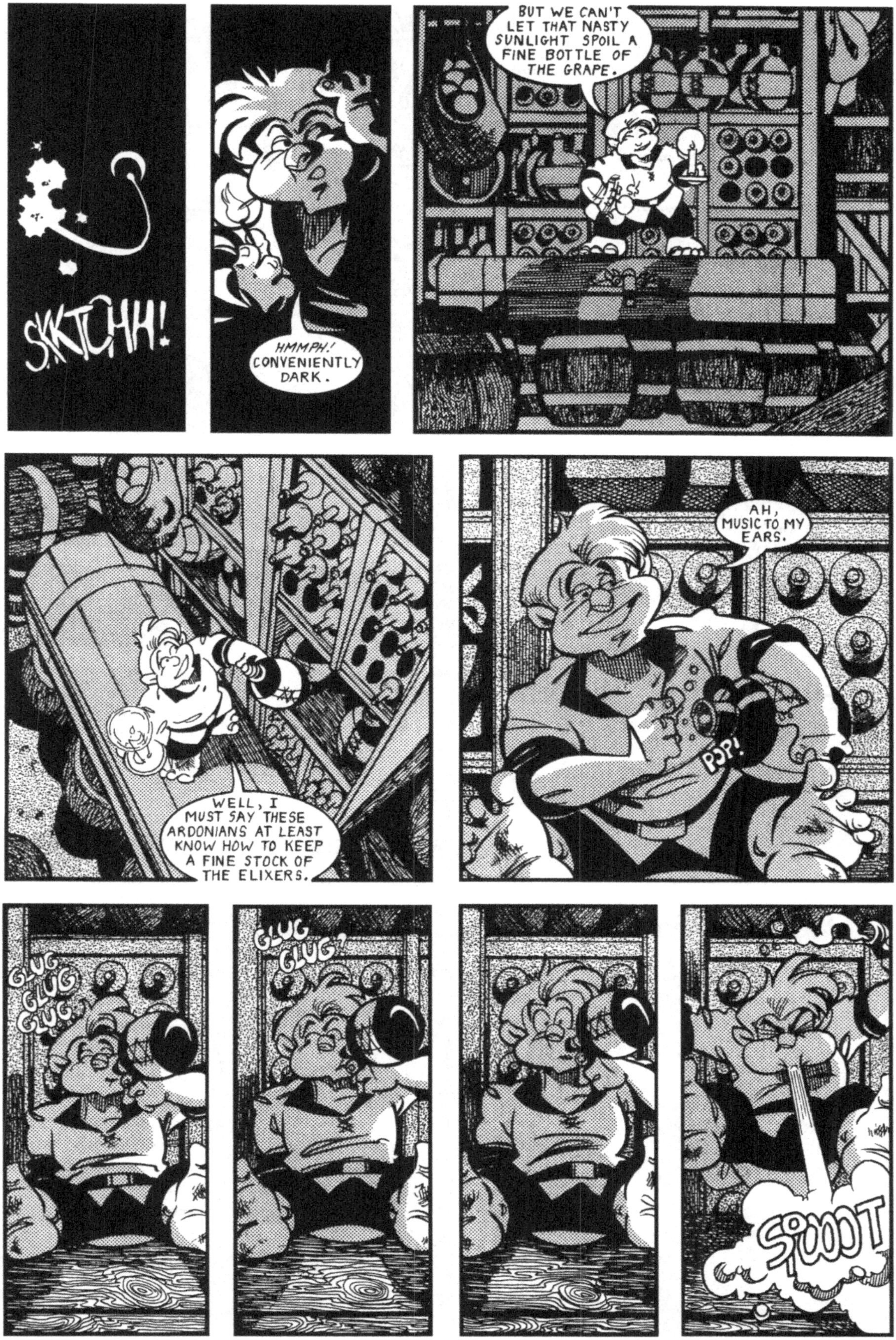
SKKTCHH!
HMMPH! CONVENIENTLY DARK.
BUT WE CAN'T LET THAT NASTY SUNLIGHT SPOIL A FINE BOTTLE OF THE GRAPE.
WELL, I MUST SAY THESE ARDONIANS AT LEAST KNOW HOW TO KEEP A FINE STOCK OF THE ELIXERS.
POP!
AH, MUSIC TO MY EARS.
GLUG GLUG GLUG
GLUG GLUG?
SPOOOT

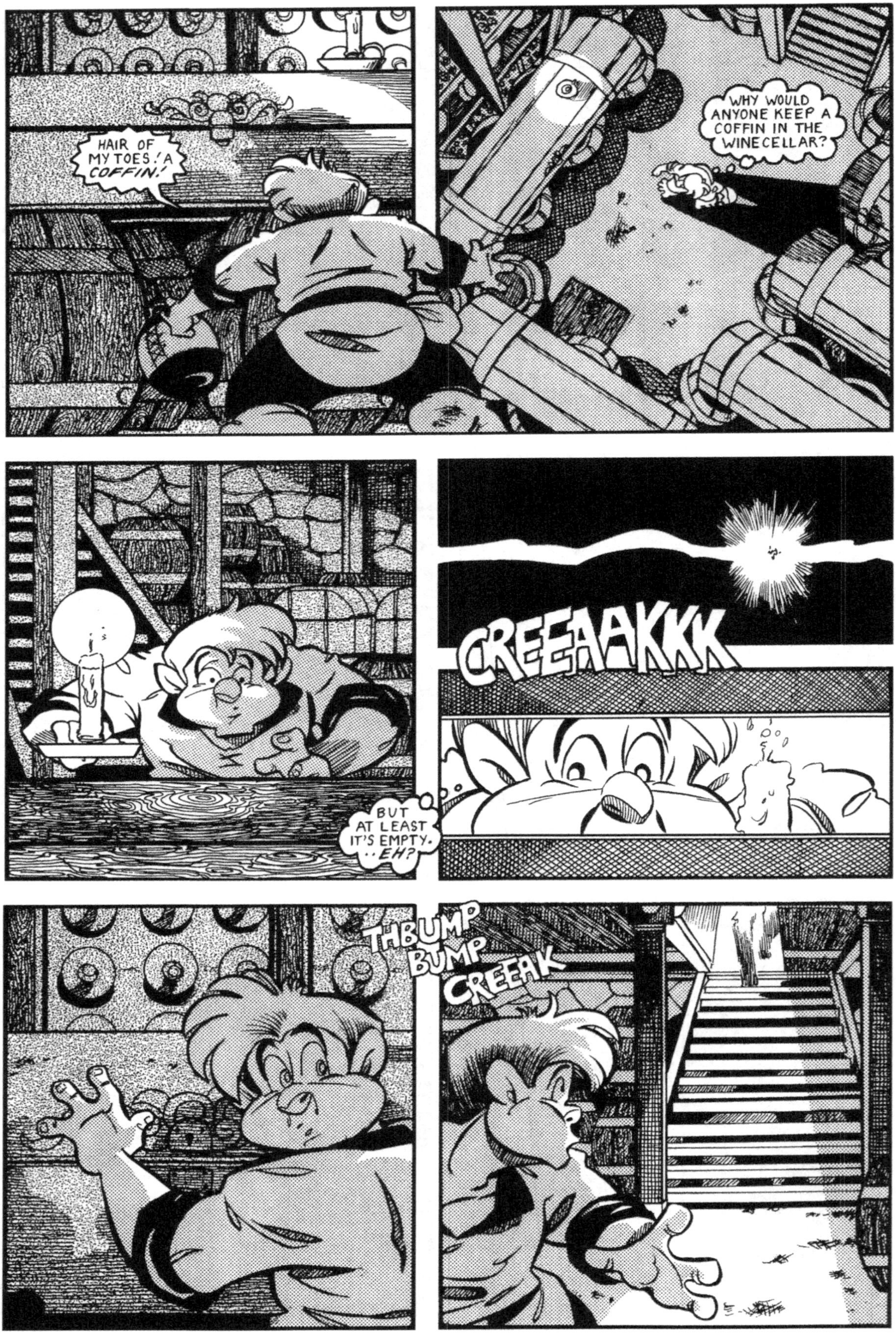
HAIR OF MY TOES! A COFFIN!
WHY WOULD ANYONE KEEP A COFFIN IN THE WINECELLAR?
BUT AT LEAST IT'S EMPTY. ..EH?
CREEAAKKK
THBUMP BUMP CREEAK

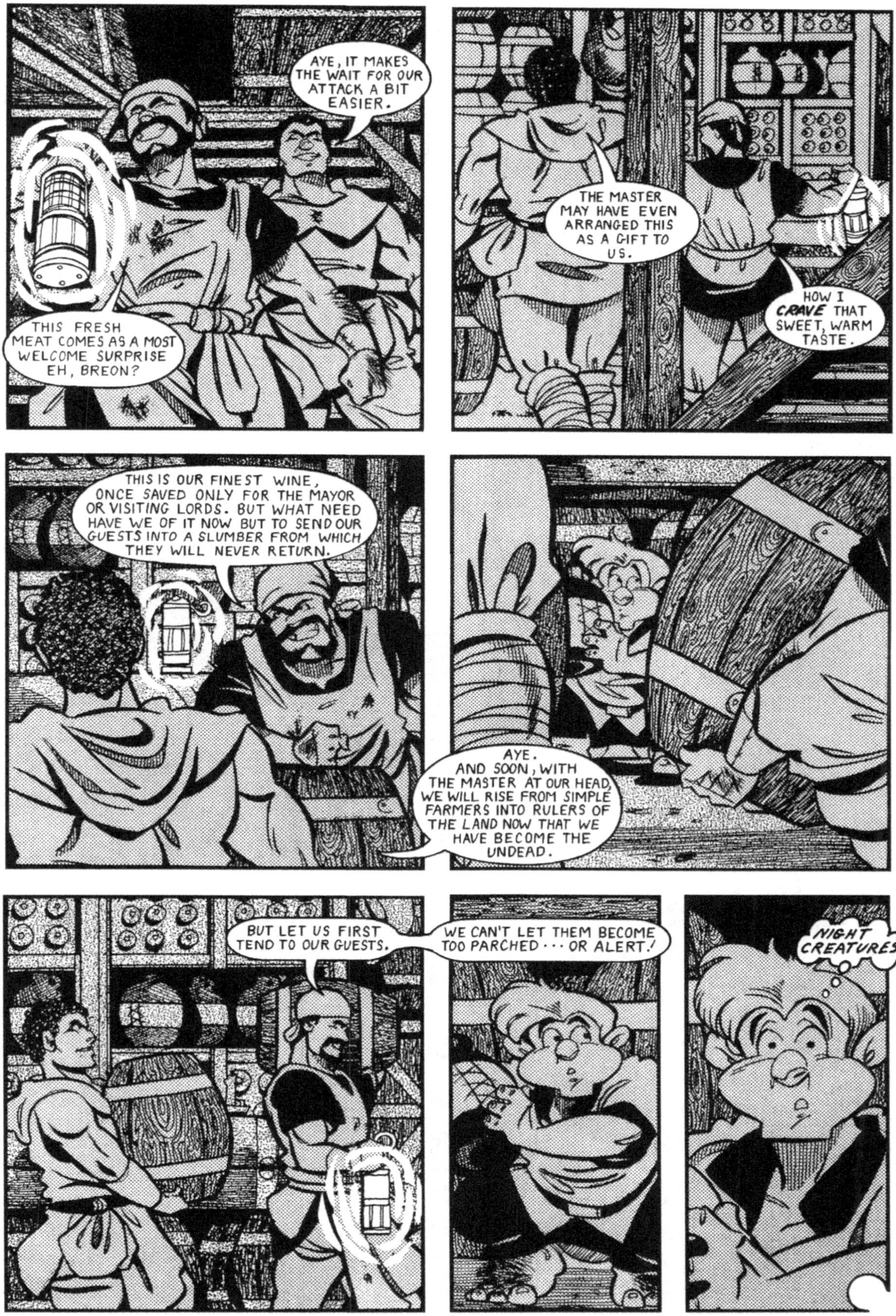
AYE, IT MAKES THE WAIT FOR OUR ATTACK A BIT EASIER.
THIS FRESH MEAT COMES AS A MOST WELCOME SURPRISE EH, BREON?
THE MASTER MAY HAVE EVEN ARRANGED THIS AS A GIFT TO US.
HOW I CRAVE THAT SWEET, WARM TASTE.
THIS IS OUR FINEST WINE, ONCE SAVED ONLY FOR THE MAYOR OR VISITING LORDS. BUT WHAT NEED HAVE WE OF IT NOW BUT TO SEND OUR GUESTS INTO A SLUMBER FROM WHICH THEY WILL NEVER RETURN.
AYE. AND SOON, WITH THE MASTER AT OUR HEAD, WE WILL RISE FROM SIMPLE FARMERS INTO RULERS OF THE LAND NOW THAT WE HAVE BECOME THE UNDEAD.
BUT LET US FIRST TEND TO OUR GUESTS.
WE CAN'T LET THEM BECOME TOO PARCHED ··· OR ALERT!
NIGHT CREATURES!

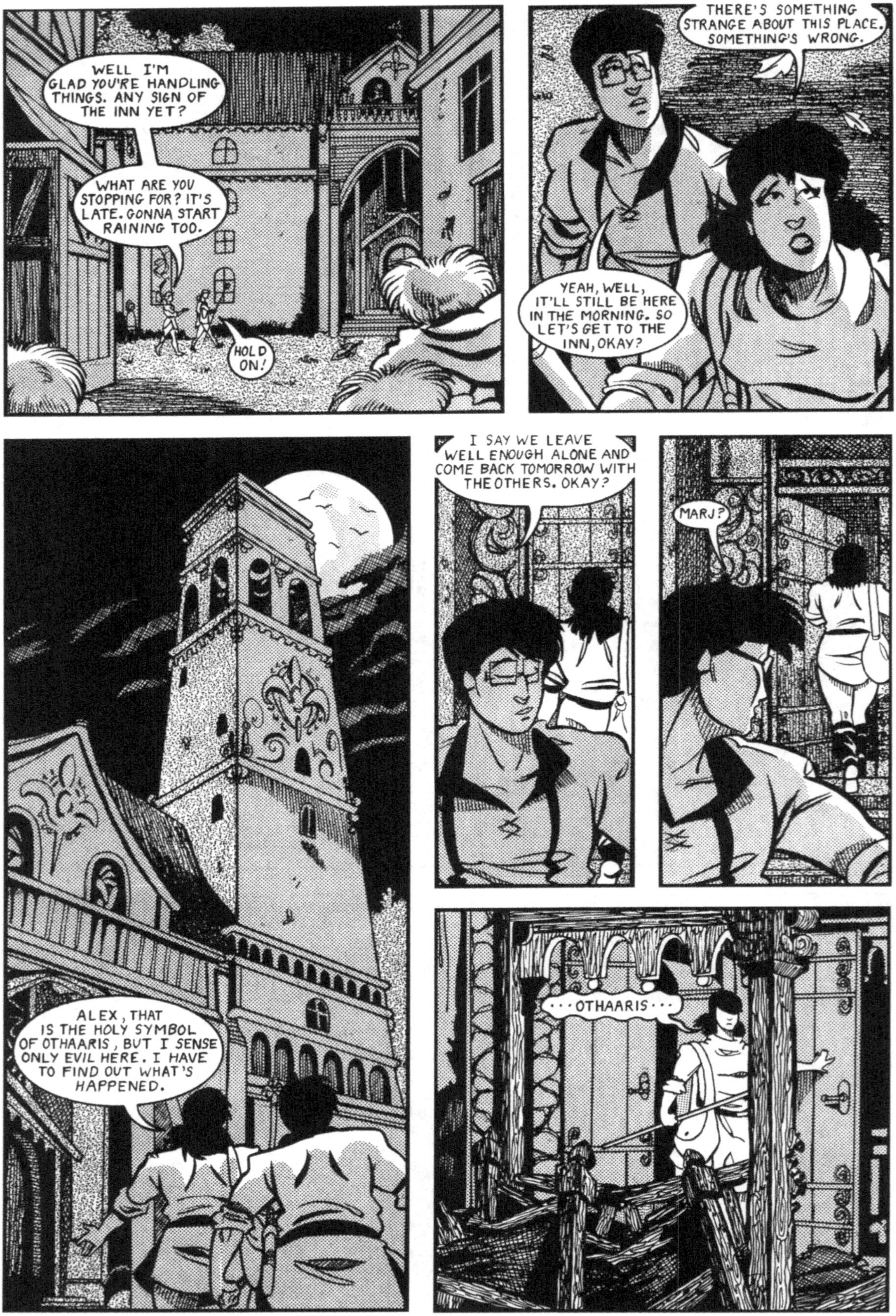
WELL I'M GLAD YOU'RE HANDLING THINGS. ANY SIGN OF THE INN YET?
WHAT ARE YOU STOPPING FOR? IT'S LATE. GONNA START RAINING TOO.
HOLD ON!
THERE'S SOMETHING STRANGE ABOUT THIS PLACE. SOMETHING'S WRONG.
YEAH, WELL, IT'LL STILL BE HERE IN THE MORNING. SO LET'S GET TO THE INN, OKAY?
ALEX, THAT IS THE HOLY SYMBOL OF OTHAARIS, BUT I SENSE ONLY EVIL HERE. I HAVE TO FIND OUT WHAT'S HAPPENED.
I SAY WE LEAVE WELL ENOUGH ALONE AND COME BACK TOMORROW WITH THE OTHERS. OKAY?
MARJ?
···OTHAARIS···

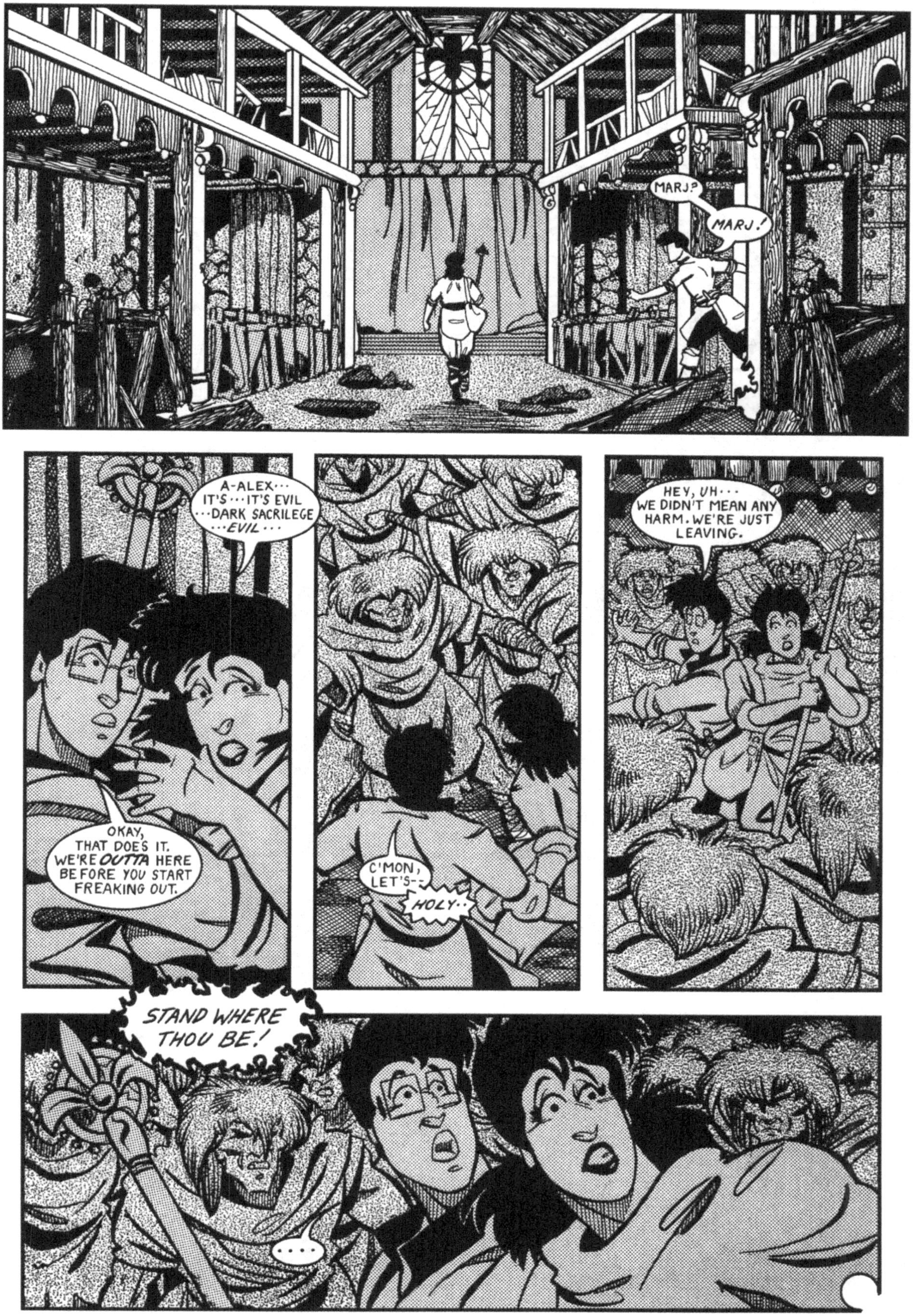
MARJ?
MARJ!
A-ALEX... IT'S... IT'S EVIL ...DARK SACRILEGE ...EVIL...
OKAY, THAT DOES IT. WE'RE OUTTA HERE BEFORE YOU START FREAKING OUT.
C'MON, LET'S--
HOLY..
HEY, UH... WE DIDN'T MEAN ANY HARM. WE'RE JUST LEAVING.
STAND WHERE THOU BE!
....

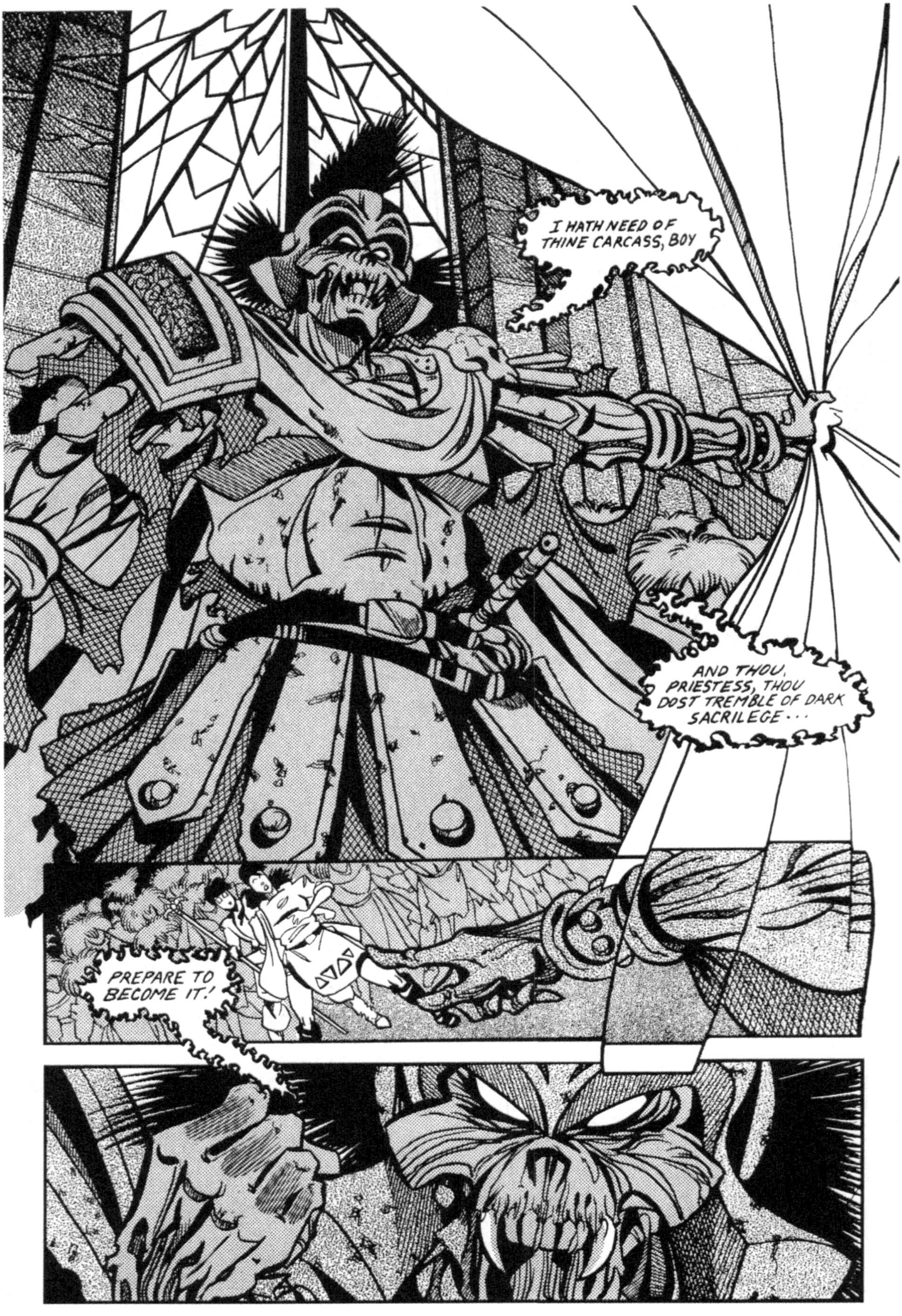

I HATH NEED OF THINE CARCASS, BOY
AND THOU, PRIESTESS, THOU DOST TREMBLE OF DARK SACRILEGE...
PREPARE TO BECOME IT!

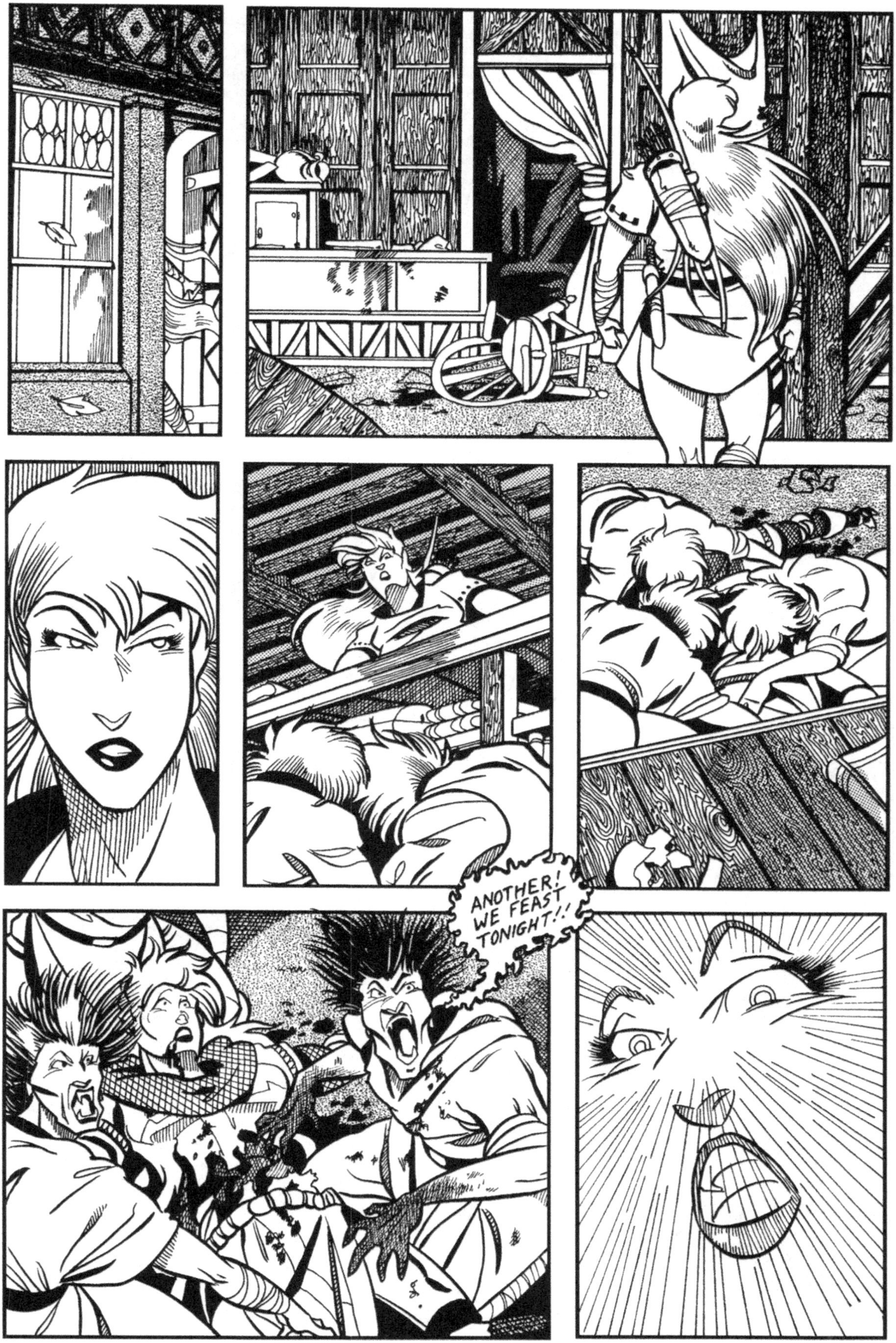
ANOTHER! WE FEAST TONIGHT!!

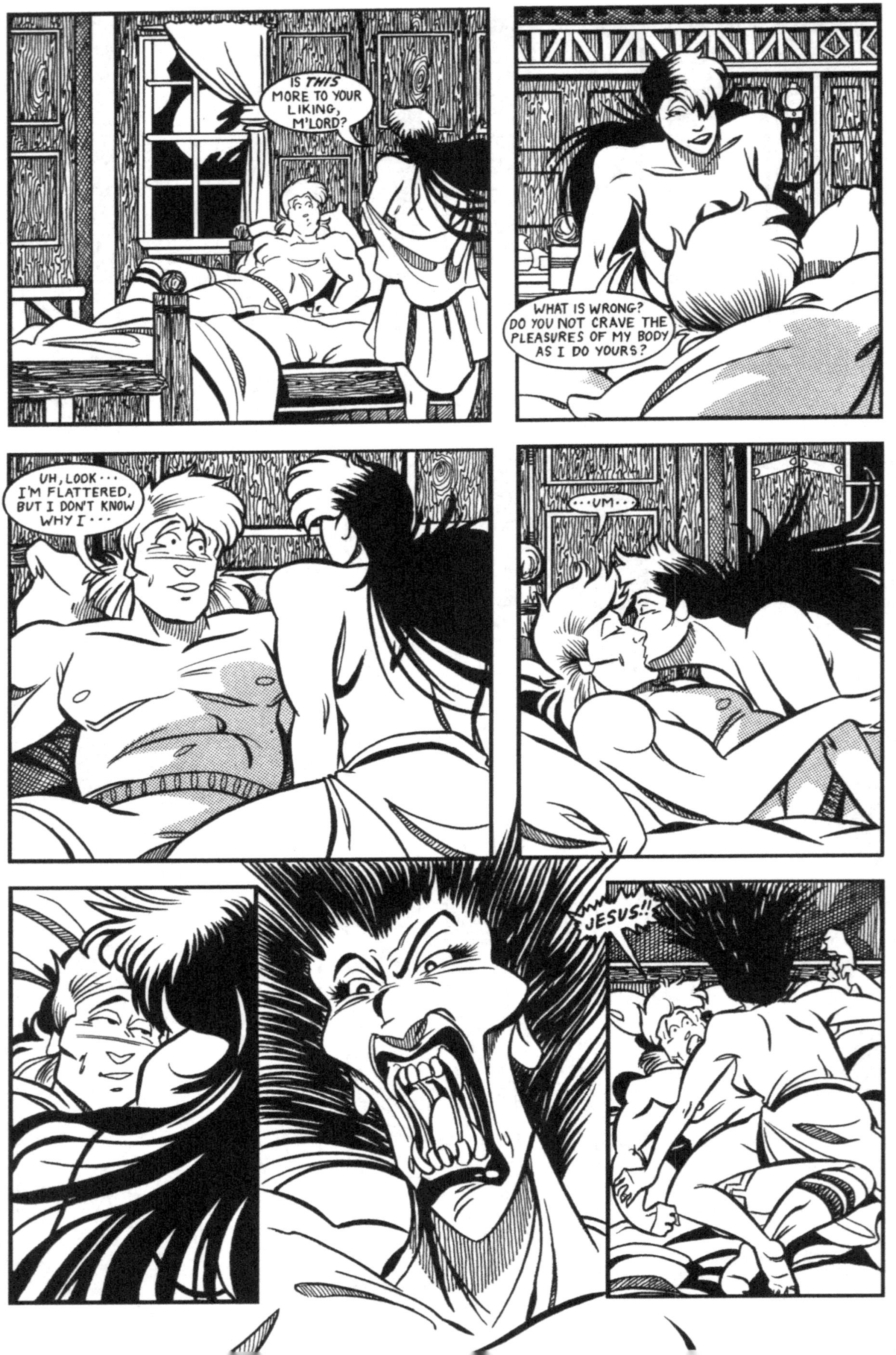
IS *THIS* MORE TO YOUR LIKING, M'LORD?
WHAT IS WRONG? DO YOU NOT CRAVE THE PLEASURES OF MY BODY AS I DO YOURS?
UH, LOOK... I'M FLATTERED, BUT I DON'T KNOW WHY I...
...UM...
JESUS!!

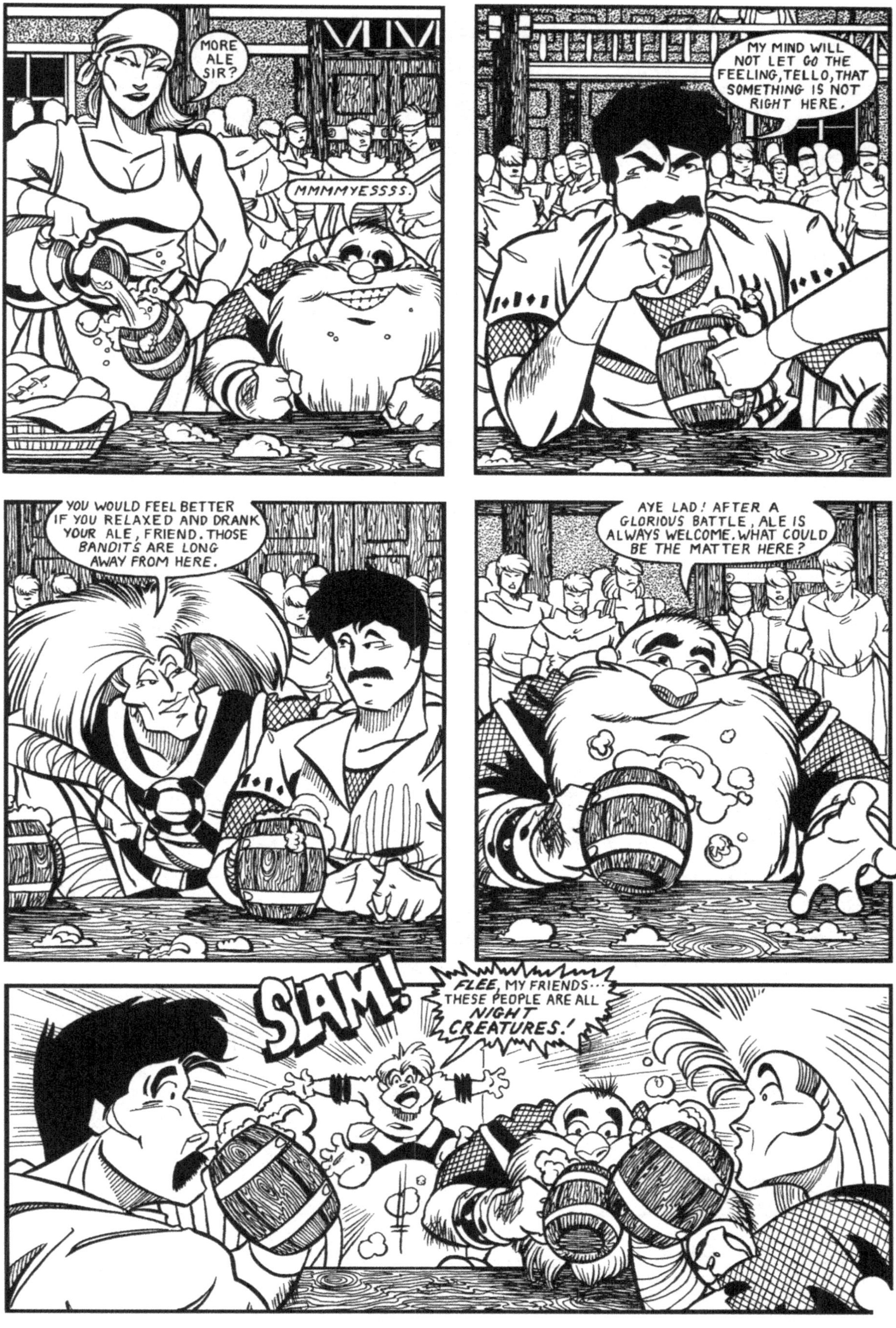
MORE ALE SIR?
MMMMYESSSS.
MY MIND WILL NOT LET GO THE FEELING, TELLO, THAT SOMETHING IS NOT RIGHT HERE.
YOU WOULD FEEL BETTER IF YOU RELAXED AND DRANK YOUR ALE, FRIEND. THOSE BANDITS ARE LONG AWAY FROM HERE.
AYE LAD! AFTER A GLORIOUS BATTLE, ALE IS ALWAYS WELCOME. WHAT COULD BE THE MATTER HERE?
SLAM!
FLEE, MY FRIENDS... THESE PEOPLE ARE ALL NIGHT CREATURES!

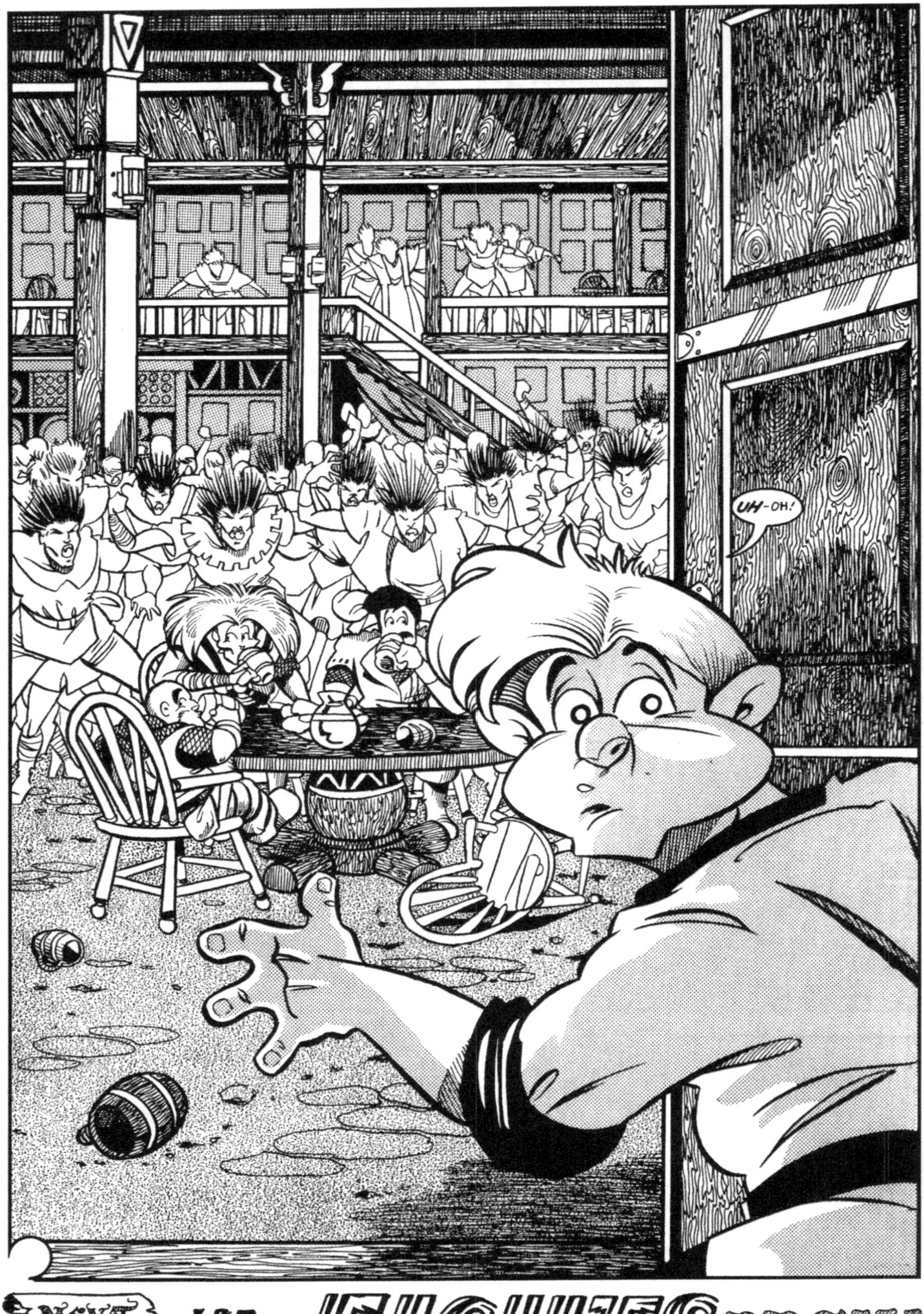
UH-OH!

NEXT ISSUE: LET THE FIGHTS BEGIN!

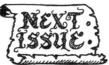

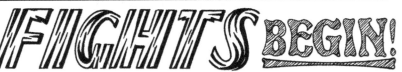

ALSO AVAILABLE FROM CALIBER COMICS

QUALITY GRAPHIC NOVELS TO ENTERTAIN

THE SEARCHERS: VOLUME 1
The Shape of Things to Come

Before League of Extraordinary Gentlemen there was The Searchers. At the dawn of the 20th century the greatest literary adventurers from the likes of Wells, Verne, Doyle, Burroughs, and Haggard were created. All thought to be the work of pure fiction. However, a century later, the real-life descendants of those famous adventurers are recruited by the legendary Professor Challenger in order to save mankind's future. Collected for the first time.

"Searchers is the comic book I have on the wall with a sign reading - 'Love books? Never read a comic? Try this one! ....money back guarantee..." - Dark Star Books.

WAR OF THE WORLDS: INFESTATION

Based on the H.G. Wells classic! The "Martian Invasion" has begun again and now mankind must fight for its very humanity. It happened slowly at first but by the third year, it seemed that the war was almost over... the war was almost lost.

"Writer Randy Zimmerman has a fine grasp of drama, and spins the various strands of the story into a coherent whole... imaginative and very gritty."
- war-of-the-worlds.co.uk

HELSING: LEGACY BORN

From writer Gary Reed (Deadworld) and artists John Lowe (Captain America), Bruce McCorkindale (Godzilla). She was born into a legacy she wanted no part of and pushed into a battle recessed deep in the shadows of the night. Samantha Helsing is torn between two worlds...two allegiances...two families. The legacy of the Van Helsing family and their crusade against the "night creatures" comes to modern day with the most unlikely of all warriors.

"Congratulations on this masterpiece..."
- Paul Dale Roberts, Compuserve Reviews

"All in all, another great package from Caliber."
- Paul Haywood, Comics Forum

HEROES AND HORRORS

Heroes and Horrors anthology provides nine rarely seen or never-before-published heroic and horrifying comic stories from the mind of veteran comic writer Steven Philip Jones.

Featured are entertaining stories with art by Octavio Cariello (The Action Bible), S. Clarke Hawbaker (Nomad), Christopher Jones (Young Justice), Dan Jurgens (Death of Superman), and many more! Foreword by Phil Hester.

"Incredibly creative...Steve's stories are masterworks of what new comics should be: absorbing and exciting and read again and again." - Clive Cussler, international bestselling author.

DAYS OF WRATH

Award winning comic writer & artist Wayne Vansant brings his gripping World War II saga of war in the Pacific to Guadalcanal and the Battle of Bloody Ridge. This is the powerful story of the long, vicious battle for Guadalcanal that occurred in 1942-43. When the U.S. Navy orders its outnumbered and outgunned ships to run from the Japanese fleet, they abandon American troops on a bloody, battered island in the South Pacific.

"Heavy on authenticity, compellingly written and beautifully drawn."
- Comics Buyers Guide

BECK and CAUL INVESTIGATIONS:
Where the Nightmares Walk
- Collects the entire Beck & Caul series for the FIRST TIME!

There is a place where evil lives. Where all of mankind's nightmares are a reality. It is the Underside. From this realm of myth and shadow was born Jonas Beck who teams up with a young woman, Mercedes Guillane and their paths meld into one...to battle evil in all its guises. Set in the voodoo influenced city of New Orleans, Beck and Caul are paranormal detectives who scrounge the streets of this dark, mystical city in order to combat and protect people from supernatural attacks and events.

COUNTER-PARTS

From best selling author Stefan Petrucha (MARVEL's Deadpool, Captain America). Think people can be disingenuous? Of course and in the future they try on new personas like hats. But when Hieronymus Jones overdoses on TPGs (temporary personality grafts), his original personality is destroyed. Now an experimental cure gives him not 1, but 6 new personalities. Each inhabiting a different part of his body. There's: Bogey, the hard-boiled right arm; Kik-li, the Kung-Fu master right leg; Jake, the self-involved torso; Buckley, the too-smart head; Don, the romantic left arm and; Tootsie, the femme fatale left leg! Together, they fight corruption & crime as one strange superhero team. Strap yourself in for one wild ride!

VELDA: GIRL DETECTIVE - VOL. 2

A unique take on the more lurid of the 1950s crime comics as if it actually existed as a Golden Age comic. More than a homage to noir films and hard-boiled detective writing of the 50s it includes in issues features such as a Velda paper doll kit & complete '52 Velda pinup calendar. Also added are vintage ads to amuse readers and shorts such as "Hawkshaw Hawk, Bird Detective" and "Neolithica: Girl of the Pleistocene" ."Velda is the kind of detective I like."- Richard S. Prather (writer, Shell Scott novels). "A pulp classic! If you like your action gritty, yet full of surprises, then you'll love Velda..." - Rick Overton (writer, Dennis Miller Show). "The Velda Comic is spectacular.." - Bob Burns.

CALIBER
COMICS

www.calibercomics.com

51226517R00076

Made in the USA
Columbia, SC
14 February 2019